Fascist Italy in the Age of Corporatism

The interwar period was marked in Europe by the rediscovery of corporatism as a possible solution to the crucial problems of modern mass society. This was the result of general changes across industrialised countries in the relationship between the state and social groups. In Italy, it took on a uniquely authoritarian shape. Fascist regime became the cradle of a new model of corporatism, a "third way" alternative to both capitalism and communism, destined to influence both political, juridical, and economic debate and similar legislative experiments undertaken by other countries, be they democratic or authoritarian.

The book offers an overview of corporatism in Fascist Italy. It examines not only the ideology but also the acts and real activities of corporative institutions (*corporazioni*). It dwells upon internal debates, the political and institutional importance acquired by corporative institutions in the Fascist regime, and the behaviour of entrepreneurial organisations and labour unions.

At the same time, the book highlights the role of Italy in the transnational circulation of the corporative ideal by reconstructing both the considerable influence of Mussolini's regime in a range of different political and geographical contexts and the way in which the authorities in Rome turned to coeval international experiences.

Alessio Gagliardi is an Associate Professor of Contemporary History at the University of Bologna. His research focuses on Fascism, anti-Fascism, and social movements in contemporary Italy. His previous books include *Il '77 tra storia e memoria* (Roma: Manifestolibri, 2017) and *L'Europa del Novecento. Una storia* (with Francesco Bartolini, Bruno Bonomo and Leonardo Rapone; Roma: Carocci, 2020). He is editor-in-chief of the scientific journal *Italia contemporanea.*

Routledge Studies in Fascism and the Far Right
Series editors: Nigel Copsey, *Teesside University, UK* and
Graham Macklin, *Center for Research on Extremism (C-REX), University of Oslo, Norway*

This book series focuses upon national, transnational and global manifestations of fascist, far right and right-wing politics primarily within a historical context but also drawing on insights and approaches from other disciplinary perspectives. Its scope also includes anti-fascism, radical-right populism, extreme-right violence and terrorism, cultural manifestations of the far right, and points of convergence and exchange with the mainstream and traditional right.

Salazar
A Political Biography
Second Edition
Filipe Ribeiro de Meneses

The Italian Far Right from 1945 to the Russia-Ukraine Conflict
Nicola Guerra

Fascists in Exile
Post-War Displaced Persons in Australia
Jayne Persian

Understanding and Countering Fascist Movements
From Void to Hope
Joan Braune

Organisation of Ukrainian Nationalists on Emigration
Its Formation and Transnational Connections in 1929–1934
Magdalena Gibiec

Fascist Italy in the Age of Corporatism
Searching for a Third Way
Alessio Gagliardi

For more information about this series, please visit: www.routledge.com/Routledge-Studies-in-Fascism-and-the-Far-Right/book-series/FFR

Fascist Italy in the Age of Corporatism

Searching for a Third Way

Alessio Gagliardi

Translated by Sergio Knipe

Routledge
Taylor & Francis Group
LONDON AND NEW YORK

First published in English 2024
by Routledge
4 Park Square, Milton Park, Abingdon, Oxon OX14 4RN

and by Routledge
605 Third Avenue, New York, NY 10158

Routledge is an imprint of the Taylor & Francis Group, an informa business

Translated by Sergio Knipe

Translated from

Il corporativismo fascista

British Library Cataloguing-in-Publication Data
A catalogue record for this book is available from the British Library

ISBN: 978-1-032-71323-6 (hbk)
ISBN: 978-1-032-71324-3 (pbk)
ISBN: 978-1-032-71326-7 (ebk)

DOI: 10.4324/9781032713267

Typeset in Times New Roman
by KnowledgeWorks Global Ltd.

Contents

Acknowledgements

This book is the result of many years of research. Throughout this time, I have had the opportunity to discuss my work with numerous scholars, colleagues, students, and friends at conferences, seminars, and courses, as well as in long friendly chats. Over time, some of these people have read draft versions of the book or individual chapters. While I cannot list them all, I would at least like to mention Giulia Albanese, Tommaso Baris, Sabino Cassese, Valeria Galimi, Guido Melis, Matteo Pasetti, Antonio Costa Pinto, Giovanni Sabbatucci, Daniele Serapiglia, Paula Borges Santos, and Irene Stolzi.

Moreover, I am most grateful to the Department of History and Cultures at the University of Bologna, which I joined several years ago. Special thanks are due to library and archive staff, who have helped me access the material I needed for my research.

For the final version of the book, I am deeply indebted to Sergio Knipe, who has translated the volume and, through his work, has helped me to clarify several points.

Last but not least, I am immensely grateful to Palgrave for agreeing to publish the book, waiting patiently for its completion, and especially to Robert Langham, who has supported this publication project from the very start.

It goes without saying that I alone am responsible for the contents of this book and for any error of fact or judgement.

This book is dedicated to my partner Chiara Tullio and my daughter Diana, who have put up far too long with the sight of piles of books lying around the house. I feel blessed to have them in my life.

Abbreviations

AConf	Archivio Storico della Confederazione generale dell'industria italiana, generally called Confindustria (Historical Archives of the General Confederation of Italian Industry)
ACS	Archivio centrale dello Stato (National Archives)
AFSDF	Archivio storico della Fondazione Ugo Spirito Renzo De Felice (Historical Archives of the Foundation Ugo Spirito e Renzo De Felice)
AGFPI	Associazione generale fascista del pubblico impiego (General Fascist Civil Service Association)
AILO	Archives of the International Labour Organization
APC	Atti Parlamentari della Camera dei Deputati (Proceedings of the Chamber of Deputies)
APS	Atti Parlamentari del Senato (Proceedings of the Senate)
ASCD	Archivio storico Camera dei Deputati (Historical Archives of the Chamber of Deputies)
BIT	Bureau International du Travail (International Labour Office)
CNC	Consiglio Nazionale delle Corporazioni (National Council of Corporations)
DAF	Deutsche Arbeitsfront (German Labour Front)
ILO	International Labour Organization
IRI	Istituto per la ricostruzione industriale (Institute for Industrial Reconstruction)
NSDAP	Nationalsozialistische Deutsche Arbeiterpartei (National Socialist German Workers' Party)
PCM	Presidenza del Consiglio dei ministri (Presidency of the Council of Ministers)
PNF	Partito nazionale fascista (National Fascist Party)
SPD	Segreteria Particolare del Duce (Special Secretary of the Duce)

Introduction

Le siècle du corporatisme (*The Century of Corporatism*) is the title of a book by Mihail Manoilescu, a nationalist and ultra-conservative Romanian intellectual and politician.[1] Originally published in France in 1934, the book enjoyed wide circulation in many countries in Europe and Latin America in the second half of the 1930s. It supported the idea that corporatism was becoming the dominant feature of European State organisation and was destined to completely replace traditional liberal or authoritarian systems: the 20th century was heralded as the "century of corporatism", just as the 19th century had been the century of liberalism. In Manoilescu's eyes, corporatism had two merits above all: it subordinated particular interests to the nation's general interests, and it allowed countries on the periphery of world capitalism to initiate a process of economic modernisation.

While Manoilescu's discourse is hardly a memorable one in terms of its analytical depth and the quality of its arguments, it nevertheless stands out because, like no other discourse before it, it portrayed corporatism not as an idea linked to specific theoretical currents or to specific national contexts, but as a systematic doctrine, capable of marking its own era and implementable almost everywhere. As we know, this "prophecy" did not come true. Yet, in the mid-1930s, when the book came out, many in Italy and the rest of Europe shared the idea that corporatism was poised to conquer the world – and that it was destined to replace liberalism once and for all.

Corporatist tendencies were widespread and cut across different political movements and institutional systems. But it is undeniable that, on an ideological level, it was above all (Fascist or para-Fascist)[2] authoritarian movements that sought to openly identify with corporatism. It was such movements that translated the fantasy of a "third way" into the vague idea of a profound upheaval in the structure of the state and the relations between politics and society in the name of a radical compression of the freedoms and autonomy of social bodies. As regards the actual implementation of corporatist ideas, for the Fascist and para-Fascist regimes, corporatism constituted a means to accomplish the repudiation of parliamentarianism, social conflict, individual rights, freedom of association, and the division of powers in order to give life to a new type of authoritarianism which represented itself as the foundation of a different system of representation, based on collective bodies rather than individuals and on the primacy of the nation.

DOI: 10.4324/9781032713267-1

Fascist Italy occupied a central place in this context from the very start. Italy provided the first example of a major European country in which a political party that had come into power set out to create a corporative state. Fascism was the political regime that most identified with corporatism, both by fuelling an endless cultural output on the subject and through numerous legislative measures and the creation of new institutional apparatuses. As already noted by Chabod in his 1950 lectures, this attempt soon attracted considerable attention from foreign observers.[3]

With the creation of corporatism, Fascism promised to bring about a profound transformation of the economy and the state: it set out, on the one hand, to subject the market and private enterprise to political control and, on the other, to create a new system of representation, completely different from the liberal system, as well as a new relationship between the rulers and the ruled.

Little of that project, however, was actually put into practice. Anti-Fascists in the 1930s and historians thereafter have emphasised the enormous gap between ideological theories, programmes, and interventions on the one hand and legislative, institutional, and political initiatives on the other. Indeed, one only has to look at the Fascist corporatists' concrete accomplishments to find more than enough evidence to support this verdict. Indeed, state intervention in the economy predominantly took place outside of corporate procedures and institutions. The construction of the apparatus, then, was marked by sluggishness and contradictions: the *Consiglio nazionale delle corporazioni* (CNC, National Council of Corporations), envisaged in the 1926 syndicalist law's regulations, was only established in 1930 and given the task of coordinating the work of the corporations – which were constituted four years later, however. Finally, the Chamber of Fasces and Corporations (*Camera dei fasci e delle corporazioni*) only saw the light of day in 1939, when the regime was entering its final phase.

But if no "corporative revolution" took place, as promised by the Fascist leaders, this does not mean that the creation of the corporatist institutions and their work was devoid of significant outcomes. First of all, one cannot underestimate the importance of the Fascist programmes and ideology, which must be considered a fundamental aspect of 20th-century politics, and not as a sham or a collection of promises. Indeed, it was mainly through the idea of corporatism that Fascism attempted to propose itself, both to the Italians and the entire world, as a "third way" alternative to both capitalism and socialism, and as a revolutionary experiment that would create a "new state" and a different model of society. While the corporatist idea today may appear mystifying, culturally fragile, in conflict with the emergence of modern mass society, and aimed at forcibly simplifying a complex reality, this does not change the fact that the corporatist perspective must have seemed credible to many. The development of this perspective allowed the Italian debate to become part of the broader consideration of the problems and changes in industrial societies that took place in much of the world during the interwar period.

The question of corporatism, on the other hand, directly relates to the central problem in modern politics: that of how to reconcile the plurality of interests present in society with the construction of the unity of state leadership. This problem was strongly felt by Fascism, which built its political and ideological project precisely on the affirmation of "total" state power and the unification of the nation. Corporatism was the instrument by which Fascism set out to relate the authoritarian and totalitarian state to the diversity and plurality of interests present in society, expressed above all by trade union organisations. The corporatist solution consisted in an attempt to make the "national interest" (naturally coinciding with the objectives of Fascism and its allies) prevail over the particular and particularistic interests present in society (classes and categories), repressing the latter's conflicting nature. The path chosen, however, was not the negation of interest groups but rather their "institutionalisation" and "fascisation", which meant recognising their political legitimacy and representation in state structures through complete assimilation into the regime. In a 1935 essay, Karl Polanyi observed: "After abolition of the democratic political sphere only economic life remains; Capitalism as organised in the different branches of industry becomes the whole of society. This is the Fascist solution".[4]

While on the ideological side, corporatism entailed the opening up of a vast and very popular reflection on how to overcome the liberal state and the capitalist market economy, on the political-institutional side, it gave rise to a double course of action: the regulation of labour relations and the regulation and management of the economy. The latter did not meet the corporatists' expectations or conform to official declarations; the former, by contrast, was fully implemented. Indeed, the regulation of labour relations was fully achieved as early as the mid-1920s, with the approval of the syndicalist system designed by Alfredo Rocco. Strikes and lockouts were banned, and trade union freedoms and the diversity of organisations abrogated in favour of the monopoly on representation granted to Fascist organisations. The goal pursued was the suppression of class struggle and the establishment of an orderly and harmonious society.

The apparatus developed by Rocco did not merely establish a highly authoritarian way of regulating labour relations and trade union activities but gave rise to a genuine system for controlling and governing relations between social classes. This system – a rigid, yet at the same time extremely "modern" one – was based on the complete "harnessing" of society, a rigid classification of the various social groups, and the placing of each individual within the specific category to which he or she belonged. The elimination of social conflict – and herein lay the system's modernity– was accomplished not by denying the division of society into classes and the legitimacy of organisations for the representation of specific interests but by bringing trade unions back into the state sphere. The "private" interest groups represented by the legally recognised Fascist organisations acquired the seal of "public" institutions. The suppression of non-Fascist organisations and the elimination of freedom of association and strikes did not therefore lead to a simple and unrealistic return to the past and to a mutual alienation between state and society. The presence of a complex organisational network was assumed to be an inescapable fact in modern mass society. In Fascism, on the other hand, the moment of destruction, violence, and repression was always inseparably welded to and superimposed on that of the construction of new norms, procedures, and apparatuses.

The regime's mobilisation of the masses therefore took place not only through unifying myths, political rituals, and the filling of living spaces with associations headed by the *National Fascist Party (Partito Nazionale Fascista,* PNF), but also by affirming a positive link between categories' specific and particular interests and the unitary, "national" objectives promoted by the regime.

Much less satisfactory for the advocates of the corporative state were the results achieved in the field of economic management. Contrary to expectations and official proclamations, the corporative bodies failed to direct and coordinate entrepreneurs' choices, to limit the power of private enterprise, and to impose the public planning of investments. But the corporative institutions were by no means irrelevant because they provided a forum to discuss measures relating to economic and industrial policies and labour and welfare issues. The formally equitable mediation between different classes and categories offered by the corporations became a means to express conflictual dynamics and demands that were otherwise repressed and condemned as illegitimate. Through corporate discussions, an undemocratic mode of mediation and negotiation between interest groups and the state took shape. Trade unionists and entrepreneurs were able to use the new procedures not only to make their case against their counterparts or competitors but also to make demands on the government. The simultaneous growth of public spending and state intervention in the 1930s and the parallel reduction of market power attracted the participation of interest groups, and it was again through the corporate apparatus – irrespective of the outcome and actual scope of the discussions – that representatives of those groups were systematically and institutionally admitted to the negotiating table.

In its general outline, this was not a completely new phenomenon. Already during the First World War and in the postwar years, European societies had increasingly come to accept the principle that economic and social welfare measures could be developed and discussed with the direct involvement of organisations representing entrepreneurs, workers, and – in several cases – the middle classes (professionals, civil servants, and small traders). The corporatist experiment, however, was characterised by two peculiar and fully innovative aspects: on the one hand, the institutional character of such involvement, and the fact that it took place in official fora and in a legally regulated manner; and on the other, the joint involvement of interest organisations in the actual decision-making process, i.e., in the formulation of laws and political decisions. While for the workers' unions – representing a sector of society that had been badly hit by Fascism – the new opportunities mostly remained on paper, and the employers' organisations were able to take full advantage of them by virtue of their bargaining power and autonomy. The corporations offered the entrepreneurial organisations a privileged means to enter the "citadel" of the state and attempt to jointly manage the shift of power from the market to public institutions while at the same time becoming involved in the process of political decision-making and administrative action.

Fascism therefore did not succeed in suppressing the conflictual framework it had inherited from the mass society of the years before the March on Rome, but rather internalised it. While apparently contradictory, it represented the specific

"Italian translation" of the new social and corporative dimension of political power that all industrialised countries – be they democratic, authoritarian, or totalitarian – were experiencing at the time, each in its own way.

In order to tackle these problems, I have decided to combine two paths of research and analysis. The first is the constant and systematic intersecting of Italian and international events: I have sought to consider the debates, reforms, and achievements of Italian corporatism as a fundamental part of the global circulation of the corporatist model in Europe and other areas of the world. The transnational dimension of Fascist corporatism is considered here an integral part of such an experience. Indeed, it constituted a source of legitimisation for the Fascist regime outside Italy. Through the corporative idea, Mussolini's government even succeeded in establishing itself as a "model" capable of inspiring both authoritarian and Fascist systems as well as democratic regimes. The second research path aims to offer a historical reconstruction of the corporative order and of the actual activity carried out by the corporative bodies. This reconstruction is consciously centred on the general functioning of the system more than on its minute effects, and on the relationship between institutions and representative organisations more than on that between institutions and social subjects. It is also an inevitably "sample-based" reconstruction, given the gaps in the sources available to historians (for many archives of the corporative bodies, the Ministry of Corporations, and the Fascist trade unions have been lost). The numerous archives I have consulted have nonetheless allowed me to bring into focus some important moments and aspects related to the corporative apparatus' activity and, through a more in-depth examination of certain discussions and procedures, to outline the overall functioning of the system.

This book stems from a study on corporatism in Fascist Italy that I published in an Italian volume, Il corporativismo fascista, *in 2010.*[5] *After some time, I decided to return to the topic in order to place the history of corporatism in Fascist Italy within a broader framework, as already mentioned. I was thus able to update my previous work in the light of a new era of corporatism studies. This historiography has examined the transnational circulation of corporatism and has delved into some national cases (especially those of Spain, Portugal, and Brazil). In recent years, by contrast, the case of Italy has remained partially in the shadows, notwithstanding certain exceptions. Another objective of this volume is therefore to make an English-language book offering a close and systematic analysis of Mussolini's corporatist State available to a wider public of readers who may not know Italian.*

The sections on Italy draw upon pages from the 2010 book, updating them and supplementing them to a considerable degree. All the sections on the transnational circulation of corporative ideas, supranational bodies, the projection of Fascism and Fascist corporatism abroad, overseas events, and comparisons with other countries are published here for the first time. Some chapters are entirely new, while others contain both original parts and some derived from the previous book.

Notes

1 Mihail Manoilescu, *Le siècle du corporatisme. Doctrine du corporatisme intégral et pur* (Paris: Félix Alcan, 1934).
2 On the concept of "para-fascism", see Roger Griffin, *The Nature of Fascism* (New York/London: Routledge, 1991), 120–145; Aristotle Kallis, "'Fascism', 'Para-fascism' and 'Fascistization': On the Similarities of Three Conceptual Categories", *European History Quarterly* 33, no. 2 (2003): 219–250.
3 Federico Chabod, *L'Italia contemporanea (1918–1948)* (Torino: Einaudi, 1961), 88.
4 Karl Polanyi, "The Essence of Fascism", in *Christianity and the Social Revolution*, eds. John Lewis, Karl Polanyi, and Donald K. Kitchin (London: Gollancz, 1935), 392.
5 Alessio Gagliardi, *Il corporativismo fascista* (Roma-Bari: Laterza, 2010).

1 The Crisis of the State, the War, and Its Aftermath

By the turn of the 20th century, an increasingly large number of people had come to regard the 19th-century model of liberal society as incapable of meeting the needs of their time. Political forces, trade unions, and intellectuals began to express increasingly strong distrust in the two pillars of the liberal model: the self-regulating market and a state based on the division of powers and the rule of law. The former largely seemed to have been overwhelmed by the establishment of large aggregates (monopolies, oligopolies, consortiums, and trusts), which were replacing competition between a range of entities through the force of their size and the drive to come together and pool resources rather than vie with each other. Governments of more economically advanced countries not only did nothing to oppose these tendencies – anti-trust laws were very limited – but actively contributed to limiting and harnessing capitalism's "animal spirits" through protectionist and neo-mercantilist policies, bailouts, and more active measures to support industrial and agricultural production. To all this, we should add the growth of socialist movements and labour unions, which openly challenged the principles of market economics and denounced the social impact of free trade. As a result, the idea of a market capable of independently (i.e. "naturally") finding a balance started appearing more and more unlikely to significant sectors of European society.

The second pillar, the liberal state, in turn, found itself facing the impact of mass society. Both in practice, wherever a liberal state had, in fact, come into being, and in the culture and imagination of the European bourgeoisie, for much of the 19th century, the liberal institutional and political model had rested on some well-defined principles: a form of parliamentary representation based on the figure of the abstract *citoyen*, the acknowledgement of individual rights (also bestowed on a "generic" and socially indeterminate individual), and the division between the various powers and the law, the latter of which was regarded as above all particular interests. These principles were seriously put to the test by the extension of suffrage, the new leading political role played by the working classes, and the establishment of structured and permanent political parties that embodied collective identities and interests. Most of all, what seemed increasingly unlikely in the age of mass politics

DOI: 10.4324/9781032713267-2

was the idea of the "neutrality" of the law and of the separation between the state and society. To quote Charles S. Maier,

> by the early twentieth century the ideal of a pristine state was difficult to maintain. It was hard to disentangle from the web of corporate interests, labor unions, and political parties that claimed the right to govern, whether in a competitive system or exclusively and without tolerating rivals. Only a century or so after the idea of a government of laws had slowly disengaged itself as the ideology of Enlightenment politics, the state seemed about to be reabsorbed as just a regime of party or of interests.[1]

In other words, already before the outbreak of the First World War, the mechanisms of social representation and political integration in Europe had come to be perceived as weak and inadequate. As far as market mechanisms are concerned, scholars and political leaders interpreted the changes introduced by the development of systems of production and economic policies in light of the ideologically charged and polarising mutual confrontation between capitalism and socialism. It was the critics of capitalism who highlighted and investigated such processes. At this stage, its defenders rather struggled, for the most part, to grasp these processes' innovative quality: they only promoted ways of regulating entrepreneurship without ever questioning the capitalist order or the principle of private property.

By contrast, the crisis of parliamentary democracy and the liberal state became the focus of an extensive and complex debate involving all the major political and cultural currents. In France, Léon Duguit, Adolphe Prins, Guillaume de Greef, Charles Benoist, and Joseph Paul-Boncour, among others, had already announced the "death of the state" at the end of the previous century – or at any rate, the death of its liberal form. Consequently, they had "taken up the banner of the representation of interests against the 'inefficiencies' or 'degenerations' of the parliamentary system".[2] In Germany and Austria the issue of the crisis of the state and of political representation lay at the centre of all plans to reform the liberal-parliamentary institutions. To consider only two of the most authoritative German-speaking intellectuals of the first half of the 20th century, both Max Weber and Hans Kelsen dwelt on this issue at length and with particular attention: the former described the progressive subordination of politics and parliamentary governments to bureaucracy's "steel cage", while the latter acknowledged the "fiction of representation", which is to say parliament's inability to serve as a genuine expression of the people's will.[3]

In Italy as well in the first 15 years of the 20th century, political theory and juridical culture showed increasing awareness of these phenomena that were underway while having trouble assessing their political and institutional consequences.[4] Scholars chiefly saw such processes as the root of the dissolution of the legal systems' uniqueness as well as sovereignty. This gave rise to a debate on the theme of the "crisis of the state", which had a crucial influence on reformulating the paradigms of political and constitutional thought. It was Vittorio Emanuele Orlando and his pupils Oreste Ranelletti and Santi Romano who were among the first to develop a commentary on this topic. Romano's 1910 study *Lo Stato moderno e la sua crisi* represents its best-known expression. Romano observes that the "crisis of the present-day state" is characterised by the convergence of two phenomena: "the progressive organising of society on the basis of specific interests, as it increasingly loses its atomistic character, and the lack of juridical and institutional means by which society itself can reflect and affirm its own structure within that of the state".[5]

In other words, the need to bring the relationship between politics and society back in order was widespread and felt at all levels. While the solutions suggested varied hugely, they all shared two aims: to regulate major economic forces and to acknowledge the institutional legitimacy of professional categories. The topic of corporatism thus became relevant again, "without having ever left the cultural horizon of the 19th century, although it had been relegated to a marginal position compared to mainstream politics".[6] In the early 20th century, corporatist ideas – while not always explicitly presented as such – were running through a wide range of intellectual currents and political traditions.

What contributed to relaunching corporatism was, first of all, political Catholicism. The last three decades of the 19th century witnessed the development of the theories of the Frenchmen René de La Tour du Pin, Albert de Mun, and Frédéric Le Play; the German Wilhelm Emmanuel von Ketteler; the Austrian Karl Freiherr von Vogelsang; and the Italian Giuseppe Toniolo. They all found a point of reference and authoritative justification in Leo XIII's encyclical *Rerum novarum* (1891). Despite some significant divergences between its various theorists, Catholic corporatism constituted an intellectual and political current that combined conservative – and sometimes openly reactionary – elements with a charitable and paternalistic view of social intervention. The shared underlying goal was to restore a harmonious society governed by a functional division of roles across the various segments of society and organised according to a hierarchical principle. The ideal of collaboration between classes and the rejection of social conflict as such was its foundational principles. Socialism was regarded as an opponent to be defeated and at the same time as the "symptom" of a weakness in the social body, of a moral crisis which needed to be faced not only by opposing and fighting socialism but also by offering some alternative solutions.[7]

Catholic corporatism, however, was not merely a reaction to socialism. All its theorists addressed the problem of overcoming the changes caused by the end of the *ancien régime* and the spread of the kind of political rights introduced by the French Revolution. They sought to defend civil society, family, and local bonds against interference from a centralised state founded on "abstract" law. At the same time, these theorists set themselves the goal of creating a bulwark against the social and cultural effects of industrialisation. The latter was regarded as the ultimate cause of a series of "degenerations" and of the departure from a "just" and "natural" way of organising society. Industrialisation was seen as having led to the spread not only of the socialist movement but also of secular and individualist liberalism.[8] The Catholic theorists of corporatism "perceived the need for intermediate institutions that help to achieve the 'decommodification' of labour. They also believed that these social bonds could help collaboration between labour and capital, and contribute to prevention and/or to smoothing unrestricted competition, which can achieve dangerous results (the reduction of wages and uncertainty are considered in particular)".[9]

Another relevant current was the nationalist one, which had emerged at the turn of the 20th century in most of continental Europe. Corporatism was here seen to provide an institutional model in accordance with the organicist objectives underlying the idea of the nation's primacy. The overcoming of trade-union conflicts was regarded as crucial for establishing harmony between society's various components and for ensuring the nation's unity; the latter, in turn, was considered an essential prerequisite for achieving a strong presence on the international stage. In this case, too, corporatism took different forms. From the late 19th century, France witnessed the rise of the *Action française*, which was founded and led for many years by Charles Maurras. This movement proposed a blend of reactionary nationalism, anti-parliamentarianism, intransigent Catholicism, the myth of traditions, an adherence to the monarchist cause, anti-individualism, and anti-Semitism. The corporatist idea was set as the foundation of an ideology centred on the re-establishment of social cohesion and the principles of hierarchy and authority. This movement combined elements drawn from both French and European anti-modernist cultures into something original.[10]

Similar experiences, partly inspired by Maurras' ideas, took shape elsewhere.[11] This was the case with the Portuguese nationalist movement *Lusitanian Integralism*, established in 1914.[12] António Sardinha, one of the leading figures within this movement, explicitly stated: "the intellectual campaign that is being led by Maurras in France is directed by *Integralism* in Portugal".[13] Likewise, the Spanish Right in the early 20th century was deeply influenced by Maurras' ideas, in keeping with the connection that conservatives and anti-liberals close to the Catholic Church and Carlism had maintained for over a century with the counter-revolutionary and Romantic thought of Abbé Barruel, Louis de Bonald, Joseph de Maistre, and the French culture of Restoration embodied by Chateaubriand.[14] In both cases, *Action française*'s influence proved particularly significant precisely in relation to corporatism. Influenced by La Tour du Pin, Maurras' radical anti-liberalism and anti-modernism were nourished by a deep distrust of the centralising and centralised state, which it regarded as an entity inevitably destined to oppress and stifle traditional institutions (the family, local communities, professional groups). The corporatism of *Action française*, *Lusitanian Integralism*, and the Spanish Right was therefore envisaged as a way of decentralising power: corporations, in other words, were intended to limit the scope and decision-making capacity of parliament and the national government. The analogies with Catholic corporatism are evident. Other nationalist movements instead took a different direction by associating the adoption of corporatism with the strengthening of the state and the centralisation of political power. As we shall see, this was the case with Italian nationalism.

The First World War provided a significant impetus for the formulation of corporatist ideas. As the conflict spread, the governments of all the warring countries were forced to develop wartime economies based on control over production and the subordination of private interests to national objectives. On account of its extent and complexity, the war of 1914–1918 could not be waged (and won) on the battlefield alone: more than any previous conflict, it required the involvement of society as a whole. To ensure production and the use of vast amounts of technologically complex weaponry, to move and feed tens of millions of soldiers, to construct endless trenches, and to ensure transportation and communication routes, a vast effort was necessary that, in every warring country, entailed the involvement not just of the army, but also of industry, agriculture, the government, and the administrative apparatus. The states engaged in the conflict had to channel most of the nation's human and material resources into war objectives; governments thus came to exercise increasing power over national life, subordinating private and public life to their war aims.[15]

To sustain this vast effort, the greatest possible compactness and cohesion in all sectors of society was crucial. This primarily affected the systems of production. Industry was required to produce arms and ammunition but also means of transport, fuel, radio and telephone equipment, clothing, shoes, helmets, gas masks, canteens, backpacks, tents, field kitchens, machines for the digging of trenches and tunnels, and all the material required to construct wooden, steel, or cement structures. To this, we should add food processing, preservation, and packaging as well as the collection of drinking water. All scientific and technological resources were deployed. Industries' productive capacity was therefore increasingly directed at meeting army needs, to the detriment of production for private consumption. No less significant was the impact on agriculture: not only was much of the produce reserved for the troops, but almost everywhere requisitions of horses, mules, and machinery were organised to ensure war transportation while the production of chemical fertilisers was reduced to focus on that of ammunition and explosives – not to mention the fact that the highest number of recruits and fallen soldiers came from the farmers' ranks. On account of agriculture's technical and productive decline, the provision of food for the civilian population became a widespread problem. To prevent the hoarding of goods and unchecked inflation, governments resorted to rationing and fixed prices, measures which further contributed to the drop in agricultural revenues.[16]

The productive effort to meet wartime needs required greater effort by workers. Strikes and ordinary negotiations were generally suspended or banned; discipline in the workplace was strengthened; a stop was put to wage rises and holidays; and work hours were increased. At the same time, to make up for the sacrifices demanded, even less liberal, if not openly authoritarian, states introduced new social safeguards and rights by adopting measures concerning the price of essential goods, rents, and work contracts. They granted subsidies and bonuses to struggling sectors (the unemployed, invalids, refugees, widows, orphans, and conscripts' spouses). They adopted new insurance policies in support of workers (particularly industrial labourers) and established new medical centres and hospitals to protect the health of the population. In this respect, the First World War marked a significant step forward in the development of social welfare systems.

In all countries, including those with democratic governments, the state increased its power to control and integrate social groups and individuals.[17]

None of the countries involved in the conflict were initially prepared to make such a colossal effort. The state was forced to take direct measures, vastly increasing its prerogatives. Liberal conceptions suddenly seemed obsolete. The state stepped into commission projects, fund enterprises useful for war aims, ensure the regular supply of raw materials, build factories, bring plants up to date technologically, distribute production among different companies, fix prices and wages, set holidays and working hours, and ensure workers' discipline and social peace. To undertake these tasks, states created new offices, administrative apparatuses, and public bodies, leading to a huge increase in staff. Head bureaucrats and army leaders increased their power as they became directly involved in managing the wartime economy. The latter also witnessed the active involvement of leading representatives of the private business and finance sectors. All warring countries thus experienced an intertwining of politics and economics, private enterprises and public institutions, civilian and military authorities, and individual and collective interests. All this was achieved chiefly at the expense of representative institutions – starting with parliament – which were confined to the margins of the decision-making process.[18]

The idea of a double crisis of the liberal system – a crisis of the self-regulating market and of the parliamentary state – was strengthened by the experience of the First World War. Corporatist ideas started circulating even more, cutting across all political factions. By this stage, what contributed to their circulation were not only political Catholicism and nationalist movements but also significant sectors of the Left. A former revolutionary syndicalist who in the early 1900s had become a monarchist and follower of Maurras, George Valois, grafted an approach influenced by his past political activism onto the corporatism of the Catholic tradition that had been adopted by *Action française*.[19] In a 1919 text, *L'économie nouvelle*, Valois outlined a corporatist system centred on workers' and employers' organisations and on an explicitly *productivist* approach. Within this framework, the state was to control the smooth running of the whole system and to ensure that all decisions would be in line with national interests. Trade unions were thus assigned a crucial role: to "nationalise" the proletariat by steering it away from any compromise with revolutionary projects, and to integrate the labour world into the national community; at the same time, however, they were to preserve their independence.[20] Valois' theoretical model was thus an original and hybrid one. In France, others made the same transition from revolutionary syndicalism to nationalism and anti-socialism (or even fascism in certain cases) under the influence of Proudhon and Sorel: let us think, for instance, of Hubert Lagardelle and Gustave Hervé.[21] As we shall see, the phenomenon found a relevant place in Italy as well.

Other forces within the socialist ranks developed their own corporatist projects. One significant experience was guild socialism, a movement that took shape in the United Kingdom in the early 20th century within the framework of non-Marxist socialism, partly as a reaction against the Fabian Society, which was regarded as overly statist.[22] The movement's guidelines were first laid out by Arthur Penty and then developed within the weekly "The New Age", published between 1907 and 1922 under the direction of Alfred Orage. In 1915, the movement adopted an organisational structure with the founding of the National Guilds League.

Guild socialism revolved around an idea of industrial democracy based on the social management of enterprises entrusted to "guilds": self-governing bodies representing the various social categories and organised according to strictly democratic criteria. The movement reached its peak during the First World War and its immediate aftermath. In those years the most prominent theorist was George Douglas Howard Cole, who made plans for a "corporate socialism" or "corporate pluralism". Guild socialism – as Cole summed it up in 1919 – "is fundamentally a challenge to the current theory of representative government, a plea for functional representation and functional democracy as against so called 'purely political democracy'".[23] Ultimately, it rested on the desire to develop a model limiting state power, in the belief that "society is a center, or rather a group of centers, of deliberation and planning".[24]

In its own way, the Russian Revolution also confirmed the decline of liberal parliamentarianism and the relevance of new systems based on forms of social representation centred on professional groups – categories – rather than individuals. The soviets elected by workers, farmers, and soldiers – precisely qua workers, farmers, and soldiers, rather than "generic" and "abstract" citizens – represented a model which met needs that were not all that different from those addressed by the theorists of corporatism, although, of course, they looked in a completely different direction. Likewise, in the immediate aftermath of the war, Europe witnessed the spread of the idea of factory councils elected by the workers, precisely on the model of the Russian soviets. This showed that working-class forces shared the need to rethink the distribution of powers by placing the organisational structures of society and individuals' professional status at the centre.

In the post-war period, corporatism was no longer merely a theory and political platform but influenced many states' laws, political choices, and administrative procedures. The measures taken during the conflict were only partly repealed after 1918. In the wake of the experience of war mobilisation, governments of the more economically advanced countries preserved policies of public intervention whereby the state took up the task of coordinating and directing relevant sectors of economic life. To achieve these objectives, new state institutions were created while promoting negotiations between enterprises and trade unions, with the government's mediation. In most countries in continental Europe, as large private organisations representing specific interests (trade unions, associations of employers and professionals) gained more and more power, the search for consensus no longer involved only elected MPs but increasingly came to entail direct negotiation between the government and the organisations in question as well. Associations representing private interests thus contributed to the formulation of political orientations in economic and social matters without having to go through parliamentary debates or any mediation by political parties.[25]

The leading role played by professional groups, which sometimes coexisted with and overrode the mechanism of top-down communication between representatives (elected MPs) and those represented (citizens), was thus becoming a fact in Western Europe in the early post-war years rather than simply a plan endorsed by intellectuals and politicians. It took the form more of "corporatist practices" than of a complete reformulation of the principle of representation and of the relationship between the state and the economy, however. As Matteo Pasetti has noted, for most of the 1920s, "any plan to *systematically* redefine the relations between politics and economics, between the state and organised interests, was to remain purely theoretical, even though traditional institutional balances were being challenged by powerful social forces and by the role acquired by mass organisations".[26] In Western Europe, despite the lack of any systemic change, cases of osmosis between public action and forms of social representation emerged in the everyday running of many governments and administrative systems. But in Eastern Europe, not even this occurred. The new Eastern European states suffered from weak administrative apparatuses and had limited autonomy as far as their national economies were concerned, insofar as much of their industrial and banking capital was in the hands of foreign companies.[27]

Even when references to corporatism were introduced into a country's constitution, they largely remained dead letter. In Germany, Article 165 of the Constitution approved in Weimar in August 1919 called for the establishment of a National Economic Council (*Reichswirtschaftsrat*) and of workers' councils. The former was given the right of legislative initiative and the right to evaluate, yet not change, any bills: it therefore had more limited powers than parliament. Although it was supported by a multitiered system of factory and district workers' councils (*Betriebs- und Bezirksarbeiterrate*) as well as by a national workers' council (*Reichsarbeiterrat*), it ended up having even less weight than what the laws provided for.[28]

The most significant example of the idea of corporatism's application to an institutional and representative system is to be found not in the structures of a nation-state but in a supra-national body: the International Labour Organization (ILO). This body was established in accordance with some of the deliberations made at the 1919 Paris Peace Conference for the purpose of improving workers' conditions and promoting social justice as the necessary foundation for the kind of harmonious system of international relations pursued by the League of Nations. In April 1919 a text entitled "Labour" was approved that was to become Part XIII of the Treaty of Versailles, and which was also incorporated into the other peace treaties. It marked the establishment of the ILO, whose members, "moved by sentiments of justice and humanity as well as by the desire to secure the permanent peace of the world", committed themselves to improving the conditions of the largest possible number of workers by fighting injustice, poverty, and deprivation. The pursuit of this aim entailed the reduction in work hours, the regulating of the work market, the struggle against unemployment, adequate wages, the protection of workers against illnesses and accidents, support for young people and women, welfare measures for the elderly and invalids, the protection of emigrant workers, the safeguarding of the freedom of association, and the ensuring of adequate technical training.[29] Through the establishment of the ILO, the victors sought not only to ensure the stability of the new international system but also to react against the shockwave of social conflicts that were affecting all countries. More specifically, these nation-states sought to meet the demand for social welfare measures put forward by their inhabitants during the conflict and to face increasing class conflict and the spectre of revolution.[30]

What makes the establishment of the ILO particularly important for the history of corporatism is its organisational structure. This organisation was based on a "tripartite" logic that called for the participation of workers' and employers' representatives. This was one of the most significant innovations introduced by the new body. The ILO was made up of different bodies: the main one was the International Labour Conference, which was held at least once a year; its members had the power to approve conventions and recommendations. Each national delegation was made up of four members, two representing the government and two appointed by professional associations to represent workers and employers, respectively. The same tripartite system was also adopted for the Governing Body, which was made up of 32 members (16 for the government, 8 for the workers, and 8 for the employers). Its task was to supervise the ILO's apparatus, organise the Conference by laying out the agenda, and oversee the ratifying of conventions by signatory states. At the Paris Conference, the choice of this organisational structure was chiefly supported by the British delegation. It reflected both the steps that countries had taken during the war to involve the representatives of sectional interests and – as we have seen – the circulation of corporatist ideas even in unexpected political and intellectual milieus.[31]

From a general perspective, tripartism responded to the need to mitigate class conflict, strip revolutionary movements of their *raisons d'être*, give rise to an international order based on stable societies, and create cross-national connections between social groups. But at the same time, tripartism also aimed to limit the power of states and the influence of national governments, and to establish a direct connection with public opinion in member states. The ILO, therefore, served as a kind of workshop to test practices that had previously only been theorised or applied in the emergency context of the war. As Daniel Maul has noted, "tripartism, then, rather than being a recognized practice adopted by the ILO on the basis of national experiences, has to be seen as something developed and practised first on the international level before being promoted as a model in the ILO's member States".[32] The founding of the tripartite ILO provided authoritative confirmation and international legitimation of the idea of an institutional system based on the direct involvement of organisations representing sectional interests and on the regulating of the relations between them.

Italy was fully involved in these dynamics. From the early 1900s, numerous cultural and political strands endorsed the overcoming of the liberal-democratic state and the creation of corporatist systems. As in the rest of Europe, a leading role in this regard was taken by the Catholic political movement and by nationalism. However, the aspiration to reform the state through the parliamentary representation of productive categories and the yearning for a way to reconcile divergent social interests cut across the entire political spectrum. These objectives, variously expressed, were also pursued by other sectors of Italian society and politics.

The reformist socialism of the early 20th century identified the representation of interests as a means to alter political balances through agreements and negotiation with its political counterpart, particularly in the field of labour legislation.[33] The socialists found this counterpart in the progressive liberal governments first led by Giuseppe Zanardelli and then by Giovanni Giolitti, who, in those years, were taking steps to bring the working-class masses closer to the state. Their most significant outcome was the creation, in June 1902, of the Supreme Council of Labour (*Consiglio superiore del lavoro*), a consultative body that entailed the full participation of workers' and employers' representatives. This new body – as the law establishing it states – was called "to examine matters concerning the relations between employers and workers; to suggest measures to improve workers' conditions; [...] to give an opinion on bills pertaining to labour legislation and, above all, those that the minister might submit to its scrutiny".[34] For socialist leaders, the Supreme Council of Labour represented "the first real incorporation of the 'labour' element into the state administration".[35] These views rested on the idea that the state could be changed through mediation between the conflicting parties. What was actually achieved was a "functional integration" between the representation of interests and political representation[36]; within the Supreme Council of Labour, "the representation of interests is only achieved and does not alter constitutional balances".[37]

Corporatism was an especially crucial element in the nationalists' ideology and political platform. In the varied context of Italian nationalism, the years leading up to the First World War witnessed the development of a markedly statist ideological approach. This was embodied by, among others, Enrico Corradini, the founder of the Italian Nationalist Association in 1910, and especially by Alfredo Rocco, its foremost theorist. Rocco supported a highly authoritarian corporatism based on the idea of the progressive integration of the masses into the state and of the reinforcement of the country's industry.[38] In the post-war period, it was precisely the nationalists, with Rocco at their head, who, on the ideological level, provided the main link between an analysis of the crisis of the state and the institutional and ideological construction of fascism.[39] We will, therefore, return to Rocco's corporatist theories in the next chapter.

The war provided various elements that could be taken to legitimise and confirm these positions, although in certain cases, their champions were weakened by the new context. This was most prominently the case with the reformist socialists, who were crushed under the weight of the maximalist current, which opposed all forms of the integration of the working class into the "bourgeois" state, and also later that minority which, early in 1921, established the Italian Communist Party, which was directly modelled after its Russian counterpart.

At first, the industrialists opposed policies that assigned a "public" role to trade unions. In the face of the post-war conflicts, however, which they saw as subversive and as a potential threat to the system, the industrialists became increasingly willing to promote solutions to limit conflict and curtail the labour movements' field of action. In the war's aftermath, many entrepreneurs looked with increasing interest to Rocco's corporatism: they envisaged a paternalistic and authoritarian approach that might integrate workers' organisations into the state "from above", depriving them of all independence.[40] This period witnessed a revival of earlier experiences and examples, as in, for example, the kind of productivist paternalism that Alessandro Rossi had promoted in the last two decades of the 19th century, based on a sort of "corporatism of the bourgeoisie".[41] The request to integrate workers' organisations was advanced within the framework of an increasingly widespread consensus with regard to protectionism: the discourse that began to circulate was centred on the defence of "national labour", and thus stripped domestic conflicts of all legitimacy. A radical opposition to the leading role claimed by the labour movement, as well as support for solutions to limit social conflicts, were also expressed by the liberals, who instead strongly rejected all protectionist policies. Particularly noteworthy is the group gravitating around the journal "La Riforma sociale", led by Luigi Einaudi: in this case, it was in the name of the principles of competition and the market economy that measures were suggested to curtail the trade unions' freedom of action and to impose measures to reconcile divergent social interests.[42]

The demand for corporatist solutions to the post-war crisis cut across the political spectrum. A call for a "transformation of Parliament through the equal participation of industrialists, farmers, engineers, and tradesmen in the governing of the country" was also made in the *Manifesto of the Italian Futurist Party* drawn up by Filippo Tommaso Marinetti early in 1918.[43] What was far more significant, besides the increasingly dynamic nationalist movement, was that strand of revolutionary syndicalism that had come to endorse the new experience of "national syndicalism" within the context of supporting Italy's entry into the war with the *Unione italiana del lavoro* (Italian Labour Union). Alceste De Ambris, Edmondo Rossoni, Angelo Oliviero Olivetti, and Sergio Panunzio, among others, promoted an ideological blend of nationalism and syndicalism from an anti-liberal and anti-socialist perspective that echoed Valois' views and upheld the need to replace class conflict with the conflict between nations. These men gave shape to a sort of "syndicalist corporatism" that sought to integrate the labour world into the national community by placing trade unions within an institutional system of corporatist decision-making bodies.[44] National syndicalism was another channel leading from the ideas and mobilisation of the war and its immediate aftermath to the Fascist movement.

The stream of countless corporatist proposals also included the plans to reform the *Consiglio superiore del lavoro* (Superior Labour Council) that were drawn up in the post-war years by governments and various social actors to ensure greater participation by the various social sectors, beyond the merely consultative role they had played until then. In May 1919, Meuccio Ruini, then the Undersecretary of Labour for the government led by Francesco Saverio Nitti, sent all entrepreneurs' and workers' organisations a questionnaire, inviting them to contribute to a deep redefinition of the Council's tasks and structure. The entrepreneurs' response was lukewarm, whereas labour unions welcomed the request and each proposed reform plan: the Christian-socialist Confederation of Workers demanded greater powers for the Council, particularly on the legislative level; the *Unione italiana del lavoro* (Italian Labour Union), which had a national-syndicalist orientation, proposed that the Council be directly assigned legislative and executive powers; and finally, the General Confederation of Labour (*Confederazione generale del lavoro*), which had a reformist socialist orientation, went as far as to ask that the *Consiglio* be turned into a second chamber, to replace the Senate appointed by the King. Despite the wealth of proposals, nothing came of this. Over the following months, other government representatives addressed the issue, yet without achieving any result. The debate and proposed reforms, however, showed just how widespread was the idea of creating an organic form of the representation of interests.[45]

The Fascist movement was soon to add its own voice to the many that were shaping political, social, and intellectual life in post-war Italy. Corporatism made an early appearance in Fascist ideology and political statements. The June 1919 programme of the *Fasci di combattimento* already mentioned the abolition of the Senate, the "creation of a technical National Council for intellectual and manual labour, industry, trade, and agriculture", and the "participation of workers' representatives in industry's technical affairs".[46] Indeed, national syndicalism had exerted an early and profound influence on Mussolini and his interventionist stance in the war years. Long before the establishment of the *Fasci di combattimento*, "Il Popolo d'Italia" had been evoking, with increasing frequency, the "new society of fighters" and – significantly – "producers".

This perspective was further confirmed after the establishment, in November 1921, of the National Fascist Party. While the programme approved at the time of the Party's establishment was marked – in its first section – by the use of liberal catchphrases ("the state must be reduced to its essential functions: maintaining the political and judicial order"), it nonetheless also addressed the issue of corporatist representation. It read:

> The State bestows powers and responsibilities on associations. It also grants professional and economic corporations the right to vote in elections to the National Technical Councils.
>
> It therefore follows that the powers and duties currently assigned to the Parliament must be restricted. Under the Parliament's sway come all problems of the individual as a citizen of the State, and of the State as an organ whose purpose consists in realizing and protecting the supreme national interest. Under the National Technical Councils' sway come all problems involving the activities undertaken by individuals as producers [...].
>
> The rise of corporations is a historical fact that Fascism cannot oppose. It aims at coordinating corporative development in the pursuit of national objectives.[47]

In referring to trade union organisations as "corporations", the document sought to stress their conciliatory character and to mark a clear break with conflictual, class-based trade unionism. The name which Fascist trade unions chose for their confederal structure in January 1922 was precisely National Confederation of Trade Union Corporations (*Confederazione nazionale delle corporazioni sindacali*). The confusion which ensued was only cleared up a few years later when the term "corporations" was reserved for public bodies for labour arbitration and the representation of workers and employers.

On the whole, the PNF's programme offered very vague and indefinite ideas and guidelines. It did little more than lay out some generic aims, such as the abolishment of class conflict, the extension of the trade unions' functions, and a radical reform of representation, which was no longer to be based on the citizen but rather on the producer. It took some time, however, for the issue of corporatism to be developed in all its theoretical and practical implications and to acquire a less ambiguous outline.

Notes

1 Charles S. Maier, "Leviathan 2.0", in *A World Connecting. 1870–1945*, ed. Emily S. Rosenberg (Cambridge-London: Belknap Press, 2012), 38.
2 See, among others, Charles Benoist, *La Crise de l'Etat moderne. De l'organisation du suffrage universel* (Paris: Firmin-Didot, 1897); Charles François, *La représentation des intérêts dans les corps élus* (Paris: Rousseau, 1899); and Léon Duguit, *Le droit social, le droit individuel et les transformations de l'Etat* (Paris: Félix Alcan 1908).
3 Max Weber, *Wirtschaft und Gesellschaft* (Tübingen: Mohr, 1922); and Hans Kelsen, *Das Problem des Parlamentarismus*, (Wien-Leipzig: Braumüller, 1924).
4 Sabino Cassese, Bruno Dente, "Una discussione del primo ventennio del secolo: lo Stato sindacale", *Quaderni storici* 6, no. 18 (1971): 943–961.
5 Santi Romano, *Lo Stato moderno e la sua crisi. Saggi di diritto costituzionale* (Milano: Giuffré, 1969), 23. Unless otherwise noted, all translations of Italian texts are my own.
6 Matteo Pasetti, *L'Europa corporativa. Una storia transnazionale tra le due guerre mondiali* (Bologna: Bononia University Press, 2016), 45.
7 Paul Misner, *Social Catholicism in Europe: From the Onset of Industrialization to the First World War* (London: Darton, Longman and Todd, 1991).
8 John Pollard, "Corporatism and Political Catholicism. The Impact of Catholic Corporatism in Inter-War Europe", in *Corporatism and Fascism. The Corporatist Wave in Europe*, ed. Antonio Costa Pinto (London-New York: Routledge, 2017), 42–59.
9 Stefano Solari, "The Corporative Third Way in Social Catholicism (1830 to 1918)", *European Journal of the History of Economic Thought* 17, no. 1 (2010): 87–113.
10 *L'Action française: culture, société, politique*, eds. Michel Leymarie, Jacques Prévotat, (Villeneuve d'Ascq: Presses universitaires du Septentrion, 2008).
11 *L'Action française et l'étranger. Usages, réseaux et représentations de la droite nationaliste française*, eds. Catherine Pomeyrols, Claude Hauser (Paris: L'Harmattan, 2001).
12 Hipólito Raposo, *Dois nacionalismo, Action e o Integralismo lusitano* (Lisboa: Ferin, 1929); António Costa Pinto, "A formação do integralismo lusitano (1907–17)", *Análise Social* 18, no. 72/74 (1982): 1409–1419; António Paulo Dias Oliveira, "Leão Ramos Ascensão e o Integralismo Lusitano", *Cultura*, 2 (2012), url: http://journals.openedition.org/cultura/1154 (accessed on 19 July 2023).
13 António Sardinha, *A prol do Comun. Doutrina&Historia* (Lisboa: Ferin, 1934), 238. See Daniele Serapiglia, *La via portoghese al corporativismo* (Roma: Carocci, 2011).
14 Miguel Ángel Perfecto, "La derecha radical española y el pensamiento antiliberal francés en el primer tercio del siglo XX. De Charles Maurras a Georges Valois", *Studia historica. Historia contemporánea*, 30 (2012): 47–94.
15 Alan Kramer, *Dynamic of Destruction: Culture and Mass Killing in the First World War* (Oxford: Oxford University Press, 2007), 331.
16 Konrad H. Jarausch, *Out of Ashes. A New History of Europe in the Twentieth Century* (Princeton-Oxford: Princeton University Press, 2015), 90–94.
17 *State, Society and Mobilization in Europe during the First World War*, ed. John Horne (Cambridge: Cambridge University Press, 1997); Lawrence Sondhaus, *World War One: The Global Revolution* (Cambridge: Cambridge University Press, 2011), 333–366.

18 Jay Winter, "L'effort de guerre", in *Encyclopédie de la Grande Guerre. 1914–1918. Histoire et culture*, eds. Stéphane Audoin-Rouzeau and Jean-Jacques Becker (Bayard: Paris, 2004), 409–420; Barry Supple, "War Economies", in *The Cambridge History of the First World War*, ed. Jay Winter (Cambridge: Cambridge University Press, 2014), 295–324.

19 Alfredo Salsano, "Georges Valois e lo Stato tecnico. Il corporativismo tecnocratico tra fascismo e antifascismo*", Studi storici* 34, no. 2–3 (1993): 571–624; Allen Douglas, *From Fascism to Libertarian Communism. Georges Valois against the Third Republic* (Berkeley: University of California Press, 1992). Significant contributions to the study of Valois have been provided by the following works by Zeev Sternhell, which have been the focus of heated debates: *Neither Right nor Left: Fascist Ideology in France* (Princeton-Chichester: Princeton University Press, 1986); *The Birth of Fascist Ideology*, with Mario Sznajder and Maia Asheri (Princeton-Chichester: Princeton University Press, 1989).

20 George Valois, *L'économie nouvelle* (Paris: Nouvelle librairie nationale, 1919).

21 Christine Bouneau, *Hubert Lagardelle, un bourgeois révolutionnaire et son époque (1874–1958)* (Saint-Pierre-du-Mont: Eurédit, 2000); Michael B. Loughlin, "Gustave Hervé's Transition from Socialism to National Socialism: Another Example of French Fascism?", *Journal of Contemporary History* 36, no. 1 (2001): 5–39; Michael B. Loughlin, "Gustave Hervé's Transition from Socialism to National Socialism: Continuity and Ambivalence", *Journal of Contemporary History* 38, no. 4 (2003): 515–538.

22 On guild socialism: Anthony W Wright, "Guild Socialism Revisited" *Journal of Contemporary History* 9, no. 1 (1974): 165–180; Anthony W. Wright, "Fabianism and Guild Socialism: Two Views of Democracy", *International Review of Social History* 23, no. 2 (1978): 224–241; Geoffrey Foote, *The Labour Party's Political Thought: A History* (New York: St. Martin's Press, 1997), 82–182; Valerio Torreggiani, "Decentralizing Political Powers: G.D.H. Cole and Guild Socialism Reaction Against the State, 1910–1920", in *The First World War: Analysis and Interpretation*, eds. Antonello Biagini and Giovanna Motta, vol. 2 (Newcastle: Cambridge Publishing Scholars, 2015), 239–252; Mariuccia Salvati, *Camillo Pellizzi. Un intellettuale nell'Europa del Novecento* (Bologna: Il Mulino, 2021), 163–172.

23 George Douglas Howard Cole, *Lecture on Guild Socialism*, 7 November 1919, quoted in Valerio Torreggiani, *Stato e culture corporative nel Regno Unito. Progetti per una rappresentanza degli interessi economici nella riflessione inglese della prima metà del XX secolo* (Milano: Giuffrè, 2018), 121.

24 George Douglas Howard Cole, *Social Theory* (London: Methuen & Co., 1920), 31. See Carlos Eduardo Suprinyak, "Pluralism and Political Economy in Interwar Britain: G. D. H. Cole on Economic Planning", in *Political Economy and International Order in Interwar Europe*, eds. Alexandre M. Cunha and Carlos Eduardo Suprinyak (Cham: Palgrave Macmillan, 2021), 249–267.

25 The main reference study is still the classic work by Charles S. Maier, *Recasting Bourgeois Europe. Stabilization in France, Germany, and Italy in the Decade after World War I* (Princeton: Princeton University Press, 1975).

26 Pasetti, *L'Europa corporativa*, 85.

27 Nathan Marcus, Stefan Nikolić, Tobias Straumann, "Economic Policy, 1918–1939", in *The Economic History of Central, East and South-East Europe 1800 to the Present*, ed. Matthias Morys (London-New York: Routledge, 2021), 190.

28 Detlev J.K. Peukert, *The Weimar Republic. The Crisis of Classical Modernity* (New York: Hill and Wang, 1987), 110.

29 *ILO Constitution*, 1919, in http://ilo.org/dyn/normlex/en/f?p=1000:62:0::NO:62:P62_LIST_ENTRIE_ID:2453907:NO (last accessed on 19 July 2023).

30 On the ILO as a response to the threat of the Bolshevik revolution, see Robert W. Cox, "Labor and Hegemony", *International Organization* 31, no. 3 (1977): 387.

31 Valerio Torreggiani, "Pluralism, Tripartism and the Foundation of the International Labour Organization", *Political Economy and International*, eds. Alexandre M. Cunha and Carlos Eduardo Suprinyak, 218.

32 Daniel Maul, *The International Labour Organization. 100 Years of Global Social Policy* (Berlin-Geneva: de Gruyter-International Labour Office, 2019), 43.
33 Gustavo Gozzi, *Modelli politici e questione sociale in Italia e Germania fra Otto e Novecento* (Bologna: Il Mulino, 1988), 256.
34 Law no. 246, 29 June 1902.
35 Attilio Cabiati, "I primi mesi di vita dell'ufficio del lavoro governativo", *La Riforma sociale* 11, no. 14 (1904): 50.
36 Charles S. Maier, "'Fictitious Bonds ... of Wealth and Law': On the Theory and Practice of Interest Representation", in *Organizing Interests in Western Europe*, ed. Suzanne Berger (New York: Cambridge University Press, 1981), 27–61.
37 Gozzi, *Modelli politici e questione sociale*, 256.
38 Mauro Marsella, "Enrico Corradini's Italian Nationalism: The 'Right Wing' of the Fascist Synthesis", *Journal of Political Ideologies* 9, no. 2 (2004): 203–224; Erminio Fonzo, *Storia dell'Associazione nazionalista italiana (1910–1923)* (Napoli: Edizioni scientifiche italiane, 2017).
39 Paolo Ungari, *Alfredo Rocco e l'ideologia giuridica del fascismo* (Brescia: Morcelliana, 1963), 32–42.
40 Giuseppe Berta, *Il governo degli interessi. Industriali, rappresentanza e politica nell'Italia del Nordovest 1906–1924* (Venezia: Marsilio, 1996).
41 Silvio Lanaro, *Nazione e lavoro. Saggio sulla cultura borghese in Italia 1870–1925* (Venezia: Marsilio, 1979), 176.
42 Adriana Lay, Maria Luisa Pesante, *Produttori senza democrazia. Lotte operaie, ideologie corporative e sviluppo economico da Giolitti al fascismo* (Bologna: Il Mulino, 1981), 258–259.
43 Emilio Gentile, *"La nostra sfida alle stelle". Futuristi in politica* (Roma-Bari: Laterza, 2009), 60.
44 Maddalena Carli, *Nazione e rivoluzione. Il "Socialismo nazionale" in Italia: mitologia di un discorso rivoluzionario* (Milano: Unicopli, 2000); Matteo Pasetti, *Tra classe e nazione. Rappresentazioni e organizzazione del movimento nazional-sindacalista (1918–1922)* (Roma: Carocci, 2008).
45 Giorgio Vecchio, ed., *Il Consiglio superiore del lavoro (1903–1923)* (Milano: Franco Angeli, 1988).
46 "Platform of the Fasci di Combattimento (1919)", in *A Primer of Italian Fascism*, ed. Jeffrey T. Schnapp (Lincoln-London: University of Nebraska Press, 2000), 3.
47 "Program of the National Fascist Party (1921)", Ibid., 11.

2 Syndicalist Authoritarianism

In the years immediately following the First World War, the wide circulation of corporativist ideas and theories throughout Europe was not matched by significant institutional reforms and achievements. As we have seen, administrative procedures and new institutional bodies based on mediation between the state and social representations spread, but there was nothing to even remotely suggest a systematic restructuring of the system of representation and the relationship between the state and the economy.

In fact, two immediate attempts were made in this direction. The first took place in Portugal even before the end of the war. There, in December 1917, a coup brought the military to power under the leadership of Sidónio Pais. The declared aim of the coupists was to put an end to political instability in the country, where parties had indeed long displayed high rates of conflict and weak governments followed one after another. Instead of creating the conditions for greater cooperation between political forces, Portugal's entry into the First World War in March 1916 had exacerbated the instability and contrasts. For these reasons, the coup targeted the 1911 Republican Constitution, which was deemed incapable of guaranteeing a strong government. Sidónio Pais' goal was therefore to implement a presidentialist turn that would reduce democratic dialectics. Elected by plebiscite as head of state in April 1918, he proceeded to transform the institutional and political system: on the one hand, he eliminated the traditional political parties and created a one-party regime centred on the Partido Nacional Republicano; on the other, he gave rise to a personalistic style of leadership (not least by combining the figures of the President of the Republic and the head of government) and forms of charismatic control of the masses. Among his various initiatives was the constitutional reform of parliament, with the creation of a partly corporative chamber.

The March 1918 reform established – alongside the Chamber of Deputies, elected by universal male suffrage – a Senate formed by mixed regional and professional representatives. 28 of the 77 senators came from professional categories: they were designated by legally recognised representative organisations, for all major sectors of the economy. As has been noted, "this partially corporative senate constituted the first case in Europe of a national institutional assembly through which representatives of socio-professional groups could take legislative initiatives".[1] Unlike what would happen a decade later with Salazar's *Estado Novo*,

DOI: 10.4324/9781032713267-3

when a corporative chamber was created with mainly consultative powers, with Sidónio Pais "the representatives of the socio-professional groups that made up the new Senate could take legislative initiatives [...]. Thus, the right of 'living forces' to have a say was established within one of the three powers that made up the triangle of the modern State's political architecture".[2] The Portuguese experiment was short-lived, however. In the last months of 1918, in order to face the growing social protests and opposition to the war, Sidónio Pais decreed a state of emergency, suspending regular parliamentary sessions. At the end of the year, the Portuguese president, who had already escaped an assassination attempt, was killed. The country thus plunged into a brief civil war between monarchists and republicans, which was followed by a long phase of political instability marked by party fragmentation, vast waves of protests and riots, popular uprisings, and growing discontent in the army. In this context, the reform of 1918 remained without any follow-up and the corporatist experiment did not continue any further.

The second attempt to establish a corporatist constitution was made a couple of years later in Fiume (the current city of Rijeka), a city disputed between the Italians and Croats. The city had belonged to the Austro-Hungarian Empire until the First World War, but the majority of the inhabitants were Italian. After the war, the Kingdom of Italy claimed its annexation on the grounds of the principle of nationality. The claim met with opposition from the Allies, however, particularly US President Woodrow Wilson, who considered it preferable to assign the city to the newly formed Kingdom of Serbs, Croats, and Slovenes. Among large swathes of bourgeois public opinion, this position triggered a certain tension with the Italian government and aroused a feeling of hostility towards Italy's former allies and towards the Italian ruling class itself, which was deemed incapable of protecting national interests. In September 1919, rebel units of the Italian army, together with groups of volunteers under the command of the poet, writer, and politician Gabriele D'Annunzio, decided to force the situation and occupied Fiume, which was then under international control, proclaiming its annexation to Italy.

After almost a year, D'Annunzio put an end to the provisional municipal government and sought to create a state institution. To this end, he entrusted one of the leading exponents of Italian revolutionary syndicalism who had arrived in Fiume, Alceste De Ambris, with drafting a constitution for what was to become a new state, the Regency of Carnaro. De Ambris saw this as an opportunity for him to "fulfil his dream: a completely new State, with a syndicalist-corporativist basis, that might serve as a model and stimulus for the creation of a new order in Italy as well".[3] This constitution had a libertarian and secular character and outlined an institutional model based on administrative decentralisation. Legislative powers were divided between two chambers, the "Council of the Best" (*Consiglio degli ottimi*) and the "Council of Corporations" (*Consiglio dei provvisori*): the former was elected by universal suffrage according to the proportional system, while the latter was composed on a professional basis, by the members of the ten legally recognised guilds into which the working population was divided (by function and productive sector). No less than four articles, out of a total of 65, were devoted to the guilds' composition and tasks. According to De Ambris' intentions, the new state was to have a strongly productivist inspiration: the leading role would be played by "assiduous producers of shared wealth", while private property was recognised, but only by virtue of its "social functions".

The constitutional experiment failed to become a reality. A few months later, around Christmas Day, Italian troops attacked Fiume and put an end to the occupation. The corporate constitution was therefore no "more than scraps of paper".[4] That document nevertheless enjoyed significant circulation, cutting across the various political and cultural currents. Conceived at first as a means of putting pressure on the government, the Fiume adventure lasted 15 months and turned into an unprecedented political experience. It would be wrong to see the occupation of Fiume as an anticipation of Fascism or of subsequent authoritarian experiences. The most diverse characters converged on the city: soldiers and politicians seeking their fortune, and nationalists, but also socialists, trade unionists, subversives, and exiles from different countries. The corporative constitution was also completely irreducible to conventional schemes: "its corporatism of Mazzini-syndicalist inspiration has very little to do with either Catholic corporatism or the future Fascist corporatism. It envisages a producers' State, in which private property does not acquire absolute value, but is justified in relation to its social utility".[5] Although the Fiume adventure turned out to be an unrealistic and ephemeral experience, the Carnaro Charter caused corporatist ideas to circulate even in environments where they had been rather marginal. And although its inspiration was far removed from the authoritarianism and state cult of Fascism, the Charter was to become an ideal point of reference, a sort of mythical precedent for corporatists linked to the regime during the dictatorship.

In Portugal and Fiume, attempts were made for the first time to introduce corporatism into the constitutional framework. Apart from these two cases, "no corporatist parliament was provided for in any of the new constitutions (more than 20, according to the French-Russian jurist Boris Mirkine-Guetzevitch)".[6] These two experiments, however, were short-lived and involved what were peripheral and marginal contexts within the broader European picture. It was not until Benito Mussolini and the National Fascist Party came to power in Italy that corporatism gradually came to be perceived not as a vague idea but as a concrete political project undertaken in one of the most important European countries.

Mussolini took office as head of government at the end of October 1922. In their first three years in power, the Fascists were faced with two converging needs: on the one hand, in the short term, they had to deal with the anti-Fascist trade unions' opposition, put a stop to social conflict, and overcome the internal tensions within the Fascist trade unions; on the other, in view of the long term they set out to create a new state and a new model of social organisation, consistent with what they had declared and theorised up until that point.

As far as the first objective was concerned, Mussolini and his men aimed to curtail the non-Fascist trade unions' actions, ultimately depriving them of all leeway, and to create conditions that might allow the Confederation of Trade Union Corporations (i.e. the union of Fascist trade unions), led by Edmondo Rossoni, to acquire a monopoly on workers' representation. The first significant step in that direction was taken with the Palazzo Chigi pact, signed on 19 December 1923 by the Rossoni's confederation and the General Confederation of Italian Industry (*Confederazione generale dell'industria italiana*, generally called *Confindustria*). The two organisations affirmed that they identified with the government's directives, which had indicated the "unanimous will to work of industrial managers, technicians, and workers as the surest means to increase the welfare of all classes and the Nation's prosperity". They consequently undertook to intensify the work of organising industrialists and workers, respectively, "in view of mutual collaboration".[7]

As far as the long-term goal was concerned, the Fascist leadership immediately sought to design a constitutional reform that would create the corporatist state. A number of commissions and working groups were set up between 1923 and 1925. In November 1923, the national technical councils were established by decision of the PNF. Headed by Carlo Costamagna, the technical councils drew up a number of very general proposals, ranging from the legal recognition of trade unions to the creation of a corporative chamber, elected "by representing the bodies and institutes concerned" and which was to be put in charge of "matters of company and professional interest". The new chamber was to stand alongside the Chamber of Deputies – to be elected by universal suffrage – and the Senate, which would perform an unspecified liaising function.[8] Costamagna's proposal, however, displeased almost everyone: the supporters of a "corporative revolution" because of its failure to abolish political representation; liberal supporters because of its alteration of the existing constitutional system; the Fascist trade unionists because it rejected one of the guiding principles of Rossoni's confederation at the time, namely that of "integral syndicalism", which envisaged a single organisation for workers and employers; and the National Fascist Party and Mussolini himself, because of the lukewarm and ambiguous nature of the innovations suggested.

In the summer of 1924, in the midst of the Matteotti crisis, more comprehensive and resolute attempts were made. On 4 September, Mussolini set up a commission of 15 members based on nominations by the PNF directorate: five senators (Giovanni Gentile, Enrico Corradini, Matteo Mazziotti, Nicolò Melodia, and Emanuele Greppi), five deputies (Gioacchino Volpe, Fulvio Suvich, Edmondo Rossoni, Pier Francesco Leicht, and Agostino Lanzillo), and five scholars (Francesco Ercole, Santi Romano, Alfredo Rocco, Silvio Longhi, and Angelo Oliviero Olivetti). The board was thus composed entirely of Fascists or pro-Fascists, with no concession to pluralism. The commission had no official character. Indeed, it was an initiative of the National Fascist Party rather than of the government. Mussolini assigned the "Solons" – as the press dubbed the commission's members – the task of renewing, not subverting, the Albertine Statute.[9] In the inaugural session's opening address, Giovanni Gentile – the leading board member – openly recalled the importance of the corporatist theme of the reconciliation of interests, although the formulas he used remained hazy and generic: "It is up to Fascism", he argued in that context, "and it will be up to us, to inform the organs designed to reconcile the trade unions' particular interests with the general interests and thus with the supreme power of the State; this kind of reconciliation pacifies the social classes through debate and the legal resolution of all conflicts, and continually reinforces the strength of the

State".[10] The commission achieved no concrete results and was dissolved a few months later. Among the suggestions it formulated in the short time it had at its disposal was to reform the Chamber of Deputies by reserving one-third of the seats for the representatives of the economic interests. Furthermore, the "Solons" proposed a reform of the trade unions which would not have entailed the repealing of freedom of association but rather the official recognition of unions, except for those not aligned with the dominant policies.[11] In place of the commission "of the fifteen", in late January 1925, a commission "of the eighteen" was appointed, again chaired by Gentile. This was no longer an initiative of the National Fascist Party, but of the government, although the distinction was now beginning to lose its meaning. The changes in terms of composition were quite small: Silvio Longhi left and economist Gino Arias, state councillor Domenico Barone, journalist Francesco Coppola, and statistician Corrado Gini joined the group.[12] What changed profoundly was the context in which the new assembly found itself operating. The transition to an explicit dictatorship, sanctioned by Mussolini's speech on 3 January 1925, made any attempt to reassure the moderate public and to stress the Fascists' alleged loyalty to the constitution superfluous.

The very objectives of this commission, however, appeared unclear. Its members all came from the Fascist ranks or from pro-Fascist forces but had different cultural backgrounds and political origins: on the one hand, the moderates continued to view the constitutional reform as a "respectful" conservative revision of the Statute; on the other, the radicals aimed to subvert the constitutional balance and create a new state.[13]

For the "eighteen" as well, the issue of trade unions and the corporative system was the decisive point. In the report addressed to Mussolini upon completion of the commission's work, Gentile maintained that "the Corporative Order is truly the most innovative idea among those that have emerged through the Commission's studies and debates". The corporatist idea was "the only one that could indicate a way to effectively contain national productive forces within the circle of State action".[14] With regard to trade unions, the "eighteen" essentially limited themselves to reiterating the conclusions reached by the "fifteen": the principle of the trade unions' legal recognition was accepted – although this was only to be granted to organisations operating within the framework of "national life" and was not to be bound to international parties – but not the idea of having a single trade union for each category. This outcome was thus another defeat for Fascist trade unionism, which aimed at achieving a monopoly on representation.

With regard to the issue of corporate representation, the discussion proved even less conclusive. Gentile's final report explicitly mentioned the difficulties and divisions: "It was therefore natural for [corporatism] to arouse doubts, perplexities, concerns, and objections even within the Commission itself. The very proponents or supporters of this idea thought about it at length before embracing it. Some of its most confident and ardent proponents and developers were radically critical of and opposed to it at first".[15] Although all members of the commission were in favour of a corporatist-based reform of representation, there were deep disagreements on how to implement it. At the conclusion of the proceedings in July, three different reports were therefore submitted. The majority report, drafted by Gino Arias, with the decisive contribution of Angelo Oliviero Olivetti, proposed that half of the chamber should be elected by the corporative bodies, while the territorial criterion should remain in force for the other half.[16] A second report, presented by Coppola, Melodia, Mazziotti, and Suvich, accused the first of reflecting "a materialistic conception, far more akin to that of socialism than that of Fascism", and thus rejected the idea that trade unions and professional bodies – regarded as pertaining exclusively to the technical field – could participate in state sovereignty and politics.[17] Finally, the third report, signed by Corrado Gini, was in favour of including corporative representatives in the Senate rather than in the chamber on the basis of a rigidly hierarchical and census-based criterion according to which each organisation would have a different weight, proportional to its importance in the life of the state.[18]

The proceedings were followed with great interest by the press and gave rise, before their conclusion and in the weeks that followed, to lively controversy.[19] At the session of 8 October, the Grand Council of Fascism considered the proposals put forward by the "eighteen" and accepted Gini's theses according to a more extensive formulation than the original one, which envisaged making the Senate elective through the votes of corporations.[20] However, this decision was not followed up and the commission's proposals were never implemented. Fascism was to struggle with the issue of corporatist representation for almost its entire existence. In 1928 it carried out a complete overhaul of the electoral system that could only be described as corporatist to a small degree (it entailed the elimination of elections, the introduction of plebiscites, and the involvement of trade unions and employers' organisations in the appointment of deputies). The government only solved the issue for good at the end of 1939, with the transformation of the Chamber of Deputies into the Chamber of Fasces and Corporations.

Even as far as trade unions were concerned, the "eighteen's" proposals remained completely unimplemented. Compared to the first two and a half years of Fascist rule, however, the idea of limiting the pluralism of trade unions and granting Fascist organisations a kind of monopoly met with increasing approval. These positions were further reinforced in mid-1925 by the resurgence of workers' unrest, which was due both to economic difficulties and inflation and to the attempts made by various anti-Fascist forces to fuel the opposition movement by advancing certain demands.

The far from pacified social situation, even in the midst of the political stabilisation that followed the 3 January speech, prompted Mussolini to try to solve the trade union question once and for all. Thus, on 2 October, at Palazzo Vidoni, the PNF's headquarters, a pact was signed between the representatives of the *Confindustria* and those of the Confederation of Fascist Corporations whereby each of the two confederations recognised the other's exclusive representation for the stipulation of contracts for employers and workers, respectively. The agreement had major consequences, especially for workers. The confederation of industrialists was already the employers' sole representative, while the Fascist corporations (as the workers' trade unions were called at that stage) had until then shared worker representation with non-Fascist organisations. The latter were thus deprived of any room for action. In this way, a decisive step was taken in the dismantling of trade union freedom, an objective which Fascism had been pursuing from its inception.

The Palazzo Vidoni pact also established the abolition of internal commissions, which were the workers' representative bodies within companies. The Fascist trade unions obtained a monopoly on representation but at the considerable cost of losing any possibility of direct intervention or initiative in the workplace. In this way a strongly authoritarian model of enterprise was affirmed, characterised by a rigid internal hierarchy and by the impossibility for workers to make claims or verify the implementation of any agreements made.

The Palazzo Vidoni pact marked a significant turning point. It delivered a decisive blow to the previous commissions' lukewarm and contradictory proposals, which had not challenged the principle of trade union pluralism; even Gentile, who had directed both the "fifteen"-member commission and the "eighteen"-member one, lost his prominent role. The promotion of state reform was then taken up by Alfredo Rocco, who was appointed Minister of Justice at the beginning of 1925. Rocco gave a strong impetus to the construction of the corporative system, starting precisely with the trade union system. The Minister of Justice tried to implement the theoretical model that he had developed over the course of the previous years, and expounded on countless occasions.

Rocco's corporatist doctrine was characterised by the absolute primacy assigned to the state. It differed profoundly from the Catholic corporative theories of, which were instead designed to safeguard the autonomy of the productive classes and categories against the power of the centralised state. Absolute statism was Rocco's true lodestar. It was to the state, and not to the people, that Rocco assigned sovereignty: individual liberties were not considered a pre-existing right of the individual but the result of a sort of "self-limitation" by the state.[21] Rocco developed his corporate doctrine very early on. Its general outline was already sketched out in his writings from the immediate post-war period.[22] His conception stemmed from a radical rejection of both liberalism and socialism, which were considered to be mirror manifestations of individualism.[23] The goal of the state was to achieve maximum social cohesion through a legal framework, and it could only be achieved by that particular form of state that was the Fascist one. Rocco wrote:

> The Fascist State is that State which achieves the juridical organisation of Society with the utmost degree of power and cohesion. And society, according to the Fascist conception, is not a mere sum of individuals, but an organism that has its own life and ends, transcending those of individuals, and a spiritual and historical value. For Fascism, even the State, which represents the legal organisation of society, is an organism distinct from the citizens, who at each moment are part of it. The State has its own life and its own ends, superior to those of individuals, to which the ends of individuals must be subordinate.[24]

This model of an authoritarian state clearly could not brook social conflict or even the presence of free trade unions. For Rocco, however, the solution did not lie in the suppression of the trade union movement but rather – as he had argued a few years before the March on Rome – in its regimentation. The trade union was a "great phenomenon of modern life" that had become inexorable and had to be judged on its own merits and not on the basis of its "degeneration". The causes of this degeneration were identified in the state's "passiveness", stemming from liberal preconceptions. The state therefore needed to behave towards trade unions as it had behaved towards medieval guilds: it needed to absorb them and turn them into its own organs.[25] Above all, however, trade unions were to be transformed from instruments of struggle for particularistic interests into a means of collaboration for the pursuit of the general welfare. To this end – as Rocco had already argued in the *Programma politico dell'associazione nazionalista* (Political Programme of the Nationalist Association) in 1919 – workers' unions and industrialists' unions were to come together into corporations "to safeguard common interests, settle disputes, and find counterbalances that satisfy not only the particular interests of the productive classes, but the general interests in terms of production".[26] Corporatism was therefore the legal and institutional system capable of ensuring the subordination of economic and social subjects to the national interests embodied by the state. Only corporations would make it possible to perfect the production process in the best possible way and avoid "useless internal competition, in order to face the struggles of world competition in conditions of maximum economic efficiency".[27] Rocco's corporatist doctrine brought together different aims and themes that cannot simply be dismissed as the wishful yearning for a medieval order or the restoration of the *ancien régime*. The denial of liberties and the elimination of social dialectics were accompanied by a modern and dynamic view of capitalism. On the one hand, Rocco openly assigned positive value to the rigid, hierarchical ordering of society: "The prevailing of the interests of the most powerful and best organised classes is a necessary social phenomenon", he wrote in *Principi di diritto commerciale* (Principles of Commercial Law) in 1928.[28] On the other, this cult of hierarchy was combined with "his immanent tendency to reshape the entire social body according to the structure of the great industrial empires that were progressively subjugating the masses".[29] The Cult of the state and "cartel rationalisation" were thus the two elements underlying Rocco's conception of corporatism. This much makes it clear that Rocco – like the vast majority of corporatist theorists – envisaged the "third way" as an alternative not to capitalism but to liberalism. Indeed, corporatism and "Fascist economics" were based on state supervision and control as much as on the competence and interests of the productive classes, according to the principle that "the productive classes do not govern themselves, they govern production, which is also in their interest, but above all in the collective interest".[30] On the contrary, the masses were not granted any autonomy or right to participate in political leadership: "the masses are eternal children", Rocco wrote in 1914.[31] Corporations were thus to serve as an instrument to integrate the masses into the state under conditions of passivity and total subordination.

Following these convictions, in the second half of 1925, Rocco took up the dossier on corporative reform. Realising that the restructuring of the system of representation was still too thorny an issue, he provisionally decided to set it aside and instead tackle the problem of the trade union system. Launched between August and September, his initiative took off in October. After a pronouncement by the Grand Council of Fascism, which called for the elimination of trade union pluralism and the right to strike, at the end of the month, Rocco presented the chamber with a bill on the legal regulation of collective labour relations, which was finally approved on 3 April 1926.[32] This law, together with two implementing decrees approved in July, established the basic principles of the Fascist syndical system:

a *The monopoly of representation.* The principle of the legal recognition of employers' and workers' associations was adopted to be granted only to associations that could "give proof of capacity, morality, and unswerving national loyalty". These associations were intended not only to protect their members' economic interests but also to provide assistance, training, and a "moral and national education". Their members had to give proof of good political conduct, and the appointment of leaders was subject to the approval of the Minister of Corporations and the Minister of the Interior. Moreover, in order to obtain recognition the associations needed the support of at least one-tenth of the workers in their sector, or of companies employing at least one-tenth of the workers. Legal recognition could only be granted to one association per category. In this way, a de facto monopoly of representation was assigned to Fascist trade unions. Even if the vast majority of workers had remained loyal to the non-Fascist trade unions, it would still have been possible to find a Fascist trade union with a sufficient number of members;
b *Collective contracts.* Legally recognised trade unions acquired the right to represent all employers, workers, or artists and professionals in the category for which they had been established, and in the territory in which they were operating, regardless of membership. Consequently, recognised trade unions could sign collective contracts valid *erga omnes*, i.e. applicable to all employers and employees within the categories to which the agreement referred;
c *Conflict control.* Strikes and lock-outs were banned and, as a result, organisations were deprived of their main and most effective means of struggle;
d *Delegation to the judiciary.* A labour magistracy was established that was in charge of resolving all disputes relating to the regulation of labour relations;
e *Corporate bodies.* Opposing representatives from each sector were to meet in "liaison bodies". The implementation decree of 1 July identified these organs as corporations; that is, state bodies tasked with reconciling disputes and promoting and coordinating production. By distinguishing between trade unions (representing specific and partisan interests) and corporations (public bodies expressing different interests), the law clarified the terminological ambiguities of previous years, mainly due to Rossoni's confederation. A second decree, on 2 July, introduced the National Council of Corporations. Endowed only with

advisory powers, it was composed of several ministers, representatives of workers' and employers' organisations, and leaders of Fascist institutions;

f *A new ministry*. The trade union system was completed with a second decree, dated 2 July, by which the Ministry of Corporations was established, entrusted with all functions in the trade union field.

The whole method of the trade union organisations' operations was immediately revolutionised and subordinated to the principles and aims of the Fascist state. The corporations, on the other hand, would take a long time to come into effect: the National Council of Corporations only came into being in 1930, at the very start of Fascist corporatism, while the creation of corporations would have to wait almost eight years.

A series of rights painstakingly acquired by workers in previous decades were erased through the Rocco Law of 1926. Fascism blocked trade union dialectics once and for all and achieved solid and pervasive control over labour relations and society as a whole. In the wake of the Palazzo Vidoni pact, this was certainly a response to the social unrest of those months, which had arisen in reaction to the rise in unemployment and the worsening living conditions of the broad masses produced by the deflationary "quota 90" policy. At the same time, it was a way of making a substantial concession to the industrialists' interests, who, in several cases, had been penalised precisely by the lira's excessive revaluation.[33] However, the new order did not arise merely as a consequence of contingent circumstances. On the contrary, it represented the consistent translation of the construction of the "bare-faced dictatorship" into trade union territory.[34] The suppression of political and associative freedoms, which was implemented in those very months, made it impossible to continue to guarantee trade union pluralism and the presence of legal and legitimate forms of social conflict. This is also shown by the general consensus that accompanied the passing of the law within Fascism and the state's upper echelons – but also in the Catholic world and among pro-Fascist liberals – notwithstanding a few unavoidable and isolated exceptions.[35] "Taken as a whole, the *legge Rocco* received widespread approval both for the reforms it introduced and for those it avoided or fulfilled only incompletely".[36] It was "neither bluff nor revolution" and, for this reason, proved attractive to large sectors of the institutional, economic, and intellectual elites at least: it foreshadowed the construction of a "strong" state; it responded to the demand for social peace coming from the productive bourgeoisie; and it did not question social hierarchies and the property-based system, postponing more radical and "revolutionary" interventions to an indefinite future.[37]

Among the many possible approaches to the question of corporatism, the one that was adopted – at least in the initial phase – was the rigidly statist approach promoted by Rocco, the main jurist and, at that stage, the Fascist state's main ideologue. As we have seen, according to Rocco's theoretical conception, corporatism had a strongly authoritarian and, at the same time, modern character. The suppression of the class struggle and the establishment of an ordered and organic society were not to be achieved by denying the constituent elements of modern industrial societies. The state had to take note of the irrepressible presence of trade unions and consequently pursue not their abolition but their absorption into its own sphere. This conception found coherent legislative application in the new Syndicalist Law, which was not simply conceived by Rocco but actually drafted by him.[38]

Rocco regarded the 1926 law as the cornerstone of the Fascist state. He argued this clearly in one of his most important political writings, where he observed that: "the reform […] that most contributed to shaping the form of the Fascist State and the concrete social content of its measures is still that which was achieved through the law on the legal management of collective labour relations and the related legislative regulations".[39] Seen in the light of these remarks, the history of Fascist corporatism appears different from how it is generally drawn: far from being the tale of an unbridgeable and profound gap between projects and achievements, and of an unequivocal failure, it represents the concrete and full implementation of one of its possible versions. At least with reference to Rocco's interpretation of corporatism, we can speak of full congruence between the intentions professed, the theory behind them, the laws passed, and the results achieved.[40]

Rocco's legislative and political initiative reflected his theories, which – as we have seen – had already begun to take shape before the post-war period. By contrast, it was little affected by the transnational spread of corporative ideas. Rocco generally attached limited importance to intellectual engagement with overseas ideas. This is demonstrated, first of all, by the scant attention he devotes – at least explicitly – to the debate outside Italy in his writings. In the 1920s, Rocco also put little effort into fulfilling his institutional obligations as a member of supranational organisations. Appointed in 1926 to represent Italy at the International Committee on Intellectual Cooperation, based in Paris, Rocco appointed a replacement for the entire year and the following one and never travelled to the French capital. The minister considered his commitments to the Italian government to be far more important than intellectual cooperation issues.[41] The situation did not change in 1928, if only to a partial extent, as Rocco was absent from more than one meeting. His presence began to become more regular from 1929, when the period of the most intense activity in the building of the new Fascist state had ended. There were several practical reasons for Rocco's attitude, such as the language barrier and the annoyance of travelling to a country, France, that he still considered hostile.[42] Above all, however, Rocco regarded domestic policy as a priority. He perceived his participation in international meetings – when he did not skip them, owing to government commitments – exclusively as a means for him to safeguard his country's most immediate interests.

According to Rocco's conception of international relations, states were organisms inevitably competing and struggling with each other. No international society or system of relations that was stable and harmonious was therefore possible.[43] The League of Nations and the international organisations that gravitated around it appeared to him to be founded on an unrealistic and anti-historical premise. In his view, participation in such assemblies could at best serve an instrumental purpose; that is, it could allow him to uphold Italian interests in an arena in which, in spite of internationalist intentions, each delegate performed a similar function for the benefit of his or her own country. What Rocco sought to uphold were Italy's national interests, and not those of Fascism, as is demonstrated by the all-too-impersonal attitude with which he presented himself at international meetings, without resorting to any explicit Fascist language.[44] Rocco's vision, and his unwillingness to commit himself on this front more than was strictly necessary, prevented him from personally promoting his achievements and corporativist project abroad.

In those years, however, much attention was paid to the figure of Rocco overseas: his theory of the state aroused considerable interest also and, above all, in its approach to trade union and corporatist matters. Some of his writings, addressing more general topics and discussing theoretical issues, were translated into other languages and circulated among European and American scholars and observers. The English version of *The Political Doctrine of Fascism*, translated in 1926, was distributed in thousands of copies and enjoyed significant circulation in the United States.[45] The attention paid to Rocco, however, was not the result of his commitment to "exporting" his theories or, more generally, his idea of authoritarian and statist corporatism. Instead, this attention reflects the importance that Rocco had acquired from the mid-1920s when he had become the main architect of the new Fascist state and corporatism.

The corporatist achievements of the 1920s were not limited to the Syndicalist Law of April 1926. As we have seen, together with the new system of regulations governing trade unions and interest organisations, the Ministry of Corporations was established. This body had very limited tasks and powers. Unlike other ministries, it did not really fulfil active administrative functions but was rather in charge of the general coordination and control of trade union associations.[46] At first, the head of the new ministry was Mussolini himself. The undersecretary was Giacomo Suardo, who in November was replaced by the younger and far more enterprising Giuseppe Bottai.

The ministry was created in order to implement the Rocco Law. In its early days, it focused on regulating and approving recognised trade unions and managing collective agreements between employers and employees. The ministry, however, soon proved to be a far more active and enterprising subject than its founding charter had envisioned. In particular, the arrival of Bottai – who became the real architect of the ministry's policy, given Mussolini's limited presence – led this institution to go beyond the tasks formally assigned to it and the severe limitations on its powers and size. The undersecretary – who would be promoted to the rank of minister in September 1929 – who was evidently supported by Mussolini, sought to make the Ministry of Corporations the driving force behind the construction of the corporative system and the renewal of the state.

The drive for innovation primarily concerned organisational aspects. Bottai attempted to make the Ministry of Corporations the "new ministry" par excellence of the Fascist state in all respects.[47] In his view, the new ministry could not "exactly be compared to any of the great State departments" and was to serve as a model for profound renewal.[48]

Particular importance was attached to the formation of its leadership group. The bureaucracy of the Ministry of Corporations was to constitute the "Fascist bureaucracy" par excellence.[49]

At least in its early days, the training and selection of the new ministry's civil servants occurred in a different way compared to other state departments: the men who were recruited shared corporatism's political aims and came from trade unions, the field of corporative studies, or the state administration. The rules established – among other things – the ministry's right to exclude from competitions anyone who was not considered to be "in line with the Ministry's special objectives", without the need to state the reasons for this exclusion.[50] Bottai brought together a team of civil servants directly interested in the implementation of corporatism. One of them was the jurist Carlo Costamagna.[51]

After the first period, however, the composition of the bureaucratic leadership ended up becoming less and less in line with its initial intentions. Bottai's advisors, chosen on the basis of their adherence to the "corporative revolution" project, mostly obtained temporary appointments, which were not always renewed in the following years. Permanent appointments were reserved, on the one hand, for officials coming from other ministerial bureaucracies or from the judiciary, and on the other for new recruits, selected through procedures that – in accordance with Italian law – continued to be based on qualifications and competences rather than on political and ideological criteria.[52] The attempt to establish a "Fascist bureaucracy" thus soon met with substantial failure. With Bottai's departure from the ministry in 1932, the plans for innovation were abandoned for good. In 1937, more than ten years after its establishment, none of the 30 directors-general, inspectors-general, and heads of division of the Ministry of Corporations had joined the state administration after 1916.[53] Seniority and the rules regulating careers were respected. The "Fascist ministry" par excellence failed to overcome bureaucratic traditions.[54]

The most radical plans for bureaucratic innovation were pushed back above all by the widespread hostility encountered from the very beginning in the rest of the public administration. The State General Accounting Office and the other ministries concerned (Finance, Interior, and National Economy) repeatedly accused the new ministry of circumventing the hierarchical order of state administrations, of setting up structures alien to ministerial traditions, and of adopting overly flexible recruitment and personnel management criteria.[55]

What fuelled the more or less direct accusations, however, was, above all, the ministry's encroachment into other fields. Bottai and the men close to him wanted to create a corporatist system that would extend beyond what had been achieved with the Syndicalist Law: a corporatism based not only on the management of labour relations but also on real management of the economy. Accordingly, the Ministry of Corporations was not to limit itself to coordinating trade union life but was to place itself at the centre of Italian economic policies. Inevitably, the other state administrations began to fear that their political space might be invaded. The Cabinet of the Interior denounced the Ministry of Corporations' tendency to arrogate to itself functions of a general nature – such as the coordination of welfare and social education initiatives or the promotion and strengthening of "national concord" – that seemed rather to be the responsibility of the head of government: the Cabinet feared that these functions might give rise to "a super-governmental body, such as the one that would actually be responsible for liaising between the

'Government' and the 'operating forces of the Nation'".[56] The most heated clash took place in 1927 with the Minister of the National Economy, Giuseppe Belluzzo, over who should have the power to intervene in industrial and production matters.[57] In this case, however, it was Bottai who prevailed. After a dispute that lasted several years, the Ministry of the National Economy was dissolved in September 1929 and its competences transferred to the Corporations, with the exception of those in the agricultural field.

After having restructured the trade union system and established the Ministry of Corporations, the Fascist leaders set to work to define more precisely and concretely the contours of the future corporative state. In particular, they set themselves the task of drafting a text that all forces within the regime could subscribe to. The result was a concise document consisting of 30 declarations: the Labour Charter (*Carta del lavoro*). Although propaganda presented it as the manifesto of corporatism and the ideological foundation of the Fascist state's social dimension, this document actually had generic and not always incisive contents. It had no normative value and never constituted an effective source of guidelines for government action. Despite this, the Labour Charter appears significant for two reasons: because of the wide political and propaganda resonance it had and because its wording reveals the state of power relations within the regime and between Fascism and the various social forces.

Renzo De Felice has accurately reconstructed the process of the Charter's formation, which took place entirely within a few months, between the end of 1926 and April 1927.[58] It all began with trade union leader Rossoni, who first launched the idea of a document setting out "the ethics and social principles of Fascism" and summarising labour legislation, and then pressured Mussolini into supporting it.[59] PNF Secretary Augusto Turati then began preliminary consultations with the leaders of the employers' and workers' confederations. He was, however, faced with opposing positions and an unwillingness to compromise. The industrialists were particularly rigid, concerned as they were that the Labour Charter could introduce excessive burdens and strengthen the trade unions' position.

It was at this point that Bottai came into play. Mussolini took the matter upon himself and delegated the Undersecretary for Corporations to draw up an initial outline. Bottai prepared a ten-point questionnaire to be submitted to all the confederations. As was to be expected, their answers reflected very different – indeed, often antithetical – conceptions and particular interests.[60] Unable to reconcile the different positions and propose a shared document, the undersecretary was forced to formulate two separate projects, one reflecting the viewpoint of Rossoni's confederation and the other that of the *Confindustria*. This is how Bottai summarised the situation to Mussolini in a letter in which he left the resolution of the matter up to the Duce: "through the Carta [Rossoni's confederation] intends to ensure *concrete* guarantees for the workers, tied to a rather overly rigid system, one that would make the *natural* development of collective contracts, conceived of as the defining institution of the syndicalist system, more difficult"; *Confindustria* instead "has tended until now to adopt an antagonistic stance towards Corporations, which are instead of crucial importance in the Fascist conception".[61] In the same letter Bottai provided some significant suggestions, which went in the opposite direction of the much-celebrated "self-government of professional categories". In his opinion, it was necessary to bear in mind "that the device of the corporative system can only partially rest on the consensus of the parties involved. Its functioning requires the decisive intervention of a political will, the action of a strong State which claims responsibility when it comes to decision-making".[62]

After an initial attempt to modify the entrepreneurs' text, Mussolini fell back on a compromise solution. The real architect of this mediation was Rocco, who – in close contact with Bottai, and probably with the collaboration of Turati and Belluzzo – drafted a third text very close to the *Confindustria*'s ideas. Rocco's text underwent some changes in its final version, designed to balance its conservative tone with some concessions to the trade unionists, whose opposition Mussolini risked facing.[63] This led to the Labour Charter's final text, which was finally approved by the Grand Council during the night of 21–22 April, together with a motion calling on the government to translate it into legislation as soon as possible.[64]

The first article of the Charter encapsulates the organicist, anti-individualist view on which corporatism was to be founded: "The Italian Nation is an organism having ends, life, and means of action superior to those of the individuals, singly or in groups, of which it is composed. It is a moral, political, and economic unity, realized wholly in the Fascist State". The social legs on which the national body was to rest were labour and private initiative. The former was regarded as a "social duty" to be protected by the state exclusively for this reason. The latter was regarded "as the most efficient and useful instrument of the Nation"; consequently, while it was recognised that an enterprise's management was the sole responsibility of its owner, entrepreneurs were declared responsible to the state for the direction of production. This was a far cry from the nationalisation of property, however. State intervention was only admitted as a supplementary measure; that is, "only where private initiative is lacking or is insufficient, or when the political interests of the State are at stake". In short, an attempt was made to reconcile Fascism's statism and anti-liberalism with the integral safeguarding of private property.

The Charter, moreover, incorporated the most important elements of the Syndicalist Law of April 1926 regarding the public recognition of trade unions, collective labour contracts, and the labour judiciary; it also reaffirmed the presence of corporations as state organs tasked with ensuring "the legal equality between employers and workers" and constituting "the unitary organizations of production", also through the issuing of compulsory rules governing labour relations and the coordination of production.

Numerous articles were devoted to labour law. In addition to setting out workers' rights and duties, they introduced the idea of the "just wage"; i.e. wages determined not only by the market but by "everyday life requirements" and work performance. The final part focused on social security and social insurance. The importance assigned to the topic was, in many respects, a novelty. As would become clear in later years, Fascism implemented "welfare policies designed to achieve broad social control over large sections of the population, to bring about processes of national integration and widespread acceptance of the regime, and to foster forms for the neutralisation of conflict and opposition".[65] The regime saw the welfare state as an instrument to achieve "a reconversion of the State towards an alternative socio-economic dimension to the liberal one".[66]

The Labour Charter was published in the *Gazzetta ufficiale*, the official collection of Italian laws. By doing so, the regime sought to give value and solemnity to the document. The Charter had no legal value, however. It was a manifesto, a kind of "white book" that set out general ideas.[67] Nevertheless, it elicited a stream of exegesis and praise that was as impressive as it was surreal: for about a decade, the Charter was constantly and obsessively evoked for the sake of propaganda and the discussion of Fascist doctrine. Despite the fact that the Charter had little actual value, the whole affair – both the preparation of the text and its final drafting – is highly revealing of the different drives within Fascism and the forces backing it. The power relations existing in society and in the regime itself did not allow the authorities at that time to go much further than what had been achieved with the Syndicalist Law.[68] It was probably because Bottai realised what fractures still permeated society, and what resistance the corporative project was encountering, that he decided to present two texts without attempting to come up with a solution that might have been more advanced in content and more effective in form. At the same time, Rocco's mediating role shows, once again, that he was the central figure in the building of the corporative state in the second half of the 1920s.

The Labour Charter sealed a series of measures deployed in the previous year (the Syndicalist Law, the Ministry of Corporations). Together, these achievements made Italy the first country to concretely move towards the realisation of corporatism. From that moment onwards, the country became a model and reference point for the rest of Europe and even other parts of the world.

Notes

1 Matteo Pasetti, *L'Europa corporativa. Una storia transnazionale tra le due guerre mondiali* (Bologna: Bononia University Press, 2016), 61–62.
2 Armando Malheiro da Silva, "Note sulla Prima repubblica (1910–26) e sulla genesi dello Stato corporativo in Portogallo", in *Progetti corporativi tra le due guerre mondiali*, ed. Matteo Pasetti (Roma: Carocci, 2006), 54.
3 Raoul Pupo, *Fiume città di passione* (Bari-Roma: Laterza, 2018), 122.
4 Dominique Kirchner Reill, *The Fiume Crisis: Life in the Wake of the Habsburg Empire* (Cambridge-London: The Belknap Press of Harvard University Press, 2020), 66.
5 Pupo, *Fiume città di passione*, 127.
6 Matteo Pasetti, "The Fascist Labour Charter and Its Transnational Spread", in *Corporatism and Fascism the Corporatist Wave in Europe*, ed. Antonio Costa Pinto (London-New York: Routledge, 2017), 63.
7 Renzo De Felice, *Mussolini il fascista. I. La conquista del potere 1921–1925* (Torino: Einaudi, 1966), 557.
8 ACS, PCM, Gab., 1924, fasc. 1.3.12.236. C. Costamagna (Deputy Secretary General for the National Technical Councils), *A. S.E il presidente del consiglio (Rapporto riservato)*, 18 December 1923; ACS, PCM, Gab., 1924, fasc. 1.3.12.236. *Il problema dei consigli tecnici nazionali. Relazione del segretariato generale per i CTN*, 10 March 1924.

9 *Il programma d'azione fascista per le riforme legislative e i limiti del compito assegnato alla Commissione dei Quindici*, "L'Idea nazionale", 9 September 1924.
10 *Gentile inizia i lavori per rinnovare la Costituzione*, "La Stampa", 29–30 October 1924.
11 Ferdinando Cordova, *Le origini dei sindacati fascisti. 1918–1926* (Roma-Bari: Laterza, 1974), 389–390.
12 Alberto Aquarone, *L'organizzazione dello Stato totalitario* (Torino: Einaudi, 1995 [1965]), 53–54.
13 Ibid., 53–60; Gianpasquale Santomassimo, *La terza via fascista. Il mito del corporativismo* (Roma: Carocci, 2006), 39–43.
14 ACS, SPD, CR, 1922–43, b. 27, fasc. 242/R "Gran Consiglio", sottofasc. 3, inserto A. G. Gentile, *A S. E. l'On. Benito Mussolini Presidente del Consiglio dei Ministri*, 5 July 1925.
15 Ibid.
16 ACS, PCM, Gab., 1931–33, fasc. 1.1.2.6163. Presidenza del consiglio, commissione per lo studio delle riforme legislative, *Relazione del Prof. Gino Arias sul problema sindacale e sull'ordinamento corporativo*, undated (but 1925); see also Perfetti, *Il sindacalismo fascista*, vol. 1 (Roma: Bonacci, 1988) 102–107.
17 ACS, SPD, CR, 1922–43, b. 27, fasc. 242/R "Gran consiglio", sottofasc. 3, inserto C. M. Mazziotti, N. Melodia, F. Suvich, F. Coppola (speaker), *Sull'ordinamento corporativo dello Stato. Relazione di minoranza*. The text of this report was never published.
18 Istituto nazionale fascista di cultura, *Relazioni e proposte della commissione per lo studio delle riforme costituzionali* (Firenze: Le Monnier, 1932), 217.
19 Aquarone, *L'organizzazione*, 54.
20 Partito nazionale fascista, *Il Gran Consiglio nei primi dieci anni* (Roma: Nuova Europa, 1933), 208–209.
21 Ibid., 45–46.
22 Giulia Simone, "L'organizzazione delle masse al servizio dello Stato. Alfredo Rocco e l'origine del corporativismo", *Clio*, 43, no. 3 (2007): 439–464; Saverio Battente, *Alfredo Rocco. Dal nazionalismo al fascismo 1907–1935* (Milano: Franco Angeli, 2005), 165–169.
23 Alfredo Rocco, "Economia liberale, economia socialista ed economia nazionale", in Alfredo Rocco, *Scritti e discorsi politici*, 1: *La lotta nazionale della vigilia e durante la guerra (1913–1918)*, foreword by B. Mussolini (Milano: Giuffrè, 1938).
24 Alfredo Rocco, "La trasformazione dello Stato", in Alfredo Rocco, *Scritti e discorsi politici*, 3: *La formazione dello stato fascista (1925–1934)* (Milano: Giuffrè, 1938), 778.
25 Alfredo Rocco, "Crisi dello stato e Sindacati", in Alfredo Rocco, *Scritti e discorsi politici*, 2: *La lotta contro la reazione antinazionale (1919–1924)* (Milano: Giuffrè, 1938), 640–641.
26 Alfredo Rocco, "Il programma politico dell'associazione nazionalista", in Rocco, *Scritti e discorsi*, 2, 479.
27 Rocco, "Il momento economico e sociale", in Ibid., 2, 586.
28 Rocco, "Principi di diritto commerciale", quoted in Santomassimo, *La terza via fascista*, 46.
29 Ungari, *Alfredo Rocco*, 27.
30 Alfredo Rocco, "Costituzioni e funzioni delle Corporazioni", in Rocco, *Scritti e discorsi*, 2, 1011.
31 Rocco, "La lezione dei fatti", in Rocco, *Scritti e discorsi*, 1, 194.
32 Adrian Lyttelton, *The Seizure of Power. Fascism in Italy 1919–1929* (London-New York: Routledge, 2004 [1973]), 266–276; Cordova, *Le origini*, 424–434; Battente, *Alfredo Rocco*, 413–425.
33 Santomassimo, *La terza via fascista*, 48.
34 Aquarone, *L'organizzazione*, 47.
35 Some echoes of this can be found in the Senate's debate on the bill. Achille Loria in particular contested the idea of a single trade union, highlighting the inconsistencies that lay behind it: APS, Legislatura XXVII, *Discussioni*, vol. IV, 4664–4665.

36 Matteo Pasetti, "Neither Bluff nor Revolution: The Corporations and the Consolidation of the Fascist Regime (1925–1926)", in *In the Society of Fascists: Acclamation, Acquiescence and Agency in Mussolini's Italy*, eds. Giulia Albanese and Roberta Pergher (New York: Palgrave Macmillan, 2012), 63.
37 Ibid.
38 Giuliano Vassalli, "Passione politica di un uomo di legge", in Alfredo Rocco, *Discorsi parlamentari* (Bologna: Il Mulino, 2005), 49.
39 Rocco, "La trasformazione dello Stato", 782.
40 Irene Stolzi, *L'ordine corporativo. Poteri organizzati e organizzazione del potere nella riflessione giuridica dell'Italia fascista* (Milano: Giuffrè, 2007), 25.
41 Giulia Simone, *Tutto nello Stato. L'itinerario politico e culturale di Alfredo Rocco*, unpublished Ph.D. thesis (Ca' Foscari University of Venice, a.y. 2009–2010), 374.
42 Simone, *Tutto nello Stato*, 379.
43 Alfredo Rocco, "La santità dei Trattati", *La Stampa*, 10 February 1932; Alfredo Rocco, "Disarmo", *La Stampa*, 21 February 1932.
44 Giuseppe Prezzolini, *L'italiano inutile* (Milano: Rusconi, 1943), 243.
45 Alfredo Rocco, "The Political Doctrine of Fascism" (Worcester-New York: Carnegie Endowment for International Peace, Division of Intercourse and Education, 1926): 393–415.
46 Aquarone, *L'organizzazione*, 136; Giuseppe Bottai, "Discorso alla Camera dei deputati (1° giugno 1927)", in *Esperienza corporativa*, ed. Giuseppe Bottai (Roma: Edizioni del diritto del lavoro, 1929), 290. B. Mussolini, "Per l'inaugurazione del Ministero delle Corporazioni", in *Opera Omnia di Benito Mussolini*, ed. Edoardo Susmel, Duilio Susmel, vol. XXII (Firenze: La Fenice, 1957), 182.
47 ACS, PCM, Gab., 1927, fasc. 1.1.2.1102. *Relazione sullo schema di un disegno di legge relativo allo ordinamento del personale e dei servizi del ministero delle Corporazioni*, 29 January 1927.
48 Bottai, *Discorso alla Camera*, 291.
49 Augusto De Marsanich, "La riforma dello Stato", *Critica fascista*, 4, no. 11 (1926): 202; Critica fascista, "Le parole e i fatti della Rivoluzione", *Critica fascista*, 4, no. 22 (1926): 411–413.
50 Royal Decree no. 898 of 28 April 1927.
51 Guido Melis, *Due modelli di amministrazione tra liberalismo e fascismo. Burocrazie tradizionali e nuovi apparati* (Roma: Ministero per i beni culturali e ambientali. Pubblicazioni degli archivi di Stato, 1988), 178.
52 Melis, *Due modelli*, 170–179.
53 Ministero delle corporazioni, *Ruoli di anzianità del personale* (Roma: Istituto poligrafico dello Stato, 1937). See also T. Cole, "Italy's Fascist Bureaucracy", *American Political Science Review*, 32, no. 6 (1938): 1143–1157.
54 Guido Melis, "Le élite nei Ministeri economici", 51, *Rivista trimestrale di scienza dell'amministrazione*, no. 2 (2005): 5–16.
55 Documents on the objections raised by the various administrations and the responses by the Ministry of Corporations can be found in ACS, PCM, Gab., 1927, fasc. 1.1.2/1102.
56 ACS, PCM, Gab., 1927, fasc. 1.1.2.1102. Ministero dell'Interno, Gabinetto, Ufficio studi e legislazione, *Disegno di legge per l'ordinamento dei servizi e del personale del Ministero delle Corporazioni*, undated (but 1927).
57 Ibid. *Riservata del ministro dell'Economia nazionale Belluzzo a S.E. Bottai, sottosegretario alle Corporazioni*, 23 September 1927. Concerning the Ministry of National Economy, see Enrica Neri, "Per una storia del Ministero dell'Economia Nazionale. Documenti e prime interpretazioni in tema di amministrazione economica (1923–1929)", *Annali di Storia moderna e contemporanea*, 4 (1998): 181–200.
58 Renzo De Felice, *Mussolini il fascista*, vol. II, *L'organizzazione dello Stato fascista 1925–1929* (Torino: Einaudi, 1968), 286–296.

59 Edoardo Malusardi, *Elementi di storia del sindacalismo fascista* (Genova: Drocchi, 1932), 159.
60 De Felice *Mussolini il fascista*, II, 291.
61 The document, dated 9 April and preserved in Giuseppe Bottai's archives, can be found in De Felice *Mussolini il fascista*, II, 292.
62 De Felice *Mussolini il fascista*, II, 292.
63 Ibid., 293–294.
64 Partito nazionale fascista, *Il Gran Consiglio*, 272.
65 Chiara Giorgi, Ilaria Pavam, *Storia dello Stato sociale in Italia* (Bologna: Il Mulino, 2021), 91.
66 Fabio Bertini, *Le parti e le controparti. Le organizzazioni del lavoro dal Risorgimento alla Liberazione* (Milano: Franco Angeli, 2004), 205.
67 Umberto Romagnoli, "Il diritto sindacale corporativo ed i suoi interpreti (Appunti per una storia delle idee giuridiche)", *Storia contemporanea*, 1, no. 1 (1970): 105–121; Umberto Romagnoli, "Il diritto del lavoro durante il fascismo: uno sguardo d'insieme", in *Korporativismus in den südeuropäischen Diktaturen*, eds. Aldo Mazzacane, Alessandro Somma, and Michael Stolleis (Frankfurt am Main: Klostermann, 2005), 225–249.
68 Renzo De Felice, *Mussolini il fascista*, II, 329.

3 Italy as a Model

The first phase in the construction of the corporative state was deeply marked by Alfredo Rocco's theories. As we have seen, the Minister of Justice was the creator and extensor of the 1926 Syndicalist Law and the main architect of the Labour Charter: with the former, Italy became the only country at that time to systematically translate the idea of corporatism into laws and political measures; and with the Charter, the Fascist elite instead tried to give shape to an official corporatist ideology as the expression not of individual intellectuals or political figures, but of a regime and a state.

Although Rocco had limited relations with foreign countries, his achievements had a wide echo outside Italy's borders and made the country the most advanced international point of reference in the debate on corporatism. The project that was being so intensely discussed in Italy was perceived by politicians and intellectuals in other countries as an interesting way of facing the kind of difficulties that the market economy and state institutions were likely to encounter in all industrialised nations. As Matteo Pasetti has correctly noted, historians have pointed to the 1930s as the period of the corporatist model's diffusion and the Italian model's transnational "success" while overlooking the fact that these phenomena were already widely at work in the second half of the 1920s.[1] The closest and most influential connections were established with the Iberian world. In Spain, Primo De Rivera's dictatorial regime initiated the implementation of a corporatist system in the mid-1920s. This step was mainly taken by the Minister of Labour, Industry, and Commerce, Eduardo Aunòs Perez: in August 1926, the *Código del trabajo* was promulgated to regulate labour relations and collective agreements. The following November the *Organización nacional corporativa* (NCO) was established, based on unitary trade union associations for workers and employers; and in September 1927, the *Asemblea nacional consultiva* was created, made up of representatives of the public administration, parties, and corporations: this was the first attempt to create a parliamentary body modelled, if only to some extent, on the principles of corporatism. As would later be the case in Italy, the new institutions encountered considerable opposition to their measures and showed deep structural weaknesses, which prevented the full realisation of a new system. Primo De Rivera's fall in 1930 brought these measures to a halt, and the corporatism experiment came to an early end. However, it is interesting to note that although the experiment in

DOI: 10.4324/9781032713267-4

question had strong local roots, owing to the obvious links with certain political and cultural currents in Restoration Spain, it was also strongly indebted to the Fascist model. Not only did the Fascists provide the initial impetus – it was Mussolini who directly advised the Spanish dictatorship's leadership to start building a corporatist system – but contacts between members of the Italian regime and Aunós Perez were frequent. Besides, Aunós Pérez himself publicly acknowledged his indebtedness to the Italian experiment.[2] The most evident result of this was a marked degree of statism, which was the main distinguishing feature of Fascist corporatism compared to the corporatist currents of the beginning of the century.[3] After the interlude of the Second Republic, the Italian model returned to exerting a direct influence on the Spanish legal system at the end of the 1930s: in March 1938, the government of "nationalist Spain" approved the *Fuero del trabajo*, which found one of its main sources of inspiration in the Labour Charter promulgated in Italy 11 years earlier.[4]

The 1927 Charter also exerted a strong influence in the other Iberian country, Portugal. The *Estatuto do Trabalho Nacional*, the 1933 text through which Salazar's Estado Novo laid the foundations of its corporative system, was largely modelled on the Italian text: it not only drew its general inspiration and some basic concepts from the Charter but also reproduced several of the Charter's articles almost verbatim.[5] This debt was openly acknowledged by some of the dictatorship's leading figures.[6] More generally, the trade union system in Portugal and the institutional apparatus for regulating social relations were largely inspired by the Italian model. In spite of some profound differences – the Estado Novo was less centralising and statist[7] – Italian sources (including both legislative texts and works by intellectuals) were not only widely circulated but also constantly studied at Lusitanian universities and by the Salazarist dictatorship's major architects.[8] Numerous lectures by representatives of the Fascist regime and Italian culture were organised in Portugal, as well as visiting periods in Rome for Portuguese politicians and intellectuals; many articles and reviews were also published on what was being done and discussed in Italy.[9] Moreover, the similarities between some of the Estado Novo's institutions and components of the Fascist state were far from negligible: from the labour judiciary to the legislation governing labour relations and the model of the extra-ministerial public body. As argued by António Castro Fernandes, one of the major ideologists of Portuguese corporatism, while imitation was to be avoided and each country was to come up with its own original developments, "through the Italian model [the Portuguese could] establish the universal values of corporatism".[10]

In Spain and Portugal, the Italian corporativist achievements of 1926–1927 thus exerted a direct influence on the initiatives of governments and legislators. Unsurprisingly, the Italian model was studied and analysed with particular attention in those two countries. The measures taken by Mussolini and the Fascist government, however, aroused immediate interest in the rest of Europe as well, and not only among far-right political organisations and intellectual circles. The main daily newspapers reported on the topic with promptness and breadth that were not usually reserved for the initiatives of Italian governments. Numerous political, legal, and economic journals began to publish the first analyses and interpretations of Italian corporatism in the following months as well.

The Syndicalist Law and the Labour Charter also had a significant impact on the International Labour Organization (ILO). What immediately stirred the waters of this Geneva-based institution was, above all, the creation of the monopoly of Fascist trade unions. Some northern European trade unions used the forum of the ILO to attack the Fascist regime: they denounced the elimination of freedom of association for workers and the outlawing of free trade unions; in particular, they argued that the trade union system devised by Rocco utterly conflicted with the fundamental principles of the organisation, and that the Italian representatives should therefore be expelled. The issue emerged, albeit marginally, as early as 1926 and acquired increasing importance over the following years. The discussion on the Italian Fascist trade unions' presence became one of the "hottest" topics addressed by the ILO, as we shall see in the next chapter.

The clashes triggered by the trade union reform, however, did not end relations between Fascist Italy and the ILO. On the contrary, they did not prevent several members of the organisation from closely following the corporatist experiment's progress. Interest in it was shown above all by the director of the International Labour Office (the office coordinating the ILO's activities), Albert Thomas. A leading exponent of French reformist socialism, during the First World War, Thomas had held important government posts as supply manager.[11] Although he did not agree in the slightest with authoritarianism and the elimination of freedom of association, he was drawn to the Fascist project of creating a new type of trade unionism. Indeed, Thomas set himself the goal of preventing class struggle from disintegrating society, and for this purpose, he considered it necessary to have (free) trade unions acting to unite workers' interests and make them compatible with the nation's general interests. Thomas set out his approach to Fascist corporatism in his 1927 annual report: without downplaying the contrasts and controversies, he acknowledged that the path taken by Italian Fascism showed great potential. On that occasion, he stated: "it seems clear that on most points Italy's social ideal accords with the social ideal expressed in the Treaty of Peace. The Italian Labour Charter, which was solemnly proclaimed on 21 April last, is in its practical provisions in harmony with the International Labour Charter enshrined in the Treaty".[12] Thomas was referring in particular to the general part of the treaty, which among other things stated that the signatories "will endeavour to secure and maintain fair and humane conditions of labour for men, women, and children" (art. 23).

That harmony and that commonality of purpose was also the fruit of the collaboration developed over the previous months. As stated in the director's report, "[t]he Office was very glad to put its available information at the disposal of the Minister of Corporations, when the latter was working on the preparation of the Labour Charter. In spite of the public discussions, daily and fruitful collaboration between the Italian Government departments and the Office has fortunately not diminished".[13]

According to Thomas, the relationship between Fascist Italy, the International Labour Organisation, and other industrialised countries in matters pertaining to trade unionism and corporatism extended far beyond the Labour Charter:

> Certainly there is no reason for overlooking the fact that, in spite of this common ideal of civilisation, serious divergencies of conception have been brought out as to the constitution of the State and the part to be played by trade unions, and that these divergencies are at any moment likely to create political obstacles. But from the standpoint of the common ideal, it is surely the Office's duty, from its international position above the conflict, to endeavour to find the elements of truth which may be contained in the different theories and which may be combined for the benefit of all.
>
> […]
>
> Such endeavours would not appeal to be, as it is too often claimed they are, in absolute contradiction with the traditions of individualism or the principles of democracy. On the contrary, it would appear that some conciliation, or at least practical cooperation, is possible in the attempt to build up a body of international legislation which would be above the different outlooks which may exist.[14]

These words of appreciation were quite significant for the Fascist regime since they allowed it to present itself to the Italians as the proponent of a reform project that was in the vanguard for Europe and the world at large.[15] The contact between the International Labour Office's leadership and the Italian government did not end there, as is evidenced by Thomas' correspondence with Giuseppe Bottai and Mussolini himself. But this is also confirmed by the numerous trips Thomas made to Italy (seven, after the March on Rome).[16] One particularly significant trip was his May 1928 visit to the Ministry of Corporations and his participation in the Congress of Fascist Trade Unions.[17]

The conflicting judgements expressed within the ILO were mirrored in the European press. On the one hand, news reports and commentaries emphasised Fascism's dictatorial nature and the lack of freedom that characterised corporatism; on the other, they discussed the novelties that corporatist legislation had introduced in the relationship between the state and trade unions and the governing of social conflict. The two lines of interpretation were divergent yet not incompatible. Everywhere, one could identify the latter approach not only in newspapers of the non-moderate, or openly pro-Fascist, Right, but also – not infrequently – in progressive, liberal, or Catholic ones. The exception, at least until the early 1930s, was the United Kingdom. Here, as we saw in Chapter 1, corporatism was already being discussed in liberal or moderate socialist circles in the aftermath of the First World War. At the same time, the statist character of Fascism's economic and social ideology made the Italian experiment less interesting in the eyes of cultures still largely imbued with free trade and far from any cult of the state: this was the case not only with liberals but with Labourists as well.[18] If we turn to the most authoritative and influential newspaper on these issues, *The Economist*, we can see how, despite its strong anti-communism, it never expressed any interest in or sympathy for the corporatist state.[19]

The "irradiation" of Fascist corporatism did not stop at the European continent's borders. Particularly in the United States, the press followed Mussolini's reforms with some attention, reproducing the same conflicting judgements. The *New York Times*' position is revealing in this respect. As John Diggins wrote, "the *New York Times* was the only important daily to characterize Fascism as a dictatorship in its editorial pages, contrasting it – at least for a few years – with the ideals of liberty and democracy". At the same time, the newspaper "endorsed corporate theory as a method of stealing thunder from the Left and of giving power to hitherto unrepresented social units".[20] According to the *New York Times*, Mussolini's conception of power and authority "has many points in common with that of the men who inspired our own Constitution – John Adams, Hamilton, Washington. The uninformed will of 'the many' is to be 'balanced' by the experience and the wisdom of 'the few'".[21]

In the United States, moreover, as early as the second half of the 1920s, numerous observers discussed the measures adopted by Mussolini's government – in several cases showing profound knowledge of the Italian situation. In a 1928 volume, *Making the Fascist State*, the philosopher Herbert W. Schneider argued that the Syndicalist Law of 1926 "has become almost equivalent to a new constitution for the Fascist state, though in itself it seems to be little more than the legal recognition of syndicates, a reform which had been carried long ago in other states".[22] Schneider outlined both a detailed reconstruction of the long process that had preceded the drafting of the law and a meticulous analysis of the law itself, examined article by article. No less thorough was his reading of the Labour Charter, whose more general political implications he grasped – without allowing himself to be influenced by propaganda – along with the effects it would have on trade unionist action:

> In general, the Charter is rightly and unanimously hailed by the fascist syndicalists as the embodiment of their reforms. It explicitly recognizes the general principles which they laid down, and the particular working out of details would in any case be more a matter of the drawing up of collective contracts than of political legislation. The Labor Confederation now has ample legal sanction for its activities and the real test of its capacity will be in its bargaining power in drawing up the contracts.[23]

The most significant aspect of the book, however, was the author's ability to grasp the different positions within the Fascist elite and the conflicts they generated. The main conflict, according to Schneider, was between the leader of the Fascist workers' unions, Edmondo Rossoni, and the Undersecretary of Corporations, Bottai:

> Rossoni, of course, championed the Charter immediately as a great achievement of fascist labor organization. It is not without significance, however, that of the two chief speeches made on Labor Day at the publication of the Charter, that by Bottai does not mention Rossoni, and that by Rossoni barely

> mentions Mussolini. Certainly the corporationism of Rossoni must be distinguished from the Ministry of Corporations. The latter is looked down upon by Rossoni as little more than a politicians' *ufficio,* whereas the fascist politicians regard this Ministry as their opportunity to subordinate syndicalist organizations to government control.
>
> Though there is no serious conflict as yet between Rossoni and Bottai, or rather, between syndicalism and corporationism, there is evidence that they are constantly diverging and that before long the issue may become serious. The revision of the Labor Charter, and the institution of government employment agencies, and of price-regulating committees, are but the first evidence that the syndicates will be increasingly subjected to the political control of the Ministry of Corporations. At present the employers' syndicates feel it more than does Rossoni, but Rossoni's tum may come soon.[24]

An ability to navigate the maze not only of corporate legislation but also of the disputes running through the Fascist state with such precision and analytical depth was not entirely uncommon among American political and social scientists. In the same year that Schneider's book came out, other volumes on the Fascist state and the corporatist system were published in the United States, although they were less original and detailed in their analysis. The topic was also the subject of books with a journalistic slant intended for a wider audience,[25] as well as of explicitly apologetic volumes.[26] Reviewing these studies in the pages of the authoritative "American Political Science Review", historian William Yandell Elliott observed that the construction of corporatism clashed with a state structure dominated by the National Fascist Party and the Grand Council of Fascism; and that, even in the late 1920s, the nature of the "collaboration" between capital and labour – beyond Mussolini's general declarations and contradictory rulings by labour tribunals – still appeared to be a vague and distant idea.[27]

The interest aroused in other countries by Italian corporatist achievements in the years 1926–1927 was not an extemporaneous event. From the March on Rome onwards, attention on the innovations introduced by Fascism was high throughout Europe. Political forces and intellectuals, especially on the Right and within the Catholic world but also among socialists and liberals, followed the initiatives of Mussolini's government with interest, even though they did not necessarily share the principles and values that marked its action.[28] Many saw Italy as a kind of laboratory in which new institutional solutions were being tested, from which inspiration could be drawn, and which could at least partly be adapted to other national contexts and different political regimes.

This interest was largely spontaneous until 1927. From the following year, however, it was the Fascist regime that promoted an increasing amount of propaganda abroad, centred precisely on the issue of corporatism.

In more general terms, it must be said that from the mid-1920s a significant part of the regime's cultural policy came to revolve around corporatism. After Bottai's appointment as undersecretary in November 1926, the Ministry of Corporations became, to all intents and purposes, a major player in that policy's implementation.

Bottai and his collaborators believed that only through a real cultural policy would it be possible to establish the building of the corporate state not only in ideological discourse or propaganda but as a real and lasting institutional reality. The ministry's cultural policy fully included corporatism among the regime's goals while aspiring to "define nothing less than the essence of the revolution, the goal towards which the new Italy was to be directed".[29] The broadness of the task and the fact that it was based on the assumption of the regime's total and all-embracing character inevitably marked a profound break with the *squadrista* mentality that continued to characterise many *gerarchi*. It is only with the birth of the Ministry of Corporations that one can therefore speak of an organic Fascist cultural policy.[30]

The ministry made a sustained and intense effort to stimulate and coordinate intellectual initiatives, and to attract and organise the most active and interesting forces that had arisen within the trade union and corporativist movement. The permanent commission for corporative studies was set up for this purpose. Most measures were taken in the field of legal theory at the beginning, while headway was slower in the field of economics. The first step was the creation, in January 1927, of the journal *Il Diritto del Lavoro*. Created with the aim of promoting study of the regime's juridical and institutional dimensions by focusing precisely on the evolution of trade union and corporative law, this journal represented the most influential forum for Fascist orientations in the juridical sphere and proved capable of involving a large number of legal scholars.[31]

The ministry also began promoting meetings and congresses with claims to scientificity and great cultural ambitions, culminating in the two conferences on trade union and corporatist studies held in Rome in 1930 and Ferrara in 1932 (see Chapter 6). It also fostered the establishment of a significant network of university chairs and schools centred on corporatism in pursuit of the double goal of "invading" academic culture – progressively leading it to embrace the new corporativist gospel – and caring for the education of the younger generations. Among the various initiatives was the establishment – at the University of Ferrara at the end of 1927 – of the first chair of Corporative Law, held by Carlo Costamagna, one of the Fascist law's main theorists; the opening – at the University of Pisa in 1928 – of the School of Advanced Study in Corporative Law (renamed School for Advanced Corporative Studies, two years later), which was long directed by Bottai himself.[32] Also part of this series of initiatives was the launching in 1928 of the ministry's journal, *Informazioni corporative* (renamed *Sindacato e corporazione* in 1933). This represented much more than an institutional body's bulletin: in addition to illustrating the ministry's activities, corporative bodies, and trade unions, the new journal sought to give an account of developments within the debate on corporatism.

All of these accomplishments were due to the action not only of the Ministry of Corporations' bureaucracy but also, more specifically, of Bottai himself: some can directly be traced back to his individual initiative. At the same time, it is likely that Mussolini's decision to put his trust in Bottai rather than any other *gerarca* was influenced precisely by the editor of *Critica fascista*'s demonstrated ability to elevate the intellectual debate's tone.[33] The undersecretary and future minister combined his activity as a cultural organiser with steady journalistic output, which remained extremely significant throughout this period. It took the form of a large number of articles and notes published in magazines and newspapers and later largely collected in volumes. It therefore seems difficult to distinguish the Ministry of Corporations' work in the years 1926–1932 from Bottai's more strictly personal initiatives – but this consideration does not apply only to intervention in the cultural sphere.

Within the framework of the initiatives just described, cultural policies and propaganda aimed at foreign countries became increasingly important. From the second half of the 1920s, especially following the drafting of the Labour Charter, the Fascist regime worked to promote awareness of corporatist ideas and Italian achievements in other countries; the greatest effort was directed at those national milieus considered most akin and receptive, namely Spain, Portugal, and France.[34] Corporatism became "a leitmotif of propaganda activity abroad, because it gave the possibility of highlighting the dictatorship's alleged 'social' and 'modern' component".[35] The Ministry of Corporations' structures were mobilised in pursuit of this aim.[36] A Commission for Corporate Propaganda Abroad was set up by the ministry in 1928 as well with "the task of preparing and implementing an organic action plan to spread accurate knowledge abroad".[37] The commission promoted numerous initiatives. Firstly, it ensured the regular dispatch of the most significant writings produced within the corporatism debate as well as up-to-date collections of legislative texts to diplomatic representations, scientific institutes, libraries, and individual scholars across the world. Secondly, it coordinated the production of material specifically designed for international dissemination. This kind of activity included the publication of the "Feuille d'informations corporatives", an information bulletin in French, which was printed at varying intervals from 1929 to 1943, as well as the translation of "official" texts on corporatism into other languages, such as: the Labour Charter, translated into four different languages; Mussolini's speeches; information and propaganda material produced by the regime's political organs; and popular works on corporatist law and economics. This activity became increasingly important in the following years, even in quantitative terms. Thirdly, the Ministry of Corporations supported the organisation of exhibitions and expositions – such as the room devoted to corporatism in the Italian pavilion at the 1929 Barcelona International Exposition – and cycles of conferences in major European cities, which saw the participation of intellectuals (such as Gino Arias and Carlo Costamagna) and politicians (such as Giuseppe Bottai).[38]

These initiatives involved many of the best-known Italian interpreters of the "corporatist gospel" and kept the Commission and its propaganda organs abroad busy for at least a decade. Given that the topic was far from obvious or easily divulged one, the propaganda campaign on corporatism was not aimed at a wide audience; rather, it was designed for intellectuals and exponents of political or trade union movements interested in such issues which were not prejudicially hostile to Fascism. As has been observed, "the regime aimed first and foremost to intercept cohorts of opinion-makers who would serve as overseas promoters of the Italian corporatist experience and contribute to putting a Fascist 'stamp' on the very idea of corporatism".[39] The regime's intentions for propaganda abroad was to use corporatism as a means to legitimise Mussolini's dictatorship on the international political stage – that is, as a sort of "Trojan horse" for Fascism in other countries.

The Italian corporativists' connections with foreign countries took the form not only of a commitment to promoting awareness of their achievements beyond the Italian borders but also of a careful – yet certainly instrumental and very tendentious – examination of what was being written and done abroad. *Informazioni corporative* (later *Sindacato e corporazione*) included sections – *Rassegna della stampa*, *Nota della quindicina*, and *Notiziario del lavoro all'estero* – that frequently featured articles on the labour and trade union policies implemented in other countries, while also providing information on particularly significant foreign articles, books, conferences, and conventions devoted to the Italian experience. The selection of writings and speeches was obviously entirely one-sided: only positive opinions were taken into account, or at any rate, views that assigned some relevance to Fascist corporatism. The aim, predictably, was not to illustrate the complexity of the debate abroad, which was also strongly marked by criticism, perplexity, and disapproval. Rather, the aim was to contribute to the construction of the regime's self-representation as the creator of a profoundly innovative experiment, destined to offer a solution to the most serious contradictions in contemporary society, and from which all other countries could draw inspiration.

Journals and magazines also provided steady contributions in this direction. Despite the hyper-nationalist climate created by Fascism, intellectuals and politicians were able to maintain – at least with regard to corporatism – an open gaze upon the outside world, showing interest and curiosity towards what was happening in other countries. Arguments about the alleged virtues and originality of the Fascist "third way" were frequently accompanied in publications on the subject by an effort to contextualise the experiment that was taking place in Italy within the broader framework of the changes occurring in Europe and the industrialised world more generally. In an article on the approval of the Labour Charter in *Gerarchia*, Mussolini's magazine, the success of corporatism was thus attributed not merely to its "intrinsic value" but also to historical circumstances: the "present moment of the social struggle in Europe", in which parliamentary democracies, the Soviet collectivist revolution, and repressive authoritarian regimes all appeared to be floundering.[40] However, the article continued, the Labour Charter's widespread resonance was accompanied by a substantial misunderstanding of its basic principles:

> While the curiosity has been great, the examination of the comments is not so comforting. We find it natural, however, that no foreigner has perfectly understood the Labour Charter's essence and value; only Fascists can fully understand it, and Fascists are Italians.
>
> The socialists and other aprioristically anti-Fascist elements regard our trade union legislation as yet another means for the dictatorship to rule [...].

> Democratic men and newspapers that conduct their business most profitably in the name of the people have based their criticism on a kind of Bismarckian paternalism […].
>
> The liberal, or rather liberalist, criticism that has been adopted by the English press in particular is concerned above all with the danger that assiduous State intervention in the trade union movement and in the many problems connected with it may lead to increased statism, stifling individual initiative.[41]

Central to this discourse was the comparison with other national experiences, including those that were politically and ideologically very different. Some clearly propagandistic texts were produced in this direction, but also more measured studies. As Giuseppe Bottai wrote in 1927, one was in the midst of "a reaction, systematic and universal in character, against liberal law's tendency – sprung from the French Revolution – to deny the laws of collective formations". However, "just as that devastating fury which demolished the very foundations of the old social order took a different course and appearance from nation to nation, depending on the different historical and political conditions", so the construction of a new system "does not follow the same paths and reach the same outcomes everywhere".[42] The aim of these comparisons was to assess similarities and differences and, above all, to bring out the superiority of the self-proclaimed "Fascist revolution".

Both by promoting abroad what was being done in Italy and by comparing their own achievements with what was being achieved in other countries, Fascist politicians and intellectuals sought not only to nurture the idea that the regime was carrying out a "revolution" in Italy but also to present corporatism as a universal model that was exportable to any context.

Notes

1 Pasetti, *L'Europa corporativa*, 125.

2 Eduardo Aunós Pérez, *Las Corporaciones del Trabajo en el Estado Moderno* (Madrid: Juan Ortiz, 1928), 35.

3 Matteo Pasetti, *L'Europa corporativa. Una storia transnazionale tra le due guerre mondiali* (Bologna: Bononia University Press, 2016), 154–177.

4 Carme Molinero, "'Sindicalisme nacional'. Una anàlisi comparativa entre Itàlia i Espanya", in *Nou Estat, nova política, nou ordre social. Feixisme i franquisme en una perspectiva comparada*, eds. Giuliana Di Febo and Carme Molinero (Barcelona: Cefid-Uab, 2005), 45–77. On Spanish corporatism's cultural antecedents, see Miguel Ángel Perfecto, "El corporativismo en España: Desde los orígenes a la década de 1930", *Pasado y Memoria. Revista de Historia Contemporánea* 5 (2006): 185–218.

5 Daniele Serapiglia, *La via portoghese al corporativismo* (Roma: Carocci, 2011), 176–182. On Portuguese corporatism in general, see *Corporativismo, Fascismos, Estado Novo*, eds. Fernando Rosas, Álvaro Garrido (Coimbra: Almedina 2012); *Construindo o estado corporativo: as experiências históricas de Portugal e Espanha*, ed. Paula Borges Santos, *Espacio, Tiempo y Forma. Serie V historia contemporánea*, no. 27 (2015); but also the numerous studies presented at the international conference *Espaços corporativos e Escalas Urbanas no Século XX*, organised by the Universidade do Minho (Braga et Guimarães, 27 et 28 avril 2015).

6 Marcello Caetano, *O sistema corporativo* (Lisboa: O Jornal do Comércio e das Colónias, 1938), 28.
7 Su questo punto, ha in misura probabilmente eccessivo, insistito la storiografia: cfr. tra gli altri Santomassimo, *La terza via fascista*, 185–186.
8 Serapiglia, *La via portoghese*, 211–216; Pasetti, *L'Europa corporativa*, 230–249.
9 On the exchanges between the two regimes, see Mario Ivani, *Esportare il fascismo. Collaborazione di polizia e diplomazia culturale tra Italia fascista e Portogallo di Salazar (1928–1945)* (Bologna: Clueb, 2008), 157–296.
10 António Castro Fernandes, *O corporativismo fascista* (Lisboa: Imperio 1938), 19.
11 Bertius W. Schaper, *Albert Thomas. Trente ans de réformisme social* (Assen: Van Gorcum & Co., 1959); Martin Fine, "Albert Thomas: A Reformer's Vision of Modernization. 1914–32", *Journal of Contemporary History* 12, no. 3 (1977): 545–564; Patrick de Laubier, "Albert Thomas (1878–1932), réformiste social", *Revue française des affaires sociales* 47 (1994): 43–52.
12 International Labour Conference, *Report of the Director* (Report of the Director-General), *10th Session* (Geneva: ILO,1927), 6.
13 Ibid., 6.
14 Ibid., 6–7.
15 Carlo Stelluti Scala, "La Carta del lavoro giudicata dal direttore dell'Ufficio internazionale del lavoro", *Il Giornale d'Italia*, 29 April 1927.
16 "Liste des voyages d'Albert Thomas en tant que Directeur du Bureau international du Travail", in *À la rencontre de l'Europe au travail. Récits de voyage d'Albert Thomas (1920–1932), 1932)*, eds. Dorothea Hoehtker and Sandrine Kotts (Paris: Publications de la Sorbonne, 2015), 321–323.
17 *Voyages en Italie*, in Ibid., 235–241. Stefano Gallo, "Dictatorship and International Organisations: The ILO as a 'Test Ground' for Fascism", in *Globalizing Social Rights. The International Labour Organization and Beyond*, eds. Sandrine Kott and Joëlle Droux (Basingstoke: Palgrave Macmillan, 2013), 161.
18 Marco Palla, *Fascismo e Stato corporativo. Un'inchiesta della diplomazia britannica* (Milano: Franco Angeli, 1991), 64–66.
19 For example, "The Corporate State in Italy", *The Economist*, 23 June 1928; "Labour Organisations in Italy"; ibid., 31 August 1929; "Fascism and Labour Problems"; ibid., 7 December 1929; and "Economics of Fascism"; ibid., 17 May 1930.
20 John P. Diggins, *Mussolini and Fascism: The View from America* (Princeton: Princeton University Press, 1972), 32.
21 "'Revolution' in Italy", *The New York Times*, 11 October 1925.
22 Herbert W. Schneider, *Making the Fascist State* (New York: Oxford University Press, 1928), 178. On Schneider's interpretation of fascism, see Katy Hull, *The Machine Has a Soul. American Sympathy with Italian Fascism* (Princeton-Oxford: Princeton University Press, 2021), 78–80.
23 Ibid., 200.
24 Ibid.
25 Edwin Ware Hullinger, *The New Fascist State: A Study of Italy under Mussolini* (New York: Rae D. Henkle Company, 1928).
26 Milford Wriarson Howard, *Fascism: A Challenge to Democracy* (New York: Fleming H. Revell Company, 1928).
27 William Yandell Elliott, *Review of Making the Fascist State* Herbert W. Schneider *The New Fascist State: A Study of Italy under Mussolini* E. W. Hullinger *Fascism: A Challenge to Democracy* M. W. Howard, *The American Political Science Review* 23, no. 2 (1929): 477–481.
28 *Rethinking Fascism and Dictatorship in Europe*, eds. Antonio Costa Pinto and Aristotle Kallis (Basingstoke: Palgrave Macmillan, 2014); *Conservatives and Right Radicals in Interwar Europe*, ed. Marco Bresciani (Oxon-New York: Routledge, 2020).
29 Salvatore Lupo, *Il fascismo. La politica in un regime totalitario* (Roma: Donzelli, 2000), 228.

30 Santomassimo, *La terza via fascista*, 101–109.
31 Sabino Cassese, "Un programmatore degli anni Trenta: Giuseppe Bottai", in Cassese, *La formazione dello Stato amministrativo* (Milano: Giuffrè, 1974), 191–2.
32 Fabrizio Amore Bianco, *Il cantiere di Bottai. La scuola corporativa pisana e la formazione della classe dirigente fascista* (Siena: Cantagalli, 2012); Andrea Mariuzzo, "Corporativismo e accademia. La Scuola pisana di studi corporativi", *Rivista storica italiana* 131, no. 1 (2019): 157–179.
33 Lupo, *Il fascismo*, 228.
34 For instance: Vincenzo Zangara, "La charte italienne du travail", *La Revue hebdomadaire*, 28 septembre 1928, 598–608.
35 Pasetti, *L'Europa corporativa*, 181.
36 On Fascist propaganda abroad, see Benedetta Garzarelli, *"Parleremo al mondo intero". La propaganda del fascismo all'estero* (Alessandria: Edizioni dell'Orso, 2004); Francesca Cavarocchi, *Avanguardie dello spirito. Il fascismo e la propaganda culturale all'estero* (Roma: Carocci, 2010).
37 Archivio storico diplomatico del ministero degli Affari esteri, *Fondo Società delle nazioni*, b. 98, fasc. 23. *Verbale della Commissione permanente per la propaganda all'estero*, 20 November 1928. Sulla commissione, Gaetano Napolitano, *La propaganda corporativa nella rivoluzione fascista* (Napoli: Pescarolo, 1932).
38 Pasetti, *L'Europa corporativa*, p. 181. On Italian participation in the Barcelona International Exposition, see *La Partecipazione Italiana all'Esposizione Internazionale di Barcellona 1929*, ed. Raimondo Targetti (Milano: Studio Editoriale Turistico, 1930); Rubén Domínguez Méndez, "El fascismo italiano y la Exposición Internacional de Barcelona de 1929", *Diacronie* 14, no. 2 (2013). URL : http://journals.openedition.org/diacronie/256 (accessed on 14th November 2023)
39 Pasetti, *L'Europa corporativa*, 181.
40 Alfredo Signoretti, "La 'Carta del lavoro' giudicata all'estero", *Gerarchia* 5, no. 5 (1927): 400.
41 Signoretti, "La 'Carta del lavoro'", 400–401.
42 Giuseppe Bottai, "L'ordinamento corporativo spagnolo", *Gerarchia* 5, no. 3 (1927): 166–172.

4 Trade Unions and Society

The government completely redesigned the trade union system with the law of 3 April 1926. Organisations representing professional interests became part of the system of state powers. Workers' trade unions were made subordinate to the "nation's interests" (as we shall see, the entrepreneurs' case was rather different). In concrete terms, this had a twofold effect: on the one hand, trade unions lost their freedom of action and were deprived of the effective capacity to represent their interests; on the other, the new order offered them a full and unprecedented degree of institutional legitimacy, since it regarded them as public subjects and no longer as private associations.

With the 1926 law, not only did the legal framework and general rules of trade union activity change for workers' organisations, but so did the apparatus, men, objectives, mentality, and methods of intervention. Non-Fascist organisations were first forced to assume a purely symbolic presence and then, within a few months, induced to disband. The process of destroying free-trade unionism and forcibly assimilating the labour world, which had begun in previous years with the Blackshirts' violence, was thus completed. Workers' representation was entirely taken over by the Fascist organisations: the numerous local and professional associations were united in the Confederation of Fascist Trade Unions, led by Edmondo Rossoni. With this new order, the source of legitimisation of trade union structures also changed: it no longer coincided with the workers, if not to a minor extent, but with the state, which was responsible for granting legal recognition and whose intervention became decisive for the governing of social dialectics. This profound change disrupted the relationship between the leaders of workers' organisations and their social base.

Large sectors within Fascist trade unionism saw the new order as too narrow a limit on their freedom of action; the constraints were not even counterbalanced by any regulation of private property and freedom of enterprise. For these reasons, numerous attacks against the Rocco Law and demands for "self-government of professional categories" were formulated by exponents of Fascist trade unions over the years. This criticism was initially veiled and kept under the radar, but in the second half of the 1930s, it would become more "vociferous", eventually leading to explicit demands for change.[1] It would, however, be wrong to identify the history of Fascist trade unionism only with its (no doubt fundamental) function of controlling and regimenting workers.[2] The nature of trade unions as mass

DOI: 10.4324/9781032713267-5

organisations, evidenced by their hundreds of thousands of members,[3] made them extremely complex bodies: on the one hand, they were an "instrument of social control and a transmission belt through which the 'mobilisation from above' of the working masses could be achieved"; on the other, they constituted a channel for the expression of workers' needs and claims, especially through the lower-level organisers.[4] In practice, there was not always full agreement between the lines of action drawn up by the national leadership and the conduct adopted at the peripheral level, in individual workplaces or categories.[5]

The workers' organisations initially had great expectations of the Ministry of Corporations. They hoped that, as a form of compensation for the abolition of the right to strike and of internal commissions, they might play a leading role in the newly created ministry, whose undersecretary Rossoni hoped to become.[6] These expectations were not fulfilled, however. The ministry's orientation soon turned out to be not very favourable to the National Confederation of Fascist Trade Unions (*Confederazione nazionale dei Sindacati fascisti*) and ended up tightening the mesh of the Rocco Law even further. This was the result of numerous demands from within the regime. At the time of the ministry's creation, the General Confederation of Italian Industry, through its secretary general, Gino Olivetti, vigorously opposed the appointment of Rossoni, who was considered too powerful and independent, and ensured that the post was provisionally taken up by Mussolini.[7] The government and the PNF's leadership also showed themselves unwilling to tolerate the independence of the trade unions; as the months went by, they expressed increasing concern about the power Rossoni had gained and a clear aversion to the confrontational speeches and practices that the trade union leaders, and Rossoni himself, authorised and legitimised.

Against the background of this general intolerance, a contrast emerged between Giuseppe Bottai, the Undersecretary of Corporations, and Rossoni: the two embodied different and very distant conceptions of trade unions and corporatism. As we shall see in Chapter 6, according to Bottai, corporatism was to be based on a statist policy and the subordination of social representation. For Rossoni, on the contrary, trade unions were to continue to play a leading and independent role. "Syndicalism", the latter argued on repeated occasions, "must be the trade unions' business. This is self-evident. The representation of the organised classes belongs to the trade unions and not to the bureaucratic organs of the State".[8] In his opinion, it would be a

> serious mistake to diminish the efficiency of syndicalism, which, *operating as it does in the atmosphere of the Fascist Revolution*, represents the breathing space for all classes and the way of training them to face their responsibilities. There is thus nothing wrong if we have more syndicalism than corporatism, since it is syndicalism that comes first and must lead to the Corporation, and not vice versa.[9]

For these reasons, at least until the early 1930s, the leading trade union leaders – Rossoni, but also Riccardo Del Giudice, Luigi Razza, Giuseppe Landi, Gherardo

Casini, and Felice Chilanti[10] – criticised the Ministry of Corporations: "the Ministry – instead of limiting itself to exercising control according to its competences – all too often likes to replace the trade union bodies in their functions and in their very *raison d'etre*", Rossoni states in a police report from April 1931.[11]

The friction between Rossoni, as well as the trade union leadership, and Bottai dates back to the early years of the Fascist government. Particularly harsh was the clash marking the final phase of the "Commission of the Solons", with reciprocal accusations of a lack of loyalty to Fascism and referrals to the PNF disciplinary court.[12] After 1926, the opposition became even more heated. As Undersecretary of Corporations, Bottai did not fail to point out the distance between what he regarded as the correct corporatist conception and the conception advocated by the trade unionists:

> The corporatist conception – he wrote in 1928 – is precisely the one whereby the State asserts itself not as a sum of individuals or trade unions, but as *an entity superior to the Trade Union, opposite and superior to the Trade Union itself*, because, according to Fascist and corporatist doctrine, the State is precisely a 'corpus' – that is, a moral person, alive and real, irreducible to its 'atoms', whether they be trade unionists or individualists.[13]

Then, in a slightly later article, Bottai stated:

> Syndicalism, as an end in itself, with pretensions to being political doctrine, must not exist, because it would cast doubt on the unitary development of productive forces, which, in syndicates or professional associations, realise the first form of corporative discipline.[14]

On several occasions, in official speeches and in the columns of *Critica fascista*, Bottai pointed to the syndicates' "trespassing tendency", which constituted an "irregular prelude to corporatist action".[15] Although this argument could be taken to refer to both employers' and workers' organisations, in reality, it was only directed towards the latter.

Bottai therefore set himself the task of limiting Fascist syndicalism, which in any case had already been largely normalised by means of strict control not only over contracts that were drawn up, both at the centre and at the periphery but also over the associations' regulations and the selection of their leaders. Much attention was focused precisely on the latter. Besides, the training of a new managerial class, suited to the regime's needs and objectives, was one of Bottai's hobby horses. The objective was, first and foremost, the implementation of strict and selective controls and the purging of politically non-aligned civil servants, as established by the Grand Council of Fascism in November 1927.[16] The presence in Fascist organisations of a significant number of old organisers, mostly from the revolutionary syndicalist milieu, even after the mid-1920s, was acknowledged by Rossoni himself.[17] But the question did not end with a generic turnover of men, which was certainly widely pursued, as it brought complex elements into play, such as the definition of the figure of a trade union leader and his tasks, the degree of autonomy from the party organs he possessed, and the mode of his selection, by appointment or election.

For Bottai, it was a matter of creating a new figure of a trade union leader: the "leader-civil servant". The "backward concept of the trade union leader, a stirrer of crowds and agitator, who organises the labour world for the purpose of conquest", had to be overcome. The trade union leader was to not only "agitate" but also "discipline", "educate", "choose", and "perfect". New tasks accompanied or replaced the old ones: "the establishment of wages, according to the possibilities of production, the normal requirements of life, and work performance"; as well as the application of labour laws, the observance of the Labour Charter, and collective agreements. These leaders were to "develop technical and moral authority at the same time" if they wished to embody "that legitimate hierarchy of values, skills, intellects, and spirits from which every piece of advice, every warning, every order can stem, with the certainty of being heeded"; in other words, according to Bottai, trade union leaders were to make up the "active aristocracy of reorganised Italian society", so as to become "the interpreters of the regime within organisations".[18]

Specifically, the undersecretary set out to sever, or at least loosen, the link between trade union leadership and the social base of those they represented. Above all, he addressed the new generations of the intellectual middle classes, to whom he suggested adopting "the new profession of trade union leader in place of other liberal professions, which are now saturated": "To the young people who are about to swell the ranks of unemployed and unemployable professionals without a profession, this new profession must be suggested, specifying its features and characteristics, and defining its development and dignity".[19]

Bottai's clear-cut position largely reflected the reality of the Fascist trade unions, which extensively drew on the reservoir of the unemployed intellectual middle classes,[20] but it clashed with Rossoni's perspective. For the secretary of the National Confederation of Fascist Trade Unions, it was essential that "the leadership of a provincial or local union [be] held not by outsiders, but by men belonging to the same category": "We have also organised the lawyers and the engineers" – he argued when speaking at the congress of the *Federazione nazionale dell'agricoltura* (National Federation of Agriculture) – "but the lawyers must lead the lawyers' unions, not the farmers', or the metalworkers' unions".[21]

In keeping with the objective of leadership turnover, the first trade union schools were set up at the end of the 1920s on the initiative of the Ministry of Corporations and the PNF for the purpose of training "new" leaders to counterbalance the enduring presence of "Corridonian" ones.[22]

The trade union reform was not limited to the formation of a new leadership group. The underlying problem was the concentration of power in a single organisation. Bottai was not the only one to take on that problem. Various forces, each with very different motives, expressed increasing dissatisfaction with Rossoni and his confederation after 1926: Turati's PNF (whose aim was to affirm the syndicalist function of the party and subordinate workers' organisations to it), *Confindustria*, minor Fascist groups, and some trade union organisers dissenting from the majority.[23] Throughout the second half of 1927 and the first months of the following year, the Confederation became the target of increasingly persistent attacks in the press.[24]

It was Bottai, however, who led the offensive in the final months of 1928 – what union leader Tullio Cianetti would refer to in his memoirs as the "fatal year" for Fascist syndicalism.[25] In a report sent to the Grand Council of Fascism in September, he openly called for the dismemberment of the organisation led by Rossoni. The existing situation, where there was only one workers' confederation and six separate employers' confederations, was considered to be incompatible with Syndicalist Law and a source of "imbalance that may make it difficult to develop that collaboration between capital and labour which encapsulates the corporatist regime".[26] These demands were accepted by Mussolini, and at the end of November, the so-called "unblocking" was approved: the confederation was dissolved and the federations that made it up were transformed into as many confederations, completely autonomous from each other (confederations of industry, agriculture, commerce, land transport and inland navigation, credit and insurance, and sea and air transport). This unblocking marked the defeat of syndicalism and completed the trade union system designed by the April 1926 law. For Mussolini it represented "a step forward on the road to corporatist achievements".[27]

There were many reasons that led Mussolini to approve the measure: to empty trade unions of their strength and subordinate them to the PNF; to limit the personal power of Rossoni, the only one potentially able – after Farinacci's exit from the scene – to play the role of "vice-Duce"; to appease the entrepreneurs, who were still uneasy about the way in which the government had handled the "quota 90" operation and worried by the trade unions' residual aggressiveness; to give a warning to the most combative trade union organisers; and, finally, to assert full control over the world of labour, not least so that they could manage wages as a real "dependent variable".[28]

The dissolution of the united confederation and the departure of Rossoni and the old leadership – with the sole exception of Luigi Razza, who was appointed head of the National Confederation of Fascist Trade Unions of Agriculture (*Confederazione nazionale dei sindacati fasci sti dell'agricoltura*) – initiated a change at the top of the unions. The arrival of new elements, from the most diverse backgrounds, led to a marked loss of prominence for cadres coming from the ranks of "Corridonian" revolutionary and national syndicalism.[29] Above all, the unblocking marked the moment of Fascist syndicalism's maximum weakness.

Divided, deprived of their means of action, and subjected to ever tighter constraints and controls, trade unions would not, however, become completely irrelevant. As we shall see later, it would take a few years for workers' organisations to recover their own role within the regime, albeit without achieving the influence and strength of the united confederation.

The Fascist regime's social compromise therefore heavily penalised the world of labour. The latter experienced a drastic worsening of material conditions which took the form of salary cuts, recruitment controls, the abolition of factory representatives, the elimination of non-Fascist trade unions, the suppression of the right to strike, and insufficient supervision of compliance with contracts and protection systems. Entrepreneurs instead managed to retain a broad organisational autonomy and full freedom of action. In contrast to the workers' unions, the employers' organisations continued to appoint their own leaders and governing bodies; moreover, they kept their relationship with their members and the entire social base substantially unchanged, and had considerable freedom to define objectives and lines of conduct.[30] Only the organisational structures were changed by the 1926 law to ensure greater centralisation. The confederations – especially the most important one, that of industry – acquired unprecedented powers of control over the officials and governing bodies of trade and territorial associations. This was matched by the extension and strengthening of the central bureaucracy, thanks also to the increased revenue guaranteed by the compulsory membership fee for companies.[31] Increased centralisation actually favoured large groups at the expense of smaller companies.[32]

Confindustria and the other employers' confederations reinforced their national dimension and, at the same time, their ties with the state. From 1926 onwards, such organisations spread more widely throughout the country, adopting a territorial structure on a provincial scale that reproduced that of the state, being centred on prefectures: there were only 16 inter-sectoral territorial units at provincial level belonging to *Confindustria* in 1925, before the Syndicalist Law, but this figure rose to 63 in 1928.[33] Such changes in organisational structure responded, on the whole, "to the State's need to have as interlocutors (and possibly as collaborators)" associations "capable of guaranteeing control over their members, securing their consent, and creating a dense network of interactions between private organisations and public institutions branching out across the country".[34]

Although the new trade union order affected the organisation and bureaucracy of confederations, federations, and territorial and trade associations, as well as the relationship between them, employers' organisations largely preserved their autonomy and their ability to represent and protect the interests of their social base.[35] One can then agree with what was claimed in the immediate post-war period in the *Confindustria* yearbook, where it was stated that, despite Fascism's corporative legislation, the confederation had "succeeded with different expedients in preserving – in its general outline, as well as in its details – its original system, tested – in a regime of freedom of association – by long and proven experience".[36] If anything, strong discontinuities with the past would emerge in the 1930s, in terms of government relations and economic policy, with the coming into operation of corporations. As we shall see in Chapter 8, however, not even those changes would significantly reduce the powers and capacities of *Confindustria* and the minor confederations.

The trade union system designed by Rocco therefore created a significant imbalance in the organisational strength of entrepreneurs and workers, respectively. This imbalance was also reflected in terms of international relations. Workers' unions immediately found themselves internationally isolated. The Fascist trade unions were not recognised by the organisations in other countries, which were mostly of a socialist, communist, revolutionary trade unionist, or Catholic orientation. The Fascist unions were accused of not constituting true associations of social representation but of rather being a direct emanation of the Fascist government, to which they were entirely subordinate. Rossoni and the other leaders of the confederations were blamed for denying Italian workers freedom in relation to trade unions, preventing them from organising themselves freely and repressing claims and conflicts to the point of banning the right to strike by law.

During the 1920s, the Italian workers' condition and the role of the Fascist trade unions were the subject of several international press campaigns, mainly by newspapers with a democratic or socialist orientation. The International Labour Organization played an important role in this denunciation. This, even against the wishes of its leaders, was the main forum for denouncing the Italian trade union system's authoritarian nature. As early as 1923, numerous representatives of workers' delegations – with the Frenchman Léon Jouhaux at the forefront – contested the presence of the Fascist trade union representative (a role that was held by Rossoni himself until 1928) on the basis of two elements: the first was the concept of "integral syndicalism" advocated by Rossoni and the other leaders, according to which trade unions should take on the representation not only of workers, but also of employers[37]; the second concerned the constant pressures, threats, and outright acts of violence to which members of non-Fascist trade unions and also many workers were subjected in order to push them to join Mussolini's organisations.[38] For these reasons, the trade union representatives demanded that Italian workers be represented not by the Fascists but by the socialist General Confederation of Labour.

The opposition became more intense from 1926 onwards. With the Rocco Law, the freedom of the trade unions was not only denied de facto through intimidation and violence but was definitively eliminated. The protest was therefore no longer directed only at trade union representatives but at the entire Italian legal system. What also sparked debate was the abrogation of the right to strike. At the first International Labour Conference, which was held after the law was passed, all the workers' representatives took a stand against the Italian trade union representative. The reasons were given by the Belgian workers' delegate, Corneille Mertens:

> Previously trade union liberty has been denied rather as a result of a number of sporadic acts; but to-day this oppression of the trade unions has been confirmed by legislative measures, that is to say, the oppression of trade unions which are not in agreement with the principles of the Government. The Workers' Group of this Conference cannot admit that the trade union organisations should be at the whim and caprice of those who happen to form the Government for the time being; they cannot admit that the right to strike should be taken away from them. The working class regards the right to strike as one of the most important rights it possesses; it represents the only weapon at its disposal for dealing with stubborn resistance to its demands.
>
> [...]
>
> Nor can the Workers' Group admit that the Fascist Corporations exercise an activity which, as the Italian Government Delegate said from this tribune, is based on principles of the most perfect democracy. We deny that those Corporations are based on democracy at all. We think that the working class should pursue its efforts through trade union organisation, without any legal or other interference.[39]

Jouhaux, in turn, presented a circumstantial analysis of the text of the law of April 1926, clearly summarising his own judgement: "I believe there is no other law in the world which contains such a denial of the fundamental principles of liberty. The whole subject would be laughable if it were not so horrible".[40] The new order not only deprived the workers of their rights, but, by depriving them of the tools for struggle and self-defence, condemned them to a sharp deterioration in material conditions, as evidenced by the drastic drop in wages.

The following year, the promulgation of the Labour Charter offered new arguments to supporters of free trade unionism and opponents of the Fascist system. According to the Dutchman Jan Oudegeest, Secretary of the International Federation of Trade Unions and Vice-Chairman of the Governing Body of the International Labour Office, and Charles Schürch, Secretary of the Swiss Federation of Trade Unions and member of the Governing Body of the International Labour Office:

> The Act of 3 April 1926 regulating labour agreements and the Labour Charter of 21 April 1927 are in violent contrast with any sane conception of trade unionism and with Part XIII of the Treaty of Versailles
>
> 1 because they prevent from participating in any trade union activities anyone who proves himself an anti-Fascist or makes any reservations with regard to the Fascist regime;
> 2 because they set up a status of privilege in favour of an association which is not open to everyone;
> 3 because they oblige even those who are not members to contribute to this organisation, even refusing them a right of supervision of the work and the financial management of the organisation;
> 4 because they prevent anyone who is not a member of the organisation which is legally recognised from appealing to the labour tribunals;
> 5 because a part of the contributions which the workers are compelled to pay to the local organisations is paid to religious and party institutions possibly opposed in tendency to the consciences of the contributors.[41]

The clash continued throughout the period in which Fascist Italy was part of the organisation, and was carried on with particular harshness until 1932, when diplomatic action by the permanent secretariat of the ILO – the International Labour Office (referred to as the *Bureau International du Travail* (BIT) in many Italian documents) – leadership ensured a relative cooling of the issue.[42] Even after Rossoni was replaced by Luigi Razza in 1929, the legitimacy of the Italian workers' designated representative was questioned every year. Precisely on the occasion of Razza's debut, a motion was proposed – but later not passed – in which it was argued that "there is no organisation representative of the workers in Italy. We sometimes hear of congresses of Fascist unions; but in reality they are nothing more than meetings of officials whose authority is derived from the Government, or the Fascist Party".[43]

The attacks on the Fascist trade unions marked Italy's relationship with the ILO but did not lead the Fascist government to abandon the organisation or to adopt a less prominent role. But it was only gradually, especially from the early 1930s onwards, that the Fascist trade unions emerged from complete international isolation following the establishment of other authoritarian regimes in Europe and the consequent construction of networks of relations with trade unions in those countries.

The situation was quite different for entrepreneurs' organisations. Italian employers, in both the industrial and agricultural sectors, had participated in collaborative experiences with their counterparts in other countries well before the 1920s, i.e. when national associations had not yet been fully set up. Landowners had already contributed to the initial establishment of a transnational network of interests in the last two decades of the 19th century. With the first "International Congress of Agriculture", which was held in Paris in 1878, and with the second, which took place in Budapest in 1885, the first attempts had been made to establish forms of cooperation between owners and agricultural entrepreneurs from different countries, through the additional participation of scholars, merchants, and politicians. Several Italians had taken part. The willingness to develop national organisations and transnational exchange networks in parallel continued in the following years.[44]

The early years of the 20th century had also witnessed the establishment of the national system for the representation of industrial enterprises in Italy, culminating in the creation of *Confindustria* in 1910. This process had developed more or less simultaneously with the other industrialised countries of Western Europe.[45] The growing organisational compactness of industrial interests on a national scale had intersected with the acceleration of industrialisation processes (an increase in the number of employees and GDP share of the secondary sector). As a result, in the years leading up to the First World War industrial interests became predominant within the business world, putting landowners' associations in second place in terms of political strength and public presence. In the 1910s, a slow process of building relationships and contacts between national employers' organisations had also begun. The Italian representatives had played an even more prominent role here. The starting point was precisely in Italy: in 1911 in Turin, during the International Exhibition of Industry and Labour, a Congress of Employers' Organisations in Industry and Agriculture was held where, for the first time, federations from Italy, Austria, Belgium, France, Sweden, and the United Kingdom discussed the need to create stable and prolonged contacts. In the aftermath of the congress, Gino Olivetti, secretary of *Confindustria*, and Jules Carlier and Jules Lecocq from the Central Industrial Council of Belgium travelled around Europe to promote the establishment of an international employers' group. The initiative met with some success. The outlines of such an association were defined and a statute prepared, which was approved at a meeting held in May 1914 in the offices of the Ironmasters' Committee in Paris, with the presence of representatives from Austria, Belgium, France, Germany, the United Kingdom, and Italy. With the outbreak of the First World War, however, the initiative came to a halt. It was resumed immediately after the end of the conflict, precisely in connection with the ILO's first initiatives. With the first International Labour Conference, which was held in Washington in 1919, contacts between industrial entrepreneurs of different nationalities resumed. It became clear to many at that time that a permanent international organisation was needed to prepare ILO meetings and conferences and to assist the national associations, which were called upon to perform more and more demanding tasks, especially in the face of the increasing organisation of workers. On 22 March 1920, the International Organisation of Industrial Employers was officially established in London.[46]

Italian entrepreneurs were therefore able to face the novelty of the Fascist government by counting not solely on favourable internal power relations but also on solid international ties. Not only did the trade union reform of 1926 not undermine organisational autonomy or freedom of action (as was also to be the case in other Fascist or pro-Fascist regimes),[47] but it did not pose any significant problems on the international level. For employers as well, the ILO was a crucial forum for strengthening relations with associations in other countries. As proof of the primacy acquired by industrialists as against agrarian entrepreneurs, *Confindustria*'s Gino Olivetti was appointed as the representative of the Italian employers. Olivetti – who held that role uninterruptedly until 1937, when Italy withdrew from the Geneva bodies – was perfectly integrated into the organisation, played a leading role in the debates that took place there, and was appreciated by the other national delegations and by the leaders of that forum. Albert Thomas publicly praised the Italian industrialists' organisational development, which he had had the opportunity to appreciate during numerous meetings in Italy.[48]

In an article published in the ILO's *International Labour Review* in 1928, Olivetti, for his part, illustrated in detail the activities and functioning of the confederation he headed and boasted of the results achieved even after the approval of the Syndicalist Law.[49] Inclusion in these networks did not prevent the Italian industrialists' representative from sometimes adopting peculiar positions: on some occasions, he sided against the other business delegations during the annual international labour conferences in order to support the Fascist government's positions, even at the cost of voting with the workers' delegates.[50] Olivetti also openly defended the Fascist government in other situations. At the annual conference of 1928, he stated:

> The introduction in the Conference of Fascist elements has at least allowed another social conception to come to life. The results are not completely revealed yet [...]. No one will have failed to notice that the problems of the constitution of States and the part played by the professional associations are developing more and more. There is not only interest in the Fascist movement, there is also the intuition that it is also destined to have an influence on public opinion and above all in the solution of certain problems such as the legal position of trade unions—problems of great importance in regard to collective agreements and the solution of labour conflicts.[51]

Then, two years later, Olivetti reassured his audience that "the social legislation existing in Italy is of an advanced character, and that effective protection is also ensured for the workers by the collective agreements which exist". On the same occasion, he reaffirmed the positive and concrete value of corporatism's fundamental theoretical principle of, namely, the objective of social harmony: "We have succeeded in establishing unity in our own country. The employers as well as the workers have accepted the Fascist discipline, and recognise that the workers are entitled to certain benefits from the industrial peace which is maintained as a result of that discipline".[52] However, as Olivetti himself noted, his mandate – unlike that of the workers' representative – was never challenged, not even after the law of April 1926 and the subsequent transformation of the Confederation of Industry (*Confindustria*) into the General Fascist Confederation of Italian Industry.[53]

All this shows both how sufficiently autonomous and representative of industrialists *Confindustria* appeared to be even abroad – and thus how sheltered it was from Fascism's centralising and authoritarian reforms – and how solid its network of international relations was. Even looking at the international reactions, it is therefore evident that in spite of its professed "neutrality", the Fascist trade union system generated a strong imbalance in relations between social forces.

The Syndicalist Law not only framed the opposing sides of employers and workers, but its effects also extended to the composite galaxy of the middle classes.[54] After all, the intermediate sectors of society were among the primary targets of the corporative project. For Fascism, the extensive presence of middle-class strata represented not only a counterbalance to the strength acquired by the proletariat but also the evident refutation of classist divisions based on the polarisation between capital and labour. Even before the March on Rome, Fascism had already sought to assign a central place in social life to the "middle classes", which – as Rossoni put it – represented a "synthesis of the functions of all classes", "more numerous than the proletariat itself and [...] the most consistent force in the Nation in terms of its intrinsic qualities".[55]

To speak of the middle classes is, of course, to refer to a social stratum whose boundaries are not easy to trace – a composite stratum that is highly varied in terms of conditions, social rank, interests, and culture. Not only do civil servants, freelancers, technicians, tradesmen, journalists, and teachers differ in terms of the situation they find themselves in, but within each category, profound differences are to be found. While this element characterises the middle classes' concrete experience, suggesting just how misleading generic simplifications can be, the 20 years of the dictatorship witnessed a sharpening of such differences. The task of framing professional categories within a trade union system, and more generally, of including them in the regime's structures, was carried out by the Fascists by disaggregating the galaxy of the middle classes and regrouping it around circumscribed and compartmentalised categories.

The April 1926 law crowned the first phase of this process. First of all, it marked out civil servants. State employees (including those of provincial administrations, municipalities, public charitable institutions, the railways, post offices, the Bank of Italy, *Cassa Depositi e Prestiti*, semi-public agencies, and public and savings banks) could not belong to legally recognised workers' associations, nor were they subject to the provisions on collective agreements and the jurisdiction of the labour courts.

Although in the preceding years, the civil servants' associative activity had taken place within the trade union movement (in 1923, the Public Employment Corporation – had been set up as a member of the Confederation of Fascist Trade Unions),[56] the Syndicalist Law established a system that was fully consistent with the regime's ideological and institutional reality. Unions of public employees were not acceptable for Fascism because they would entail the opposition of a "part" (public employees) to the "totality" represented by the state, the guardian and guarantor of the general interest. A number of civil servants' organisations were therefore set up, linked to the PNF and lacking the trade unions' prerogatives. Among these organisations, the General Fascist Civil Service Association (*Associazione generale fascista del pubblico impiego*, AGFPI) was the one with the highest number of members. The *Associazione* – which was only open to employees who had proven their loyalty to the Fascist regime – was assigned welfare functions, mainly through after-work activities, and so-called "moral" and "cultural" tasks, such as fostering "the formation of a solid civil and national consciousness among its members", promoting all sorts of initiatives aimed at "perfecting knowledge of problems related to the services and professional improvement of its members", and carrying out "propaganda in favour of the fundamental principles of Fascism as regards the organisation and functioning of the State and all public administrations".[57] By contrast, the association could not try to influence – through demands and disputes – matters related to occupational requirements or salaries; above all, unlike the workers' unions, it could not fulfil any contractual function.

The framing of public employees within the corporatist state, as formulated by the new law, was thus based on politicisation without unionisation. In practice, however, it was to prove difficult to conform to such a rigid design. From the end of the 1920s onwards, the Fascist associations of public employees progressively became subject to tensions similar to those marking the workers' unions, albeit to a less harrowing extent and in a manner that was only subtly conflictual: on the one hand, they acted as a transmission belt bringing members and representatives closer to the PNF and the regime; on the other, as a channel through which, despite everything, public employees' needs, expectations, and demands were expressed.[58]

The work of the AGFPI was part of the more general process of the "national unification of civil servants" pursued by Fascism. Employees of the state, provinces, municipalities, public charities, semi-public institutions, and savings banks could or were expected to join the association. The representation of all these categories of civil servants, who had hitherto been subject to different legal regimes and framed within different organisations, was now concentrated in a single association. Thus the same programmes, watchwords, and organisers addressed what had hitherto been distinct and separate categories. The civil servants consequently appeared "unified more by their legal status as civil servants than by the Fascist Idea (by definition, at this point all civil servants are Fascists insofar as they serve a Fascist State)". And it was through this unification, and through the strengthening of the employees' sense of belonging to their professional category, that their incorporation into the Fascist regime and the structures of the corporative state took place.[59]

While for civil servants the Fascist system, despite its contradictions, interrupted the unionisation process that had been developing over the course of the previous years, it actually promoted an acceleration as far as the union organisation of professionals is concerned. The Fascists showed an interest in this sector of society early on. From the beginning, they proved themselves capable of receiving positive feedback throughout the country, not least owing to the lack of intervention by socialists and Catholics. In 1920 the Fascist Trade Union Corporation of Intellectual Professions was set up, with Dino Grandi as one of its first organisers; by the end of 1924, it encompassed 910 trade unions with 57,200 members, excluding the medical sector, which was organised through the *Corporazione sanitaria* (Healthcare Corporation).[60] This focus on the realm of the professions was fully confirmed after the March on Rome when trade union action was accompanied by legislative measures. In 1923-24, the Mussolini government granted legal recognition to those professions that lacked it, also providing for the creation of registers for them.[61]

The first phase of this process ended in 1926. The Syndicalist Law significantly strengthened state control over the professions, with registration being prohibited for those who carried out public activities contrary to the "higher interests of the nation". For these reasons, according to Gaetano Salvemini, about 2,000 lawyers were struck off the registers.[62] The orders, colleges, and professional registers were kept alive, but these were flanked by a single trade union representation for each category that was valid for all, members and non-members alike, and tasked with protecting the interests of the represented and providing assistance and instruction. The trade unions then had the power to appoint half of the members of the orders' councils and, for professions without their own orders or colleges for which registration was in any case required, to exercise the functions of guardianship of the register and control of its members.

These very prerogatives marked the beginning of the process of stripping existing orders and associations of all powers to the benefit of the Fascist trade unions. The professional orders constituted autonomous institutions, free from control by the Fascist ones. They were hence considered incompatible with the regime's discipline, since "even apolitical people" took part in the election of leaders, without there being any certainty as to "their ability, their morality and, worse still, their faith in the nation".[63] For those professional categories that had obtained legal recognition following the law of April 1926, the moral and material protection of representatives was entrusted solely to the trade unions. In the case of "older" professions, the replacement of the orders with trade unions occurred later: in 1934 for lawyers, in 1935 for doctors, and in 1938 for all other professions, with the exception of notaries, who were only put on a par with the other categories in 1940.[64]

The new situation obviously favoured the growth of professional unions. Membership increased considerably, thanks to the influx of new members from all categories, while the organisations expanded across all provinces. The National Federation of Intellectual Trade Unions (*Federazione nazionale dei sindacati intellettuali*) obtained legal recognition as a member of the Confederation of Fascist Trade Unions. At the end of 1928, the federation was recognised as a separate confederation, called the National Confederation of Fascist Trade Unions of Professionals and Artists (*Confederazione nazionale dei sindacati fascisti dei professionisti e degli artisti*). It brought together the organisations representing all professional and artistic activities, with the exception of those engaged in the employ of the state.[65]

By taking over functions previously fulfilled by the orders, the trade unions progressively found themselves invested with a dual function. On the one hand, they were charged with defending the economic and professional interests of their members and improving their status, which, in concrete terms, meant: the protection of educational qualification, the extension of social security legislation, the defence of professionals from the plethora of new graduates – and, therefore, from the threat of unemployment or underemployment.[66] On the other hand, trade unions had to ensure the close connection between the functions of the professions and the state sphere.[67] The principle had been laid out by Rocco with regard to the professions of lawyer and legal representative, but his considerations can be extended to the other categories: "professional orders, even the noblest and most traditional ones, such as the bar associations, are but part of the body of the State; they have public functions which they exercise in the name and on behalf of the State, whose control they therefore cannot escape".[68] Fascism extended legal recognition to technicians (engineers, architects, and accountants), affirming for the first time their social utility and enhancing their credentials, as had been the case for legal professionals in the post-unification period.[69] In the name of the professions' public relevance, Fascism strengthened government control over accessing and practising all professions, including both "old" and "new" ones; in 1938, it then extended registration requirements to all professional categories. The trade unions were therefore called upon to guarantee the "restoration of state sovereignty" over the professions.

The outcome of this authoritarian unionisation was the strengthening of the professionals' adherence to the Fascist state: an adherence mediated by an intense sense of belonging to their category. Even more so than for other sectors of society, the professionals' inclusion in the regime's structures was achieved by strengthening the link between individuals and the interests of their specific group. Despite the progressive standardisation of legislation and the creation of a unitary confederation, the level of membership and participation in trade union organisations as well as the party differed significantly across categories. This can be seen from the varying membership in trade unions: at the end of the 1930s, the percentage of members out of the total number of representatives ranged from 63% for accountants to 85% for journalists and notaries, from 62% for lawyers and procurators to 77% for doctors, and from 59% for industrial technicians to 76% for surveyors and 81% for pharmacists.[70]

The unionisation and corporatisation of another middle-class sector, small traders, were achieved in yet a different way. Contrary to what is generally believed, the category of shopkeepers – a particularly large one in Italy – had not initially been a staunch supporter of Fascism. It had expressed "an unexpected degree of political autonomy and consistently upheld it as long as the times permitted it", i.e. until the complete suppression of political and associative freedoms.[71] This did not amount to genuine ideological anti-Fascism but rather to the "correct perception of the support that big industry and big traders had shown Mussolini". This show of support "aroused strong mistrust in small traders and well-founded concerns that in the future they would be prevented from personally protecting their own interests, which were often at odds with those of pro-Fascist big business".[72]

Their fears were fully confirmed. With the reorganisation of the trade union system brought about by the law of April 1926 and the measures of the following years, the interests of retail were sacrificed to those of larger trade businesses. The General Confederation of Italian Commerce *(Confederazione generale del commercio italiano)* – established in 1919, adhering to the Fascist trade union movement of February 1923, and largely influenced by big business – became the National Fascist Confederation of Merchants (*Confederazione nazionale fascista dei commercianti*) and obtained a monopoly on representation. Founded in 1921, the National Confederation of Small Industrialists, Merchants, and Shopkeepers (*Confederazione nazionale piccoli industriali, commercianti ed esercenti*, PICE) had over 30,000 members, mainly small shopkeepers, but did not win legal recognition: it was definitively disbanded in 1928.[73]

The new organisation representing trade interests thus enshrined a clear hierarchy between the different categories and groups. Despite being by far the largest sector in terms of employees out of all the ones included the confederation, retail trade was assigned only one federation out of nine – and this was still in the process of being set up in 1933. At least until that date, the specific problems in the retail sector found no direct expression in the confederation's governing bodies. This weakness was compounded by the fact that "small businesses" could not count on any representatives of their own, as a direct expression of their category, in key positions within the organisation.[74] This had a major effect on the organisation's own activities. Faced with the punitive legislation against small retailers passed at the end of 1926, which, among other things, introduced restrictions on licences and the possibility of revoking them, the confederation – influenced by big business – did not oppose such measures but acquiesced to the defeat of small businesses.[75] Besides, in 1928, Ferruccio Lantini, the secretary of the Confederation of Merchants, noted that one of its main objectives was to "supervise" retail sales and to stimulate the activities of high-end commerce, particularly international trade.[76]

The new trade union system therefore did not only include "producers". Alongside employers and workers in the industrial and agricultural sectors, a precise legal status was assigned to the middle classes: in some cases (the intellectual and professional middle classes), their function was enhanced through a process of Fascist unionisation; in other cases (small traders and civil servants), the imposition of a subordinate status for these professionals meant the loss of prerogatives and the ability to defend themselves.

Fascism intended to offer an original solution to the problems that all economically advanced countries were facing. The unionisation of civil servants had been a subject of heated debate everywhere, both before and after the First World War. Faced with growing conflicts and demands, politicians and jurists began to argue that state employees could not be treated like private employees in legislative and contractual terms; that the "general interest", embodied by the state, could not be subordinated to the freedom of action of partial groups and private associations.[77] As we have seen, Fascism cut the knot by denying the possibility of unionisation. Democratic states, on the other hand, tried to maintain a precarious balance between guaranteeing the freedom of association and limiting employees' partial rights.

The professional world posed new challenges to the political authorities. Over time, different models had emerged for the regulation and legislative framing of professions: from the more liberalist and pluralist (UK) to the more centralist and statist (Germany and Italy). The quantitative growth in the number of professionals, specialisations, and functions, and the fact that many of these activities (e.g. legal or health professions) performed an unquestionable social function, imposed the need to redefine the relationship between the state and professionals. The issue had already been discussed at the turn of the century but became especially relevant in the inter-war years. The authoritarian unionisation imposed by the Fascist regime therefore did not only respond to the need for control but intended to offer an organic solution to problems felt everywhere: the solution radically reinforced the statist approach that had long characterised Italian legislation concerning the professions.[78]

What seems less original are the measures concerning small traders: in this case, state intervention was driven by punitive intentions (towards a social sector that was not initially supportive of Fascism) and the pursuit of social control and economic rationalisation. The new trade union hierarchies aimed, on the one hand, to control a sector – small trade – which constituted a point of reference and connecting element for urban society and, on the other, to incentivise the more modern and advanced sectors by promoting the first processes of concentration in the distribution sector, via an analogy to what was happening in other industrialised countries. This policy was actually short-lived: by the end of the decade, the Fascist government had already launched measures to defend and protect the interests of small businesses, thereby distinguishing itself, at least to extent degree, from other large European countries, with the partial exception of France.[79]

With the Syndicalist Law, the regime therefore sought to offer solutions to face changes in social structures and forms of association that were affecting all industrialised countries. These solutions, of course, reflected Fascism's authoritarian and anti-democratic principles and its plan to create a totalitarian state. In the pursuit of full domination over the various social groups and their incorporation into the state, the management, or creation, of a vast network of trade union associations proved decisive. This operation – it bears repeating – was conducted through a combination of violence, control, and official recognition. Yet, a profound paradox emerges here which marked the entire experience of the dictatorship and its totalitarian project. It is true that through its ideas Fascism sought to unify the post-materialist and warlike community of the "new Italians", no longer contaminated and weakened by divisions and infighting. However, the entry of the masses into the regime's institutional system was achieved not only by affirming their subordination to the totality represented by the state but also by organising, breaking up, and regrouping those masses into multiple distinct groups, each expressing specific interests. In this way, not only were the legal boundaries of the various socio-professional categories determined more rigorously but by bringing them entirely within the public sphere through their legal recognition, it was acknowledged that their plurality was an undeniable fact and, at the same time, a presence of fundamental relevance in the "new state".

For factory workers or field labourers, landowners or entrepreneurs, professionals or retailers, joining a trade union organisation representing their professional category was no longer an experience linked only to specific and private interests: in some way, it was a political experience. Along with state recognition, each organisation received the seal of the Fascist state (each confederation was required to include the adjective "Fascist" in its name). Joining a trade union and participating in its activities therefore meant joining and participating in organisations that, by law and in practice, constituted a component of the regime's associative system.

In legitimising participation in union life, this process ultimately also legitimised the sense of belonging to one's own social group: not to the "class", whose relevance was indeed denied by Fascism in the name of the principle of corporatist concord, but to the "category". Fascism's corporatist policy distinguished and separated the various categories. At least as far as trade union organisation was concerned, it was addressed more to factory workers, textile workers, agricultural labourers, and shop assistants than to "salaried workers"; more to mechanics, chemists, landowners, and commercial companies than to the "landowning and entrepreneurial class"; more to lawyers, notaries, engineers, journalists, small traders, and public employees than to the "middle class". The experience of Fascist unionisation was accomplished through the progressive breakup of organisations: the role of the highest unifying bodies (the confederations) was gradually downplayed, while the function of the category federations was emphasised.

In short, the order that Fascism sought to impose on the social body, first through the syndicalist system and then through its corporative institutions, "did not exclude, but on the contrary presupposed, the rigid separation (between workers and clerks, between field labourers and industrial workers, between manual labourers and intellectual workers), the esprit de corps, category claims, and parochialism. The *whole* entailed the *particular*".[80] The public life of a substantial part of Italian society therefore occurred not only through the Fascist nationalisation process led by the PNF and oriented towards the celebration of the cult of the Duce and the regime but also through membership and participation in professional associations which were strictly divided from one another.

It remains to be ascertained to what extent and how, in the Italians' concrete experience – inevitably with profound differences across social strata and geographical areas – integral belonging to the national community and subordination to a state that aspired to be totalitarian could be integrated with the preservation of a sense of belonging to a specific group, with particular interests. What clearly emerges, even on an initial examination of the institutional scaffolding created in 1926, is the partial and inadequate nature of those interpretations that see totalitarianism as the annihilation of the plurality of classes and interests for the purpose of fragmenting society, depriving it of independent judgement and conscience, and thus making it more easily controllable.[81] The mechanisms of correlation between individuals and the state would appear to have been complex and diverse and based not only on atomised masses but also on a highly organised society.[82]

The functioning of the corporative institutions would fully confirm this tendency. In the 1930s, within a weakened corporative framework, professional organisations were nonetheless to act as forces that at least partly escaped the state-centred and monistic order of Fascism.

Notes

1 Giuseppe Parlato, *La sinistra fascista. Storia di un progetto mancato* (Bologna: Il Mulino, 2000), 239.

2 For an analysis of Fascist trade unionism focusing on its repressive aspect, see Domenico Preti, ed., "Per una storia del sindacato fascista negli anni trenta", in *Economia e istituzioni nello Stato fascista* (Roma: Editori Riuniti, 1980), 261–386; see also the "classic" work, Ernesto Rossi, *I padroni del vapore* (Bari: Laterza, 1955).

3 We do not have reliable data on trade union membership. The official data does not appear sufficiently reliable, nor do the sources enable accurate estimates. In 1927, however, before the "unblocking", official estimates credited the Fascist workers' unions with over 2 million members: Ferdinando Cordova, *Verso lo Stato totalitario. Sindacati, società e fascismo* (Soveria Mannelli: Rubbettino, 2005), 76–77.

4 Alberto De Bernardi, *Operai e nazione. Sindacati, operai e stato nell'Italia fascista* (Franco Angeli: Milano, 1993), 17.

5 This is Togliatti's well-known thesis: see Palmiro Togliatti, *Corso sugli avversari. Lezioni sul fascismo*, ed. Francesco M. Biscione (Torino: Einaudi, 2010). Some remarks that go in this direction are also to be found in Alberto Aquarone, Maurizio Vernassa, "Introduzione", in *Il regime fascista*, eds. Alberto Aquarone and Maurizio Vernassa (Bologna: Il Mulino, 1974), 27–30; and Leonardo Rapone, "Il sindacalismo fascista: temi e problemi della ricerca storica", *Storia contemporanea* 13, no. 4–5 (1982): 635–696.

6 Lyttelton, *The Seizure of Power*, 271.

7 Olivetti noted the objections from the Confederation of Industrialists in a letter to Mussolini dated 1 May 1926. This letter, preserved in the Historical Archives of the *Unione industriale* of Turin, has been partially published in Mario Abrate, *La lotta sindacale nella industrializzazione in Italia 1906–1926* (Milano: Franco Angeli, 1967), 459.

8 Edmondo Rossoni, "Riflessioni sulla Rivoluzione Fascista. La corporazione come Idea", *La Stirpe*, March 1931, 99. See Renzo De Felice, *Mussolini il duce*, I. *Gli anni del consenso 1929–1936* (Torino: Einaudi, 1975), 16–17; Santomassimo, *La terza via fascista*, 94–95.

9 Edmondo Rossoni, "Il sindacalismo e l'economia eroica del fascismo", *La stirpe*, May 1930, 226.

10 See, among other sources, the texts featured in the anthological section of Giuseppe Parlato, *Il sindacalismo fascista,* vol. II, *Dalla «grande cris»i alla caduta del regime (1930–1943)* (Roma: Bonacci, 1989), 187–263.

11 ACS, SPD, CR, fasc. W/R, "Rossoni Edmondo", sottofasc. 2. Rapporto di Ps, *Esplicite dichiarazioni di Rossoni sull'attuale situazione sindacale e corporativa*, 4 April 1931. This was an "interview" with Rossoni in relation to his article "Riflessioni sulla Rivoluzione Fascista".
12 ACS, SPD, CR, 1922–43, b. 4, fasc. 64/R "Giuseppe Bottai", sottofasc. 2. *All'On. Presidente della Corte di disciplina e d'onore del Partito Nazionale Fascista*, 18 April 1925; Giuseppe Bottai, "Il caso Rossoni", *L'Epoca*, 15 April 1925; Bottai, *La «Corporazione di Stato» proposta dai Diciotto, L'Epoca*, 19 April 1925.
13 Critica fascista, "Lo Stato senza aggettivi", *Critica fascista* 6, no. 7 (1928): 123.
14 Critica fascista, "Chiarificazione necessaria", *Critica fascista* 6, no. 9 (1928): 162.
15 Giuseppe Bottai, "Discorso al Senato" (31 May 1928), in Bottai, *Esperienza corporativa*, 70.
16 Partito nazionale fascista, *Il Gran Consiglio nei primi dieci anni*, 288–291.
17 "Le direttive dell'organizzazione tracciate dall'on. Rossoni", *Il Lavoro d'Italia*, 5 May 1928.
18 Giuseppe Bottai, "Discorso alla Camera dei deputati" (15 March 1928), in Bottai, *Esperienza corporativa*, 229–230.
19 Bottai, "Discorso alla Camera dei deputati" (15 March 1928), 230.
20 Aquarone, *L'organizzazione*, 193, 210–211.
21 "Le direttive dell'organizzazione tracciate dall'on. Rosson*i", Il lavoro d'Italia*, 5 maggio 1928.
22 ACS, SPD, CR, 1922–43, b. 30, fasc. 242/R "Gran Consiglio", sottofasc. 6, inserto B. *Relazione Bottai*, no date (but September 1929).
23 De Felice, *Mussolini il fascista II*, 329; Cordova, *Verso lo Stato totalitario*, 100–101.
24 Angelo Oliviero Olivetti, "Le corporazioni e la loro formazione naturale", *Il Diritto del lavoro*, January 1928; "Sindacati e burocrazia", *Corriere della sera*, 3 November 1927; and A. M. [Arnaldo Mussolini], "Complementi necessari", *Il Popolo d'Italia*, 17 November 1927.
25 Tullio Cianetti, *Memorie dal carcere di Verona*, ed. Renzo De Felice (Milano: Rizzoli, 1983), 151.
26 ACS, SPD, CR, 1922–1943, b. 30, fasc. 242/R "Gran Consiglio", sottofasc. 6, inserto B. *Relazione Bottai.*
27 Benito Mussolini, *250ª riunione del Consiglio dei ministri*, in *Opera omnia di Benito Mussolini*, ed. Edoardo Susmel, Duilio Susmel, vol. XXIII (Firenze: La Fenice, 1957), 260.
28 De Felice *Mussolini il fascista II*, 326–36; Perfetti, *Il sindacalismo fascista I*, 155–65; Cordova, *Verso lo Stato totalitario*, 82–106.
29 See Ornella Cilona, "La Confederazione fascista dei lavoratori dell'industria negli anni Trenta", *Annali della Fondazione Luigi Einaudi* 22 (1988): 267.
30 Gian Carlo Jocteau, "Gino Olivetti: la Confindustria e il corporativismo. Il ruolo dell'ideologia nel sindacalismo padronale italiano", *Annali di storia dell'impresa* 8 (1992): 367.
31 Luca Lanzalaco, *Dall'impresa all'associazione. Le organizzazioni degli imprenditori: la Confindustria in prospettiva comparata* (Milano: Franco Angeli, 1990), 138–141.
32 Roland Sarti, *Fascism and the Industrial Leadership in Italy, 1919–1940. A Study in the Expansion of Private Power under Fascism* (Berkeley-Los Angeles-London: University of California Press, 1971), 79–88.
33 Lanzalaco, *Dall'impresa all'associazione*, 133.
34 Ibid., 143.
35 The president of *Confindustria*, Antonio Stefano Benni, voiced his reservations about certain details of the law and the implementing decree: ACS, PCM, Atti 1919–36, 1927, b. 297, fasc. 3/5. Benni's letter to Mussolini on the degree of implementing the Syndicalist Law, 1 May 1926.
36 *Annuario. Confederazione generale dell'industria italiana*, 1 (1947), 235.

37 Address by Léon Jouhaux, in *International Labour Conference, Fifth Session* (Geneva: International Labour Office, 1923), 171–177.
38 "Objection of the 'Confederazione Generale del Lavoro' with regard to the nomination of the Italian Workers' Delegate", in *International Labour Conference, Sixth Session*, vol. 1 (Geneva: International Labour Office, 1924), 533. On the complaints raised by the CGDL, see Andrea Panaccione, "'L'operaio italiano': Un sindacato nell'emigrazione e il suo giornale", *Economia & Lavoro* 40, no. 2 (2006): 119–120.
39 Address by Corneille Mertens, in *International Labour Conference, Eighth Session* (Geneva: International Labour Office, 1926), 169–170.
40 Address by Léon Jouhaux, in *International Labour Conference, Eighth Session*, 173.
41 "Statement on 'Freedom of Association' in Italy", in *International Labour Conference, Tenth Session* (Geneva: International Labour Office, 1927), 498.
42 Renata Allio, *L'organizzazione internazionale del lavoro e i sindacati fascisti* (Bologna: Il Mulino, 1973); Antony Evelyn Alcock, *History of the International Labour Organisation* (London: MacMillan, 1971); and Roberto Virzo, "The Influx of International Law Scholars in the Constitution-Making Process", in *A History of International Law in Italy*, ed. Giulio Bartolini (Oxford: Oxford University Press, 2020), 401.
43 "Minority Report", in *International Labour Conference, Twelfth Session* (Geneva: International Labour Office, 1929), 675.
44 Alexander Nützenadel, "A Green International? Food Markets and Transnational Politics, c.1850–1914", in *Food and Globalization Consumption, Markets and Politics in the Modern World*, eds. Alexander Nützenadel and Frank Trentmann (Oxford-New York: Berg, 2008), 160–165.
45 Richard W. Gable, "Birth of an Employers' Association", *The Business History Review* 33, no. 4 (1959): 535–545; Tony Adams, "Market and Institutional Forces in Industrial Relations: The Development of National Collective Bargaining, 1910–1920", *The Economic History Review* 50, no. 3 (1997): 506–530; and Alan McKinlay, "From Organised to Disorganised Capital? British Employer Associations, 1897–2010", in *Global Anti-Unionism Nature, Dynamics, Trajectories and Outcomes*, eds. Gregor Gall and Tony Dundon (London: Palgrave Macmillan, 2013), 39–62.
46 Rolf Birk, Nils Maack, "International Organisation of Employers", in *Handbook of Transnational Economic Governance Regimes*, eds. Christian Tietje and Alan Brouder (Leiden: Brill-Nijhoff, 2009), 177–178.
47 *Enterprise in the Period of Fascism in Europe*, eds. Harold James, Jakob Tanner (London-New York: Routledge, 2017).
48 AILO, *CAT* 1/28/1/4. *Voyage officiel Italie-Espagne*, May 1928; ibid., *CAT* 1/32/2. *Note personnelle*, 17 March 1932.
49 Gino Olivetti, "Employers' organisations in Italy", *International Labour Office* 18, no. 4–5 (1928): 483–508.
50 Gallo, *Dictatorship*, 158.
51 Address by Gino Olivetti, in *International Labour Conference, Eleventh Session* (Geneva: International Labour Office, 1928), 206.
52 Address by Gino Olivetti, in *International Labour Conference, Fourteenth Session* (Geneva: International Labour Office, 1930), 238.
53 Address by Gino Olivetti, in *International Labour Conference, Tenth Session*, 85.
54 On the problem of the relationship between the middle classes and the State in inter-war Europe: Jonathan Morris, "Introduction. The European Petite Bourgeoisie 1914–1945: Encounters with the State", *Contemporary European History* 5, no. 3 (1996): 279–283. On the Italian case: Alessio Gagliardi, "Valorizzare 'il terzo elemento'. Classi medie e organizzazione corporativa nell'Italia fascista", *Rivista Storica Italiana* 131, no. 1 (2019): 128–156.
55 Edmondo Rossoni, "Forze di governo", *Il Lavoro d'Italia*, 4 May 1922.
56 Mussolini himself fully acknowledged the corporations' merits as trade unions: Benito Mussolini, "Fascismo e sindacalismo (1925)", in *Opera omnia di Benito Mussolini*, eds. Edoardo Susmel and Duilio Susmel, vol. XXI (Firenze: La Fenice, 1956), 333–334.

57 "Statuto dell'Associazione generale fascista del pubblico impiego", annex to RD 23 February 1927, *Gazzetta Ufficiale*, 1927, no. 57.
58 Alessio Gagliardi, "Il sindacato negato. Gli impiegati pubblici e l'organizzazione dello Stato fascista", in *La sindacalizzazione del pubblico impiego. Dalle origini delle rappresentanze alla Funzione pubblica CGIL*, ed. Pasquale Iuso (Roma: Ediesse, 2006), 233–288.
59 Mariuccia Salvati, *Il regime e gli impiegati. La nazionalizzazione piccolo-borghese nel ventennio fascista* (Roma-Bari: Laterza, 1992), 203.
60 Giacomo Di Giacomo, *L'organizzazione sindacale dei lavoratori intellettuali* (Milano: Imperia, 1924), 29.
61 Gabriele Turi, "Le libere professioni e lo Stato", in *Libere professioni e fascismo*, ed. Turi (Milano: Franco Angeli, 1994), 25.
62 Gaetano Salvemini, *Under the Axe of Fascism* (London: Victor Gollancz, 1986), 102.
63 Costantino Chiaria, "La scelta non può essere dubbia", *Il lavoro d'Italia*, 30 January 1930.
64 Turi, "Le libere professioni", 30.
65 PNF. Ufficio stampa, *Venti anni*. II. *L'ordine corporativo e la difesa sociale* (Roma: 1943), 181.
66 For example, in the case of the legal professions, see Antonella Meniconi, *La «maschia avvocatura». Istituzioni e professione forense in epoca fascista (1922–1943)* (Bologna: Il Mulino, 2006).
67 Gabriele Turi, "La presenza del fascismo e le professioni liberali", in Istituto lombardo per la storia del movimento di liberazione in Italia, *Cultura e società negli anni del fascismo* (Cordani: Milano, 1987), 11–30; Turi, "Le libere professioni".
68 Alfredo Rocco, *La trasformazione dello Stato. Dallo Stato liberale allo Stato fascista* (Roma: La Voce, 1927), 31.
69 Maria Malatesta, "Professioni e professionisti", in *Storia d'Italia. Annali*, 10, *I professionisti*, ed. Malatesta (Torino: Einaudi, 1996), XXI.
70 Fernando Coscera, *Professioni e arti nello Stato fascista* (Roma: Trinacria, 1941), 41.
71 Vera Zamagni, *La distribuzione commerciale fra le due guerre* (Milano: Franco Angeli, 1981), 87–88.
72 Zamagni, *La distribuzione commerciale*, 88.
73 Jonathan Morris, "The Fascist 'Disciplining' of the Italian Retail Sector", *Business History* 40, no. 4 (1998): 138–164; Morris, "Contesting Retail Space in Italy: Competition and Corporatism 1915–60", *The International Review of Retail, Distribution and Consumer Research* 9, no. 3 (1999): 291–306; and Mara Anastasia, *Interessi di bottega. I piccoli commercianti italiani nella crisi dello Stato liberale 1919–1926* (Torino: Zamorani, 2007).
74 Anastasia, *Interessi di bottega*, 211–212.
75 Zamagni, *La distribuzione commerciale*, 96.
76 Confederazione Nazionale fascista dei commercianti, *Secondo Consiglio Nazionale (Roma 12 13 dicembre 1928)* (Roma: F.lli Pallotta, 1929), 144.
77 On the British case, for example, see J.W. Bowen, "Trade Unionism in the Civil Service", *Public Administration* 15, no. 4 (1937): 419–432.
78 Konrad H. Jarausch, *The Unfree Professions: German Lawyers, Teachers, and Engineers, 1900–1950* (New York-Oxford: Oxford University Press, 1990); Charles E. McClelland, *The German Experience of Professionalization; Modern Learned Professions and Their Organizations from the Early Nineteenth Century to the Hitler Era* (Cambridge: Cambridge University Press, 1991); *Lawyers and Vampires. Cultural Histories of Legal Professions*, eds. W. Wesley Pue, David Sugarman (Oxford-Portland: Hart Publishing, 2003); and Maria Malatesta, *Professionisti e gentiluomini. Storia delle professioni nell'Europa contemporanea* (Torino: Einaudi, 2006).
79 Joseph Jones, "Vichy France and Postwar Economic Modernization: The Case of the Shopkeepers", *French Historical Studies* 12, no. 4 (1982): 542–546; and Jonathan

Morris, "Retailers. Fascism and the Origins of the Social Protection of Shopkeepers in Italy", *Contemporary European History* 5, no. 3 (1996): 287.

80 Maurizio Degl'Innocenti, *La società unificata. Associazione, sindacato, partito sotto il fascismo* (Manduria-Bari-Roma: Lacaita, 1995), XXIII.

81 See, among many others, Hannah Arendt, *The Origins of Totalitarianism* (New York: Harcourt, Brace and Co., 1951).

82 Emilio Gentile, *La via italiana al totalitarismo. Il partito e lo Stato nel regime fascista* (Roma: Carocci, 2001).

5 The Great Depression and the Rise of Corporatism

The phase of stabilisation and increasing prosperity that Europe and the whole industrialised world experienced after the early 1920s came to a more or less abrupt halt at the end of the decade. The turning point was an event that took place in the United States. In October 1929, a wave of selling on New York's Wall Street Stock Exchange caused shares to plummet. Large financial institutions suffered huge losses, while small savers saw their fortunes evaporate, in many cases losing everything. Panic swept through the banks, causing account holders to withdraw their deposits. In order to defend their interests, the banks demanded the repayment of loans, which reduced the capital available on the markets. The situation had immediate repercussions on the real economy: companies had to face, on the one hand, a reduced availability of capital and, on the other, a drop in consumption levels among those who had lost their savings; the decrease in sales, in turn, led to a drop in production, a loss of working days, redundancies, and cutbacks in the purchase of raw materials and machinery, thus triggering a spiral of further contractions. Given the high degree of interconnectedness among national economies, the crisis soon involved almost the whole industrialised world, starting with Europe.

The collapse of the New York Stock Exchange had a resounding impact and came as a real shock to public opinion, the ruling classes, and economic actors. Yet, in spite of a recurring narrative that traces the economic crisis to the black days on Wall Street, clear signs of the growth cycle's exhaustion in the second half of the 1920s were already visible in the United States, where the increase in sales and profits had been slowing down since the early months of the year, as well as in Germany, which had been grappling with a reduction in capital flows from overseas since 1928. The origin of the crisis lies not in the stock market crash but in a more complex process that was closely linked to the changes experienced by international capitalism over the course of the previous two decades.

In the years leading up to the First World War and the 1920s, first in the United States and then in the more advanced areas of Western Europe, new ways of organising work based on greater labour intensity, combined with an abundant flow of investments, had ensured sustained production growth. Profits had increased at the expense of workers' consumption shares, which had grown less than the production levels. A growing imbalance had thus arisen between

DOI: 10.4324/9781032713267-6

the overabundant production of goods and the markets' capacity to absorb them. During the second half of the 1920s, the risk of overproduction was postponed by the stock market boom and the spread of consumer credit. The imbalance was not resolved, however. On the contrary, the formation of a "bubble" in the US economy, which also dragged the European economies into this growth process, further aggravated the initial imbalance. In the US, there was a sharp slowdown in the first half of 1929, and the bubble burst in October 1929. The close integration of the two sides of the Atlantic, which was further strengthened by the international payments system that had been established with the Dawes Plan of 1924, almost immediately pulled Europe in, which was already facing internal contradictions. In 1931, some major banking institutions in Germany and Austria declared bankruptcy.

The financial crisis and the real crisis were thus closely intertwined and indeed constituted two aspects of the same phenomenon. A crisis of unprecedented proportions began. The collapse of national income and industrial production continued until 1932–1933. The fall in production was not the only consequence. The drastic contraction of world trade, which was reduced in value by more than half, as well as falling prices and the drop in employment levels, were no less significant. The great mass of unemployed workers, the social fact that most marked this decade, not only created vast strata of new poor populations in the heart of the most economically advanced countries but was at the origin of a progressive destabilisation of the institutional and political framework of democratic states through the rise of authoritarian and radical right-wing movements.

In the first phase, the national governments and central banks of almost all capitalist countries adopted – albeit in different contexts – policies that were in line with tradition. In the shared conviction that market mechanisms would spontaneously regain their equilibrium, they did not promote any specific forms of state intervention. Instead, at least in the first two years, they pursued a balanced budget, even via cuts in public spending, and defended the anchoring of their currencies to the gold standard, even at the price of an increase in the value of money. In other words, in a situation already marked by falling demand and prices, they applied economic policies that produced deflation and austerity, further worsening all domestic economic indicators. At the same time, after the first few months, some of the largest economies chose to cope with the collapse by reducing their ties to international markets and trying to unload the costs onto other countries. In order to protect domestic production against foreign competition and global market fluctuations, they chose to adopt protectionist policies. First came the United States – which introduced a new customs tariff in 1930 – followed by the European states. European exports plummeted by 60% in value. Some Eastern European and Balkan countries (particularly Poland, Czechoslovakia, Yugoslavia, Hungary, and Greece), Austria, and Spain saw particularly catastrophic results, far worse than the continental average.[1] About two years after the Wall Street Crash, the international monetary system also entered into crisis. In order to defend themselves against speculative attacks and boost their exports, many countries chose to escape the system of common rules and devalue their currencies to reduce the relative cost of their exports. The decisive step in this direction was taken by the United Kingdom, which in September 1931 decided to abandon the gold standard.[2]

Overall, these choices not only failed to boost production, incomes, and consumption levels but actually worsened and prolonged the collapse. In order to bring a halt to the collapse and usher in the first signs of a reversal of the cycle, it was necessary for the ruling classes of the industrialised world to realise that the path they had followed up to that point had been ineffective, if not harmful. In light of this, they began to reformulate their economic paradigms and intervention strategies. At the same time, public confidence in the market's ability to regulate itself and spontaneously produce a new equilibrium and a return to growth was irrevocably shattered. From 1932 onwards, many governments gradually moved away from the dictates of laissez-faire economics and initiated policies based on a sharp increase in state intervention. No longer pursuing a balanced budget, they began to finance investments and public works to create new jobs while at the same time strengthening welfare and social security policies to support those hardest hit by the crisis. The aim of these interventions was not only to help those individuals who were struggling the most in the short term but also to encourage an increase in wages and consequently of consumption so as to stimulate companies to return to investing and hiring new staff, thus triggering a virtuous circle that was supposed to spark a recovery process. In such a way, state funding was expected to drive the recovery of the private economy with a positive multiplication effect. The idea of the "multiplier" (a calculation mechanism to measure the increase in national income due to increased public spending) was developed by the British economist John Maynard Keynes in those very years. In his 1936 work *The General Theory of Employment, Interest, and Money*, Keynes summed up the fundamental lines of the new economic policy based on the use of public expenditure to support domestic demand, as well as on the need for the state to pursue the goal of a drastic and ideally complete reduction in unemployment rates.

The less orthodox orientation of the new economic policies adopted – as exemplified by the New Deal in the United States and the public works programme launched by Adolf Hitler – helped to substantially reduce unemployment, but not a return to pre-1929 levels. In 1932–1933, however, the most dramatic phase of the crisis ended almost everywhere and a period of very slow recovery began.

Among politicians and economists, the idea took root that the balance between the state and private initiative had to be completely rethought. In other words, the conviction spread that the current transformations in the organisation of work, the increased size of companies, and the consequent growth in production had rendered the market's self-regulating action less effective, meaning that the authorities were called upon to play a more prominent role. Both in practice and in theory, through governments' initiatives and intellectuals' theories, this new leading role of the state took many different forms, ranging from mild measures to regulate imports and exports or competition to policies for planning production in individual sectors, the nationalisation of industrial and financial companies, and the creation of vast public enterprise complexes, such as the one established in Italy under the control of the Institute for Industrial Reconstruction (*Istituto per la ricostruzione industriale*, or IRI).[3] All these initiatives remained fully within a capitalist market economy in which price and investment dynamics were mainly entrusted to the decisions of private individuals. One exception was the USSR, which in the early 1930s experienced Stalin's implementation of a "revolution from above" that, within a short time, would give rise to a model of modernity that was an alternative to capitalism through the centralised planning of production and the forced collectivisation of the countryside. The wide range of more or less innovative measures also included a great revival of corporatism.

This development was perfectly mirrored by Fascism's cultural programme as well as its economic policies.[4] Mussolini's writings and speeches provide a very clear testimony to this. In an address to the Senate late in 1930, Mussolini examined the origin of the crisis. Numerous factors had created the conditions for an economic collapse. The "mother of all explanations", however, was the "imbalance [...] between production and consumption":

> The watchword for the Americans was, "Mass production, mass consumption." This formula was wrong, as they themselves have realized. Wrong, because production is done by machines and consumption by men. It was a logical formula, from a purely mechanical point of view, but all it took was a small hitch to make it collapse. American prosperity was tied to the assumption that production and consumption would march in lock step. What if consumption gave signs of fatigue? Then the jockeys, like on a race track, would spur the horse of consumption. How? With high salaries But since high salaries were not enough, then with sales on payment plans, production cut to the extreme and finally wild advertising that created an unhealthy inflationary mindset. When consumption started showing signs of fatigue, a full crisis broke out.[5]

The "Duce of Fascism" endorsed an explanation of the international depression in terms of overproduction, identifying the Fordist equilibrium created in the United States after the First World War as the main originating factor. His analysis had clear political implications, as it was a critique of the industrial developments promoted by the leading democracy and of the negative role played, in his view, by consumer society.

Hence, Mussolini wondered whether that system of production had unleashed forces that the market was no longer able to control, and thus "whether an economy that had already experienced restrictions in the workplace, would also have to be restricted inside states and state federations".[6] If it was market forces that had led to the crisis, it was up to the state to get out of it:

> It is not a question of whether or not the government should intervene. That would be a waste of time. When a private company reaches beyond certain limits, it is no longer a private but rather a public company. A craftsman's business may be private but when an industry, a credit institute, a business, a bank, controls billions and employs tens of thousands of people, how can

> one think that its success or failure is the personal affair of the director of that business or the shareholders of that industry? No. At that point it becomes part of the national interest. The state, the political expression of the legal, moral will of the nation cannot remain on the sidelines. It would sow ruin.[7]

In any case, there were no "heroic remedies", no immediate and universally applicable solutions. In the international context – and this was Mussolini's political conclusion – Italy had certain advantages over the major industrial powers. The first was the Italians' "capacity to resist". This was a paradoxical and certainly bizarre argument: the ability to cope with the crisis was traced back to Italy's "not yet overly developed" national economic system. According to Mussolini, "[f]ortunately [the use of this adverb is truly striking] the Italian people are not used to eating many times a day. Since they have a modest standard of living, they feel suffering and shortages less".[8] This "negative" advantage was combined with a "positive" one, namely the Fascist state, which "has organized all interests and framed all national factors into categories so the government can intervene and not allow itself to be surprised by events".[9]

Mussolini briefly returned to the subject about two years later, in October 1932, when opening the celebrations of the ten-year anniversary of the March on Rome. His analysis was still open to different conclusions. If the current crisis were to prove to be a "crisis *within* the system", i.e. an economic downturn, it would resolve itself in a short time (but here, Mussolini glossed over the fact that the depression had been going on for at least three years). If it instead proved to be a "crisis *of* the system", it was bound to trigger a profound transformation of the structures of society and the mechanisms for regulating the economy ("a transition from one stage of civilisation to another"). In any case, there were no easy and immediate ways out, no "miraculous remedies". The only certainty, according to Mussolini, was that the unlimited growth of state intervention, far from being the solution, would create enormous problems: "Where they have sought to stretch capitalism even more by turning it into State *capitalism,* the result has been extreme distress".[10]

Finally, Mussolini took up the issue a year later, in November 1933, within a broader and more comprehensive address on the great economic crisis of the 1930s, its effects, and the solutions to be adopted. This address was significantly anticipated by an interview in the French newspaper *Echo de Paris*.[11] In his speech, Mussolini first of all answered the question raised the previous year, namely whether the current crisis was a "crisis *within* the system" or a "crisis *of* the system": "Today my answer is that the crisis has sunk so deeply into the system that it has become a crisis of the system. It is no longer an injury, but a constitutional disease. We can now assert that the capitalistic mode of production has been superseded, and with it the theory of classical economic liberalism which explained and defended it".[12]

Mussolini traced a concise history of capitalism to support his argument, distinguishing three periods. The first, from 1830 to 1870, is the dynamic and vital period of the Industrial Revolution. Development is guided by the law of free competition, which translates the principles of the struggle for the survival and selection of the fittest into the economic sphere. The lives of states also conform to the same rules.

From 1870 one begins to detect "the first symptoms of fatigue and of deviation in the capitalist world".[13] The vitalism of competition is gradually replaced by the search for accommodation for mediation; the drive towards change is replaced by the defence of what is already in existence: "The era of cartels, syndicates, combines, and trusts began".

The First World War marks the beginning of the third stage: "supercapitalism". The new system is characterised by three elements: firstly, the unchecked proliferation of goods produced and the spread of the illusion of their immediate accessibility – in other words, "the utopia of unlimited consumption". Secondly, the standardisation of products and human activities, starting with labour. This is a consequence of the fact that only the uniformity of practices, measures, and timings, i.e. their predictability, can enable large-scale planning. It is precisely this large scale, this large dimension, that constitutes the third characteristic element. Enterprises continuously grow in size, becoming "monstrous, babelic", as everything becomes "abnormal";[14] they come to control ever-larger masses of workers, mobilising enormous capital and previously unthinkable quantities of raw materials and products; consequently, they cease to be "an economic fact" and become "a social fact". Having grown too large, enterprises cannot govern themselves, nor can they resolve their difficulties on their own; and this failure is bound to have disastrous consequences. For this reason, enterprises can no longer do without the state. This is proof of the final, systemic crisis reached by capitalism: unable to self-regulate and develop because it has abandoned the principles of competition and struggle, capitalism can only end up under the complete control of the state, giving rise to "total state capitalism, which is nothing less than state socialism in reverse".[15]

Having outlined the history of capitalism in somewhat catastrophic terms, Mussolini dwelt on the specificity of the Italian situation and how it fitted within the general picture. If one looked at technological progress and the most widespread practices, Italy could be considered a capitalist nation; but if one analysed employment and income statistics, and the weight of the different categories, a different picture emerged. The country's social and economic structure was extremely complex, and far removed from the polarisation between capitalists and proletarians that Marx had indicated as a sign of capitalist development. Only a small share of the workforce and national income could be traced back to industry; large enterprises were still very few in number, while the intermediate sectors (sharecroppers, small landowners, professionals, retailers, and public and private employees) were substantial. Mussolini continued:

> In my opinion Italy should remain a country with a mixed economy with a strong agricultural sector at the root of everything. Actually the revival in industry as of late is due, in the unanimous opinion of all acquainted with these matters, to the good crop harvests of the last few years. Then there is sound small and medium-sized industry; banks that do not speculate; commerce that fulfills its irreplaceable task of supplying commodities rapidly and reasonably to consumers.[16]

In short, insofar as it had not followed the dictates of mass production, Italy had first remained sheltered from the excesses of unbridled capitalist growth and the limitless spread of consumption; consequently, it had suffered less than other countries from the effects of the systemic crisis.

The belief that the Italian economy had managed to avoid the Great Depression's blows continued to circulate for quite some time after 1945, both among the public and in early historiographical reconstructions. However, more detailed chronologies and increasingly rigorous and mature studies have long revealed that Italy was fully in line with international economic trends.[17] All major indicators were negative in the early 1930s. But it is also true that the collapse was less severe than in other more advanced economies. From 1929 to 1932, industrial production plummeted by 14%: a significant fall, but certainly a limited one compared to Germany's 39% or France's 26%.[18] This figure was the consequence of two factors: the Italian economy, unlike others, was not coming from a period of accelerated development but from a long phase of slow growth[19]; moreover, as Mussolini himself observed, areas that are generally less affected by cyclical trends, such as the agricultural sector and the less innovative areas of the tertiary sector, weighed much more heavily than elsewhere: suffice to say that agriculture accounted for 30% of the total revenue in Italy, while in the United States it accounted for only 9%, in the United Kingdom for 4%, in Germany for 20%, and in France for 22%.[20]

Mussolini then added an element which constituted the fundamental argument of his speech: the relative resilience of the Italian economy was to be attributed not only to its productive and employment structure but also, to a decisive extent, to Fascism and its corporatist system. It was precisely corporatism that had prevented the total subjugation of social and political life to the logic of production by ensuring a more balanced development; and it had reaffirmed the principle of the superiority of spirit over matter:

> Corporativism means a regulated economy and therefore also a controlled economy, for there can be no regulation without control.
>
> Corporativism supersedes socialism and supersedes liberalism by creating a new synthesis.
>
> [...]
>
> This is why Corporate economics rises at a particular moment in history when the two concomitant phenomena of capitalism and socialism have given all they had to give.
>
> We inherited everything that was still alive in either of them.
>
> We rejected the liberal theory of the economic man, and we rose up every time labor was referred to as a commodity.
>
> Economic man does not exist. Man is complete He is political, economic, religious, a saint, and a warrior.[21]

Consistent with Mussolini's speeches, the crisis years saw the Fascist government give renewed impetus to cultural reflection on corporatism and institutional reforms. On the cultural level, the first half of the 1930s constituted the phase of greatest commitment and liveliness, at first partly owing to Bottai's action as Minister of Corporations. Above all, major reforms were carried out in that period following the 1926 trade Syndicalist Law. In 1930, the National Council of Corporations, already provided for in the 1926 law's implementation decrees (see Chapter 2), was established after several years of waiting; four years later, in 1934, corporations were established. The edifice of the corporate state was thus finally constituted. We will examine the actions of these bodies in the following chapters. Meanwhile, it should be noted that the reforms of the 1930s shifted the focus of intervention from the governing of trade unions (control over organisations representing particular interests, achieved by legal means) to the governance of the economy to create a new balance between the state and society.

Not least in light of these novelties, at the beginning of the 1930s, the regime's (domestic and overseas) propaganda and its leading intellectuals staunchly maintained that Italy was moving towards the so-called "corporative revolution". The talk about possible achievements outside Italy, by contrast, sounded uncertain and contradictory. As we have seen, Mussolini – followed by all the regime's leaders and intellectuals – was convinced that corporatism constituted a historical alternative both to the "supercapitalism" originating from the United States and to Soviet socialism, i.e. that it constituted a genuine model for the state and the economy. On several occasions, however, he had emphasised that corporatist experiments were taking place in a country, Italy, that had unique characteristics: it enjoyed both the advantages of a relatively delayed development and the presence of the only political system, Fascism, capable of regulating society in his view. This created an obvious contradiction: was corporatism a universal model, exportable to other countries, or could it only be realised in a specific and particular context such as Italy's? In the already quoted speech of November 1933, Mussolini argued:

> Let us ask ourselves one last question. Can corporativism be applied to other countries? We are bound to ask ourselves this because the same question is being asked in every country making an effort to study and to understand.
>
> There is no doubt given the general crisis of capitalism, that the corporate solution will come forth everywhere. If the system is to he carried out fully, completely, integrally, and revolutionarily; three conditions are required.
>
> A single political party so political discipline may coexist with economic discipline and for the bond of a common fate to unite everyone above contrasting interests.
>
> This is not enough. Besides a single political party there must be a totalitarian state, a state that may transform and uplift the people by absorbing their energy, interests, and aspirations.
>
> But even this is not enough. The third and last and most important condition is to live in an atmosphere of strong ideal tension.
>
> We, in Italy, live in such an atmosphere today.
>
> That is why, step by step, we will give force and consistency to all our achievements, why we shall translate all our doctrine into action.

> Who can deny that the fascist era is an era of great ideal tension? No one can deny it. This is an age in which arms are crowned by victory, institutions renewed, land redeemed, and new cities founded.[22]

Mussolini thus fascistised corporatism; in other words, he considered the corporatist system an integral part of the Fascist state model, which could not be applied to a democratic state. This became the dominant theme of Fascist propaganda abroad, which was significantly reinforced in those very years. Pointing to corporatism as the only possible way out of the current crisis, it proposed Fascism not as a typically Italian achievement but as a new political model that could also be adopted in other countries.

Mussolini had laid the first foundations for this approach in 1930: in a speech delivered on 27 October, he declared that "Fascism as an idea, doctrine, and realisation, is universal", and that therefore one could "envisage a Fascist Europe, a Europe that models its institutions on the doctrines and practice of Fascism".[23] The effort to spread the "Fascist gospel" outside Italy had begun in the second half of the 1920s with propaganda on corporatism, as we have seen in Chapter 3. In the early 1930s, in the new intellectual climate dominated by the Great Depression – and thanks to the efforts of Bottai, who had been appointed Minister of Corporations – this propaganda became even more intense and systematic. The production of materials and initiatives on corporatist issues greatly increased, directly involving prominent intellectuals and political leaders. In this way, the international public was given direct access to the words of the major architects of the corporatist reforms, allowing it to appreciate their theories but also to take note of the range of conceptions that animated the debate among the regime's higher echelons. In 1930 a double issue of the journal *Rassegna italiana* was published entitled *Lo Stato mussoliniano e le realizzazioni del fascismo nella nazione* (*Mussolini's State and the Accomplishments of Fascism in the Nation*).[24] This volume, featuring contributions by numerous government and state figures as well as representatives of private enterprise, was also intended for international circulation: the following year, it was translated by Plon in France, with a preface by the Maurrasian Charles Benoist, by Benn in United Kingdom, and by MacMillan in the United States (with some changes to the index).[25] As the various reviews show, what attracted the attention of the non-Italian public were, above all, the essays by the leading politicians involved, the ministers Rocco and Bottai, who offered precisely an insider's description of the corporative state. Not only that but reading the two contributions one after the other clearly revealed the differences between their conceptions. On the one hand, Rocco, in reviewing "the transformation of the State" (this being the title of his speech), attributed enormous significance to the 1926 trade union reform, which he had personally drafted:

> the syndicalist reform [...] has solved, completely and simply, the gravest problem of our times –a problem which has troubled humanity for more than a century. Not only the question of how classes might live peacefully together and by what legal means the inevitable conflicts between them might

> be settled, but also the problem of the better organization of production and the better distribution of wealth, have been solved by this reform. Unlike the old organizations which arose outside the State and lived outside it, our new syndicates form part of the State, and are for the State elements of force and of prestige. But, besides all this, the syndical and corporative organization of the nation has given a new order to Italian society, which is no longer based on the individualistic atomism of the French Revolution philosophy, but on a truly organic conception of society, which cannot ignore the qualitative differences existing among its component parts. Italian society is, in fact, reorganized on a professional basis, that is to say, on the basis of the productive function exercised by each individual.[26]

On the other hand, Bottai clearly stated that he still considered the 1926 law to be insufficient. It had enabled the creation of an unprecedented syndicalist state. Now, however, at the beginning of the 1930s, the time was ripe for the real "corporative revolution":

> The distinction, therefore, between syndicalism and corporativism, although one is completed by the other, is clear and profound, and to neglect it would be a source of equivocation and of misunderstanding. It is a distinction both of organs and functions. While the recognized syndicalist associations are 'juridical persons, the corporations', on the other hand, are organs of State administration. So, while the syndicalist function is strictly connected with the syndicates, the corporative function belongs only to the State. By its corporative activity the State acquires a new and typical function which, though it may seem to be a part of its administrative function, yet constitutes at least a very special phase of it.[27]

Bottai was the Fascist leader most committed to promoting the spread of the regime's projects beyond its national borders. He trusted that the exporting of the Italian model would foster the "corporative revolution" in Italy.[28] Hence, his commitment to participate in official congresses, but also through his own contributions in the international intellectual debate. In the 1930s, he consistently looked at Germany, both before and after the Nazi rise to power,[29] and then broadened his gaze to American events after the launching of the New Deal (as will be seen in Chapter 7).

Besides the publications in the various European languages directly promoted by the Fascist authorities, numerous volumes were independently published abroad by sympathisers or scholars interested in the corporative experiments that were being conducted in Italy. *Bibliografia del fascismo*, a periodical bulletin by the National Federation of Professionals and Artists (*Federazione nazionale dei professionisti e degli artisti*) that collected and classified publications on Fascism published in Italy and abroad (in the latter case gathering information from embassies and consulates), listed countless texts on corporatism.

What also proved important, alongside these publications, was the participation of the regime's representatives in international organisations. I have already emphasised the relevance of the International Labour Organisation in previous chapters. The Italian delegates repeatedly celebrated the corporatist state in the early 1930s, presenting it to the other delegations as the only effective answer to the contradictions highlighted by the crisis. Bottai, too, as Minister of Corporations, spoke at the annual International Labour Conference on several occasions. Central to his speeches was criticism of the ILO's approach, which tended to address social policy issues without considering the possibility of changing economic policies. For Bottai, instead, the former could not be separated from the latter. As he observed in April 1932, this was "the lesson which may be learned from the crisis". The government, entrepreneurs, and workers were to overcome this contrast. It was necessary, on the one hand, to involve the workers in the management of economic activities and, on the other, to make the entrepreneurs responsible for the development of society. This was the direction in which the Fascist government was heading: "The Italian corporative system is following this course prudently but firmly. [...] The opposition between economic policy and social policy is thus being converted in our country into fruitful collaboration".[30]

Other international events also became a vehicle for Italian corporatist propaganda. This was the case, for instance, with the two conferences on "The State and Economic Life", organised respectively in Rome in 1932 and London in 1933, under the aegis of the League of Nations' International Committee on Intellectual Cooperation. On both occasions, Rocco presented papers on Fascist corporatism in which he detailed ideas, laws, and institutions, always attracting considerable attention from his interlocutors and the foreign press.[31]

The regime's effort to export its model of corporatism met with widespread interest among broad sectors of public opinion, as well as the intellectual and political world, in other countries. What still lay at the centre of this transnational reception in the early 1930s was corporatism understood as a system to ensure social pacification and overcome class conflict. As a new model for regulating and governing the economy – something the regime was beginning to come to grips with in the early 1930s – corporatism nonetheless remained on the margins of public discourse, even in this phase.

The Italian regime's propaganda accompanied general trends that were emerging in European politics in those years. From the beginning of the 1930s, an increasing number of southern, central, and eastern European countries gave themselves over to authoritarian movements that were more or less openly pro-Fascist. Out of the ruins of fragile democracies, regimes and systems of government arose that looked at Mussolini's Italy with sympathy, if not with admiration and a spirit of emulation. Against this backdrop, the European continent witnessed a proliferation of attempts to give rise to corporatist experiments.

The first country to move in that direction after Italy was Portugal. In May 1926, a coup d'état put an end to the parliamentary republic that had emerged some 15 years earlier in the country. A long transitional phase followed, led by a military junta and inspired by the Italian example, which ruled under the banner of the total repudiation of parliamentary democracy. In 1933, a complete reform of the institutional and constitutional set-up was approved: this marked the birth of what its creators called the *Estado Novo* (New State) under the leadership of António de Oliveira Salazar. A fundamental cornerstone of the reform was corporatism. The attempt made 15 years earlier by Sidonio Pais (see Chapter 2) was resumed and further developed. According to the new constitution, Portugal was to become a "unitary and corporative republic". More specifically, a *Câmara corporativa* (Corporative Chamber) was established, composed of representatives of various social interests and local administrations, and given the task of offering opinions on all projects and proposals presented by the legislative chamber, the National Assembly. In practice, the powers of the new body were rather limited, both because they were restricted to advisory functions and because the entire institutional framework was entirely subordinated to the head of government. But the importance of this innovation cannot be underestimated: the *Estado Novo* was the first state in inter-war Europe to adopt a corporatist constitution which provided for the political representation of social interests. In this respect, Portugal also anticipated Italy, which would only endow itself with a corporative chamber – the Chamber of Fasces and Corporations – in 1939.

The *Estado Novo*'s corporative character did not end there. The constitution also introduced the principle of regulating the relationship between capital and labour. It recognised the need for the state to supervise competition, preventing it from degenerating, and to foster collaboration between the different subjects of production. It also attributed a "social function" to property, capital, and labour. More concretely, it regulated collective labour agreements, provided for the establishment of special courts for labour disputes, and prohibited strikes and lock-outs.

The similarities to the Italian model are already evident from these brief outlines. Making the source of inspiration for Portuguese corporatism even more explicit, in September 1933, the Salazar government issued the *Estatuto do trabalho nacional*: the theoretical manifesto of the economic-social side of corporatism, largely based on the Italian Syndicalist Law of 1926 and the 1927 Labour Charter (see Chapter 2). Article 1 – "The Portuguese nation is a *moral, political,* and economic union, the aims and interests of which are superior to those of the individuals and groups composing it" – faithfully reproduced the first article of the Labour Charter. The succession of themes also indicated a direct filiation: the *Estatuto* recognised private initiative, to which it nonetheless attributed the obligation to regulate economic life according to the goals indicated by the political authorities; it established the need to eliminate all forms of parasitism to guarantee the lowest prices and the highest salaries; it established the objective of social peace within a society ordered according to hierarchical principles; it declared any act blocking or disrupting economic activity to be punishable; and, finally, it provided for the creation of a labour magistrature. Above all, the *Estatuto do trabalho nacional* and the subsequent implementing regulations designed an extremely articulated trade union system which, for each category, was composed of separate organisations for workers, employers, and self-employed professionals. The state legally recognised only one organisation per category, to which it granted the monopoly of representation.[32]

The Portuguese regime was soon followed by other authoritarian ones. As Matteo Pasetti has observed in his most systematic study on the transnational diffusion of corporatism, "after the 'revival' registered at the end of the Great War with the flourishing of largely short-lived projects and experiments, and the affirmation of a new model in the mid-1920s with the centrality acquired by the Italian prototype, from 1933 onwards numerous experiences of a similar sort followed one another on the Continent, which on the whole seemed to give a strong boost to the spread of a corporative standard".[33] Almost all European states that took on an authoritarian political organisation in the 1930s adopted, in the social and economic spheres, legislation and institutions inspired by the principles of corporatism. This was the case with Dollfuss' Austria, Piłsudski's Poland, Metaxas' Greece, the authoritarian regimes of the Baltic states, the monarchical dictatorships of Bulgaria and Romania, Tiso's Slovakia, Franco's Spain at the end of the decade, and during the Second World War, Vichy France.

Each of these cases presented peculiar characteristics stemming from the cultural, legal, and institutional traditions of the country, as well as the specific political and ideological climate at the time. It is at the same time possible to point out some recurring elements which have already been identified in relation to the Portuguese model. The first is the establishment of a corporate chamber, replacing or operating alongside the traditional representative assembly. Everywhere, the new assemblies had very limited, if not entirely irrelevant, legislative powers. The importance of these experiments cannot be underestimated, however. With the new chambers, the principle of corporatist representation, based on social categories and organised interests as opposed to individual wills, was incorporated into the constitutional charters. The second recurring element is the absorption of trade union organisations into an authoritarian framework. The aim of suppressing social conflict was pursued not by eliminating workers' and employers' organisations but by imposing a single trade union, whose action was strongly constrained and regulated under public law. The third element is the systematic use of rhetoric centred on the primacy of politics over economics. Although in none of the countries mentioned were significant restrictions on private property ever adopted or freedom of enterprise ever undermined, official speeches and propaganda campaigns in those regimes proposed corporatism as a way of overcoming economic liberalism and the market economy. Finally – and this is the fourth recurring element – all the corporatist experiments of the 1930s were profoundly influenced by the Italian model. The ideas and many of the practical achievements of the Mussolini regime since the mid-1920s were always seen as an example to be followed and adapted to individual national contexts.[34]

Given this picture, Germany represents a notable exception. The debate on corporatism in the Weimar Republic had been intense and widely followed ever since the post-war period. It was above all within the framework of this debate that the reorganisation of the state and the relationship between politics, the economy, and society were discussed. As will be recalled (see Chapter 1), the Weimar Constitution already provided for the presence of bodies for interclass cooperation. Although these institutions proved a failure within a few years, this did not spell the end of their political-legal consideration. The Great Depression sparked further theoretical elaborations and debate; and in those very years, the corporative system inaugurated in Mussolini's Italy became an object of increasing interest.

In the early 1930s, numerous German scholars published books and articles on the Fascist experiment: those linked to democratic or communist currents expressed strong criticism, while those taking a conservative, nationalist, or pro-Fascist stance saw the Italian regime as a model of the authoritarian corporate state.[35] Particularly noteworthy among the latter scholars is Erwin von Beckerath, probably the greatest expert on Fascist policies – he was also among the participants at the Conference on Syndicalism and Corporatism Studies (*Convegno di studi sindacali e corporativi*) in Ferrara and the Volta Conference in Rome, both held in 1932[36] – and Hans Reupke, one of the most active in introducing ideas based on the Fascist model into the National Socialist Party.[37] Scholars associated with the far right also visited Italy and established ties with various Fascist intellectuals, including Guido Bortolotto, Delio Cantimori, Giuseppe Renzetti, and Arnaldo Volpicelli.[38]

When Hitler came to power, the public debate on the corporatist option was therefore well underway and the Fascist prototype held a certain degree of ideological fascination for the NSDAP, although it was far from unanimously endorsed. The new government's first interventions in the trade union field seemed to replicate Mussolini's model, if anything stressing its more coercive aspects. Trade unions were dissolved, their assets confiscated, and all members integrated into a new unitary organisation that was created in May 1933: the German Labour Fron (*Deutsche Arbeitsfront*) led by Robert Ley. This plan was soon abandoned, however. In 1934, the DAF was affiliated and subordinated to the party: the latter was put in control of the organisation, whose officials all belonged to the NSDAP. Moreover, the DAF was deprived of the power to negotiate labour relations, which was assigned to "national labour trustees" appointed by the ministry. The DAF was thus only left with the task of imposing "social peace" through the regimentation of labour into a huge and eminently political apparatus, but it could not carry out any form of mediation between the government and the social interests represented, nor could it intervene in economic policy choices. Corporatist logic was soon replaced by the idea of the *Betriebsgemeinschaft* ("business community"), according to which the entrepreneur acted as a little *Führer* and the employees as his followers, and as "soldiers of labour" serving the company for the greatness of the Reich.

According to Franz Neumann – who in 1942 published *Behemoth*, one of the very first systematic analyses of the Nazi state – a corporative structure similar to the Italian one "was particularly dangerous to the regime in the field of labor because, by articulating the working class into bodies distinct and separated from the employers, it implicitly recognized the differences created in society by the division of labor".[39] The construction of the National Socialist system thus followed another path, which had as its ideological cornerstones the *Führerprinzip* and the concept of *Volksgemeinschaft* (which indicated a classless and racially homogeneous community) rather than the myth of the corporate state: "Corporativism and National Socialism" – Neumann argued – "are incompatible. For National Socialism, the primacy of politics is decisive".[40]

Notes

1 Charles H. Feinstein, Peter Temin, and Gianni Toniolo, *The World Economy between the World Wars* (New York: Oxford University Press 2008), 96.
2 Patricia Clavin, *The Failure of Economic Diplomacy. Britain, Germany, France and the United States, 1931–36* (Houndmills-Basingstoke-Hampshire-London: Palgrave Macmillan, 1996).
3 See Guido Melis, *La macchina imperfetta. Immagine e realtà dello Stato fascista* (Bologna: Il Mulino, 2018), 467–496.
4 Sarti, *Fascism and the Industrial Leadership in Italy*, 94–133; and Gianni Toniolo, *Storia della Banca d'Italia*, vol. 1, *Formazione ed evoluzione di una banca centrale, 1893–1943* (Bologna: Il Mulino, 2022), 525–300.
5 Benito Mussolini, "The Economic Policies of the Regime (1930)", in *Economic Fascism: Primary Sources on Mussolini's Capitalism*, ed. Carlo Celli (Edinburgh, VA: Axios Press, 2013), 150–151.
6 Mussolini, "The Economic Policies of the Regime", 151.
7 Ibid., 153.
8 Ibid., 152.
9 Ibid., 152–153.
10 Benito Mussolini, *Primo discorso per il decennale* (16 October 1932), in *Opera Omnia di Benito Mussolini*, ed. Edoardo Susmel, Duilio Susmel, vol. 25 (Firenze: La Fenice, 1958), 136.
11 Henri De Kerillis, "M. Mussolini croit a 'l'internationalisation' du fascisme. Il annonce qu'il va changer la constitution de l'Italie", *Echo de Paris*, 7 October 1933.
12 Benito Mussolini, "On the Corporate State (1933)", in *Economic Fascism: Primary Sources*, 181.
13 Ibid., 184.
14 Ibid., 186.
15 Ibid., 187.
16 Ibid., 191.
17 *L'economia italiana nel periodo fascista*, ed. Pierluigi Ciocca, Gianni Toniolo (Bologna: Il Mulino, 1976); Gianni Toniolo, *L'economia dell'Italia fascista*, Roma-Bari, Laterza, 1980.
18 Feinstein, Temin, and Toniolo, *The World Economy*, 96.
19 Alberto Baffigi, "National Accounts, 1861–2011", in *The Oxford Handbook of the Italian Economy since Unification*, ed. Gianni Toniolo (New York: Oxford University Press, 2013), 172–173.
20 Feinstein, Temin, and Toniolo, *The World Economy*, 57.
21 Mussolini, *On the Corporate State*, 195.
22 Mussolini, *On the Corporate State*, 196–197.
23 Benito Mussolini, *Messaggio per l'anno nono* (27 October 1930), in *Opera Omnia di Benito Mussolini*, vol. 24, 283.
24 "Lo Stato mussoliniano e le realizzazioni del fascismo nella nazione", ed. Tommaso Sillani, *Rassegna italiana politica e letteraria*, 13 (1930), no. 144–145.
25 *L'état mussolinien et les réalisations du fascisme en Italie: études et documents*, ed. Tommaso Sillani, Preface by Charles Benoist, (Paris: Plon, 1931); *What Is Fascism and Why?*, ed. Tommaso Sillani (London-New York: Benn-MacMillan, 1931).
26 Alfredo Rocco, "The Transformation of the State", in *What Is Fascism and Why?*, 23.
27 Giuseppe Bottai, "The Corporative State", Ibid., 36.

28 Nicola D'Elia, *Giuseppe Bottai e la Germania nazista. I rapporti italo-tedeschi e la politica culturale fascista* (Roma: Carocci, 2019), 28–29.

29 Giuseppe Bottai, "Die Grundsätze des Faschismus", *Der Querschnitt* 10, no. 11 (1930): 709–713; Giuseppe Bottai, "Die Faschistischen Korporationen", *Europäische Revue* 8 (1932): 695–701; Giuseppe Bottai, *Grundprinzipien des korporativen Aufbaus in Italien* (Köln: Petrarca-Haus, 1933).

30 Address by Giuseppe Bottai, in International Labour Conference, *Record of Proceedings, International Labour Conference, 16th session* (Geneva: ILO, 1932), 204. See also the address by Giuseppe Bottai in International Labour Conference, *Record of Proceedings, International Labour Conference, 11th session* (Geneva: ILO, 1928), 218–219.

31 On the address at the 1932 conference: "Il Congresso della Cooperazione Intellettuale. Il sistema corporativo italiano illustrato dal Ministro Rocco", *La Stampa*, 26 May 1932. The address at the London conference, delivered with Alberto Asquini and Gaetano Azzariti and published under the title "I rapporti fra capitale e lavoro", had been published in Commissione nazionale italiana per la cooperazione intellettuale, *Lo Stato e la vita economica. Relazioni presentate alla seconda Conferenza internazionale di studi su lo Stato e la vita economica, Londra, maggio-giugno 1933-XI* (Padova: Cedam, 1934), 27–60.

32 José Luís Cardoso, Nuno Estêvão Ferreira, "The Corporatist Chamber of the 'New State' in Portugal: Organized Interests and Public Policy", in *Corporatism and Fascism*, ed. Antonio Costa Pinto (London-New York: Routledge, 2017), 174–197; *Corporativismo Fascismos Estado Novo*, eds. Fernando Rosas and Alvaro Garrido (Coimbra: Almedina, 2012); Daniele Serapiglia, *La via portoghese al corporativismo* (Roma: Carocci, 2011).

33 Pasetti, *L'Europa corporativa*, 249 (my transl. from the Italian).

34 Pasetti, *L'Europa corporativa*, 249–260.

35 Klaus Neumann, "Inter-War Germany and the Corporatist Wave, 1918–39", in *Corporatism and Fascism*, 125–131.

36 Erwin V. Beckerath, *Wesen und Werden des faschistisches Staates* (Berlin: Springer, 1927); Erwin V. Beckerath, "Il fascismo e la Germania", *Gerarchia* 12, no. 10 (1932): 872–877.

37 Hans Reupke, *Das Wirtschaftssystem des Faschismus. Ein Experiment der Planwirtschaft auf kapitalistischer Grundlage* (Berlin: Hobbing, 1930).

38 Pasetti, *L'Europa corporativa*, 262.

39 Franz Neumann, *Behemoth: The Structure and Practice of National Socialism, 1933–1945* (Chicago: Ivan R Dee, 2009), 415.

40 Ibid., 232.

6 The Second Half of the 'Corporative Revolution' (1930–1933)

The beginning of the corporatist boom in Italy coincided with Giuseppe Bottai's rise as head of the Ministry of Corporations. Together with Rocco, Bottai was the representative of the regime's higher echelons who was most committed to the realisation of the corporative state. Bottai's conception of corporatism differed profoundly from Rocco's. Starting from his unquestioning faith in the one-party regime and his conviction that party pluralism in a mass society inevitably produces an unhealable rift in the social body, Bottai supported the idea that debate between different positions within Fascism should be allowed, if not promoted and organised.[1] So, whereas for Rocco, corporatism was a tool to reaffirm the state's monolithic unity and its superiority over society, for Bottai, it was to be the pivot of a Fascism established "on a popular basis".[2]

Within this framework, corporatism acquired the function of an instrument for governing and regulating the social dialectic and confrontation between social interests and the state. Particularly revealing, in this respect, is what Bottai stated at the Conference on Corporatism Studies in Ferrara in 1932: "Class struggle exists. It is necessary to come to the Ministry of Corporations to see how it presses at all our doors, to see how alive and passionate it is, and how only from its fervour a harmony is born that is not a governmental, exterior order, but an interior order of individuals and categories".[3] Bottai conceived of the corporations as an instrument to seek concord and harmony between the various social interests and to make social groups participate in state life. According to Bottai, the corporative order was intended to assign "recognition and a personality to the economic forces; a moral, legal, and political personality to the social categories", and thus "to consider the interests of categories a public interest". In other words, corporatism meant

> acknowledging the profound political value of social life, bringing it into the mainstream of political life, and thus making society and the State coincide. The corporative principle is therefore the principle of the organisation and personification of economic forces, enabling them to consciously participate in the life of the political community.[4]

Society's active participation in the destiny of the state, not its passive integration, was the principle on which Bottai's conception hinged. At the risk of

DOI: 10.4324/9781032713267-7

oversimplifying things, it could be said that while Rocco developed the most coherent version of a fully authoritarian corporatism, Bottai attempted to formulate a totalitarian corporatism.[5]

Consistent with this conception of corporatism as a source of ideas and intellectual energy, after becoming minister in September 1929, Bottai intensified – in addition to propaganda abroad (see Chapter 5) – the Ministry of Corporations' cultural policies aimed at the Italian public. From 1929 to 1932 – a period that coincided with the most acute phase of the economic crisis – countless volumes were published on the subject, including both broadly political books and those providing specific analyses in the economic and legal spheres. A number of journals were founded explicitly devoted to corporatism and directly promoted by the ministry (the most significant being *Archivio di studi corporativi*), and increasing space was assigned to the subject in newspapers. The Ministry of Corporations endeavoured to direct the education of the younger generation: it created university chairs of "Corporative Law" and "Corporative Economics", and in 1931 it founded the Collegio Mussolini in Pisa to support students from the local *School* for Advanced Corporative Studies. A significant number of lectures and conferences also took place, culminating with the two conferences on trade union and corporative studies organised in Rome in 1930 and Ferrara in 1932. These two events were attended by dozens of scholars who were among the leading voices in the corporatist debate of the time: economists such as Celestino Arena, Lello Gangemi, and Rodolfo Benini; jurists such as Carlo Costamagna, Francesco Carnelutti, Santi Romano, and Guido Zanobini; and philosophers such as Ugo Spirito and Arnaldo Volpicelli. Various leading figures of the regime also attended, starting with Bottai. It was precisely at the Ferrara conference that Spirito laid out the "proprietary corporation" thesis (a vague attempt to rethink forms of corporate ownership), undoubtedly the address that provoked the most heated and exasperated reactions in the 20-year debate on corporatism.[6]

On a political and institutional level, Bottai's project translated into an attempt to bring about a reform of the state and the administrative system. Corporatism was seen as the instrument to implement economic planning policies in a non-socialist society.[7] The creation of corporatist apparatuses was seen by Bottai, first and foremost, as a means to free the Fascist state from the conditioning exercised by economic power and to subordinate the economy to political objectives. The main achievement in the early 1930s in this direction was the establishment of the National Council of Corporations (*Consiglio Nazionale delle Corporazioni*, or CNC).

The Council saw the light at the end of a long tunnel. Although one of the decrees implementing the 1926 trade union law had already provided for its establishment, it was not until the summer of 1928 that Undersecretary for Corporations Bottai submitted a concrete proposal to Mussolini. This was discussed by the Grand Council of Fascism on 7 March 1929, then submitted for consultation to the trade union organisations, and was discussed again – in a modified version – by the Grand Council on 9 April 1929. It was examined by the ministries concerned, approved by the Council of Ministers on 30 September, and discussed in the Chamber of Deputies (17–21 December) and in the Senate (12–15 March

1930). It finally became law on 20 March 1930. The main inspirer and promoter of this measure was Bottai, who in the midst of this long legislative process had succeeded Mussolini as Minister of Corporations in September 1929, a role he would fill until 1932.

According to the law establishing the National Council of Corporations, the presidency of the new institution was to be assigned to the head of government and, in his absence, to the Minister of Corporations. The Council consisted of three institutional levels: (1) the seven divisions (liberal professions and arts; industry and handicrafts; agriculture; commerce; land transport and inland navigation; maritime and air transport; and banks), whose members were designated by the professional organisations, in equal numbers for employers and workers; (2) the general assembly, in charge of intervening in cases that affected the entire syndicalist and corporative system, and composed of all the members of the divisions, the Ministers of Corporations and Agriculture and Forestry, the secretary and deputy secretaries of the National Fascist Party, representatives of the public employees' associations, the presidents of some public bodies, and ten "experts" appointed by the ministers,[8] for a total of 150 people; and (3) the Central Corporative Committee (*Comitato corporativo centrale*), which was much smaller in size: it consisted of the same government and PNF representatives as the general assembly, and a smaller number of representatives of economic and social interests. Its function was to stand in for the general assembly and conduct ordinary business in the recesses between sessions.

The CNC was assigned a consultative function in relation to trade union matters, labour legislation, and any issue affecting national production. The Council was also endowed with legislative powers; in particular, it could issue laws to regulate collective economic relations between the various productive categories. According to some jurists, these were "corporative laws in the true sense", i.e. those not concerning "labour relations" between employers and workers but "horizontal" relations between producers.[9] The law, however, specified that any legislative initiative by the CNC was subject to the will of the associations directly affected by the decisions. The fact that this legislative power depended on the will of the subjects that were to be administered by this legislation significantly limited the scope of the new body's action. This element also bears witness to the extremely cautious approach that was adopted towards private enterprise when building the corporative system.

The question of legislative power was the most controversial element of the new body.[10] Already during the debate on the bill in the Chamber of Deputies, a conflict emerged between the deputies from the entrepreneurial categories, who were in favour of the solution then adopted, and those from trade unionist ranks, who instead favoured a Council with full powers which was capable of governing the national economy. This was a very important issue because it contributed to defining the boundaries of freedom of enterprise, the ability of corporate bodies to intervene, and, more generally, the state's actual powers in the economic and social fields. Unsurprisingly, the debate in the chamber was one of the most open during the years of the regime, and it was unusually heated, by contrast to the dull and regimented routine of parliamentary life under Fascism.

Significantly, the discussion was driven by the leading exponents of the two fronts, namely Luigi Razza, president of the National Confederation of Fascist Agricultural Trade Unions – who was at that time probably the most combative and authoritative exponent of Fascist syndicalism – and Antonio Stefano Benni, president of *Confindustria* (the Confederation of Italian Industry). According to Razza, the Council needed to have full regulatory powers and not be subordinated to the consent of the associations concerned. Only in this way could it avoid being overwhelmed by the "immaturity" and "selfishness" of professional associations; this "selfishness" was "easier to overcome in the case of workers' organisations" and "less easy to overcome among the leaders of employers' organisations".[11] Razza's openly "classist" tones accompanied a precise political plan: for the trade unionists, a CNC with full regulatory powers would provide an institutional platform through which to take part in decisions on economic and social issues, after they had been deprived of the right to strike and ousted from workplaces.[12]

The opposite stance was taken by the entrepreneurs. *Confindustria* president Benni argued that the "stimulus to private enterprise" is what was "most needed by a dynamic country, full of willpower and with a necessity to expand such as Italy".[13] Consequently, the National Council of Corporations' task could only be to promote private enterprise, "to put every producer in a position to develop his capacity and means in an increasing, and increasingly better, way by orienting them and putting them into the country's service".[14] Ultimately, for Benni, these were the "fundamental canons" of Fascism. Strengthening the Council's legislative power could therefore only lead to the imposition of agreements that would soon prove to be useless or harmful: "If, as some have said, it were possible for a higher body [...] to establish what and how much should be produced, what should be sold, and how and at what price, it is easy to see that private enterprise would not be stimulated, but restrained and arrested".[15] The solution adopted in the end fully reflected the position of the industrialists and other employers' organisations.

The parliamentary debate had brought out in an unusually clear way the presence of different and irreconcilable positions within Fascism and among the social forces supporting it. This problem was grasped, and authoritatively highlighted, by Giovanni Gentile. Commenting on that debate "in the heat of the moment", Gentile posed the problem of the existence of a "dual soul" in Fascism. On one side, there were those who tended to assign the Council – and every other corporative body – the power to issue legal norms; opposing them, there were those who wanted to reduce those bodies to mere technical instruments of the state to render private economy compatible with public interests. On the one hand, there was a tendency "to deny the ethical substance of the State, and therefore the State itself; on the other, to deny its economic content".[16] Gentile referred to these two positions as that of the "syndicalists" and that of the "conservatives", respectively. In his view, they were more than two tendencies, but were rather "two different souls" which emerged "in spite of strong discipline and sincere devotion to the Leader, in every fundamental political question", making the divergence and disagreement felt: simplifying things, they could be defined as "the left-wing tendency and the right-wing one".[17] The corporatist question thus clearly revealed the plurality of positions and points of view within the Fascist state.

As was to be expected, the establishment of the Council of Corporations was greeted by a flood of celebratory speeches but also viewpoints on the actual nature of the new body. Mussolini defined the CNC as the "high command of the economy", the "thinking brain that prepares and coordinates [things]".[18] Many wanted to see the Council as the prefiguration of a new legislative chamber, replacing the "anachronistic" Chamber of Deputies.[19] According to Sergio Panunzio, the creation of the Council could even be considered the most important reform implemented until that time because it established the state's "corporative function" alongside the traditional legislative, juridical, and administrative functions. Carlo Costamagna instead believed that equality between the social classes had now been achieved through a common subordination to the state, "an affirmation at the same time of political power and social justice".[20]

According to other observers, the CNC's action would also have important repercussions overseas. Filippo Carli started from the analysis of the economic crisis, which he traced back to the imbalance between supply and demand and the inadequacy of the domestic market. In order to launch a recovery, it was necessary to improve Italy's position in the international markets by completely reorganising its foreign trade system through the active participation of all the categories involved: "This is the great problem of exports", argued Carli, "and the National Council of Corporations is the right platform for fully addressing the problem".[21] In a more in-depth analysis, Giuseppe De Michelis argued that the new institution was to ensure the Italian economy's expansion in overseas markets by defending its interests within official international organisations (such as the economic commission of the League of Nations and the International Labour Organization, within which De Michelis served as a delegate of the Italian government). These organisations were increasingly tending to deal with issues pertaining to the relations between the economic forces operating on world markets. The establishment of the CNC could therefore enable Italy to create a "united front" of all the forces of Italian society to best defend their interests in international relations.[22]

All contributions more or less explicitly touched upon the idea that the CNC was a wholly original body in Europe, and therefore an Italian and Fascist achievement. Other European countries also had a National Economic Council, but in theory, none of these councils had the same powers and representativeness as the Italian. As we saw in Chapter 1, in Germany, such a body was even provided for in the Weimar constitution. In France, a National Economic Council was created in early 1925, but it was conceived as a think-tank that could at best propose non-binding solutions to the public authorities. Reporting directly to the government, it provided for the representation not only of workers' and employers' organisations but also of consumer cooperatives and purchasers' associations, mayors' associations, users of public services, and even representatives of families. Almost at the same time as the creation of the CNC, in January 1930, the Economic Advisory Council was established in the UK. Like its French counterpart, it was under the prime minister's authority and could only give opinions; but unlike the French council, it was only composed of government-appointed ministers and experts and did not include social representatives. Italian commentators emphasised the superiority of the National Council of Corporations. When the law was passed, the journal *Politica Sociale* featured a lengthy dossier on the situation in other countries, including the Soviet Union.[23] According to Alberto De Stefani, the German National Economic Council, the French National Economic Council, and the British Economic Advisory Council, to mention only the main ones, were merely "amorphous products", "lacking legislative powers".[24] They were incapable of dealing with economic problems because they did not have a trade union structure under them and were not an actual state organ. Those institutions – wrote the jurist and magistrate Silvio Longhi – operated within liberal systems in which the whole fabric connecting the individual and the state had been eliminated; they could therefore not rely on the presence of organisations representing the interests of professional categories. Even in those cases in which trade unions were recognised, this recognition was passively accepted by the state rather than granted: "So when economic councils are created in liberal states, this is a kind of experiment, an attempt to put two heterogeneous things together".[25] For this reason, "such councils are but academies: looked upon with indifference from above, looked upon with suspicion from below".[26] Within this framework, Longhi argued, Italy had come last compared to other nations – but last in the old league and first in a new one. "It did not occur to people that the originality of the present institution is not chronological, but of substance; it consists in its constitutional position. And this becomes apparent in its very name".[27] Only in the Fascist state, and only through the National Council of Corporations, was it possible to overcome the dualism of trade unions and the state. This opinion was also shared by Gentile, among others, according to whom the antithesis in question was being resolved "not by the old methods of suppressing one of the two terms, but through their reconciliation within the corporative system of the State".[28] Similar remarks were put forward in the following years by other authors and other journals, including the authoritative *Giornale degli economisti*.[29]

Despite the debate's celebratory tone, from the outset, the National Council of Corporations revealed certain frailties, which did not escape the notice of more balanced observers. Emphasising the dependence of the Council's legislative power on the will of the organisations, important jurists such as Mariano D'Amelio and Guido Zanobini saw the new body as nothing more than a "college of *arbitratores*" or a subject with a mere "regulatory function".[30] When presenting the law establishing the CNC to the chamber, the Minister of Corporations, Bottai, attempted to conceal the new institution's limitations and to block any expressions of disappointment by invoking the "necessarily experimental attitude" and the "uncertainty" inherent in "almost all, indeed all, revolutionary legislation".[31]

Limits were set on the CNC's activity not only by the constraints placed on its legislative power but also by its place in the Fascist state's articulated structure. Like any new institution, the Council was part of a dense web of public powers that were interdependent and, at the same time, hierarchically subordinate to Mussolini. It was dependent on the head of government, who was president of the new body and who, in addition to actively participating in the formation of the corporative laws, gave his assent to the trade unions' requests or ministerial proposals and made the laws compulsory through their publication in the *Gazzetta ufficiale*. Dependence on the head of government has often been presented by historians as a clear sign of the Council's structural inability to function and of its character as a fictitious institution with no real powers.[32] In reality, dependence on Mussolini was an unavoidable fact in the Fascist regime. In the dictatorship of the head of the government and one party, every segment of the institutional apparatus and society had to be framed within a hierarchy that had the Fascist leader at its apex, regardless of whether or not this link was sanctioned by a special law. It is hardly surprising, then, to find that many corporatists endorsed and enthusiastically welcomed the corporatist organs' direct link with the head of government.[33]

Another characteristic feature of the council was the range of social interests that received corporate representation. This was based on a two-party structure, with employers on one side and workers on the other, each with an equal number of representatives. Civil servants, technicians, and the category of "professionals and artists" were given a marginal presence. Corporatism thus ended up reproducing a rigidly bipolar image of society, precisely the kind of image which Fascism – with its insistent calls for the nation's unity and the overcoming of class struggle – sought to deny.

The employers' and workers' organisations dominated the CNC, with a total of 85 members out of a total of 150. As far as the former were concerned, the major leaders of the employers' organisations and some business leaders were members of the Council. As we have seen, the employers' confederations, unlike the workers' confederations, had not been subjected to Fascism's repression and – apart from a few formal tributes (such as the inclusion of the adjective "Fascist" in the name), some forced changes in organisational structure, and rare vetoes regarding individual leaders – they had retained most of their organisational autonomy. The figures on the board were therefore a direct expression of the categories represented. For *Confindustria*, the most powerful and most influential of all confederations, we find the names of the general managers, Giovanni Balella and Felice Guarneri, and of the industrialists at the head of the organisation at that time, Gino Olivetti and Antonio Stefano Benni, along with Alberto Pirelli, the head of the Association of Joint Stock Companies (*Associazione fra le società per azioni*, also called *Assonime*).

The situation of the workers' organisations, however, was different. With the "unfreezing", there had been a significant turnover at the head of the trade unions, and the old leaders had been replaced by figures who were not always competent or sufficiently experienced. It was not uncommon to find PNF officials, public administration executives, senior militia officers, professors, and "experts" in corporate economics. Among these figures, however, there was no lack of "pure" trade unionists, often coming from the experience of revolutionary and national syndicalism. Scrolling down the list of Council members, we find the leader of the agricultural workers, Luigi Razza, the most charismatic figure in Fascist trade unionism at the beginning of the 1930s; Riccardo Del Giudice, Fascist trade unionist of the first hour; and Giuseppe Landi, who was in the Trade Workers' Union. The last two were destined to rise to the top within other categories.

A source of great expectations when it was first established, the CNC did not live up to its initial ambitions. Suffice to say that while the Council was significantly restrained and limited in its legislative role, it hardly ever made use of this power in the sphere of "economic relations". It only ever issued two laws, and these were not exactly decisive ones for the destiny of the Italian economy: the first law regulated the sale of milk in Rome, while the second one defined the legal nature of the relationship that bound insurance companies to insurance agents.[34] The General Assembly only held two debates on economic relations. The most important debate was the one on customs policies and foreign trade in November 1931. The debate was heated and involved a large number of people, but it was in many ways an "academic" discussion, since the government, some two months earlier, decided on a 15% increase in duties for various categories of goods. Precisely, the fact that the National Council of Corporations held a plenary session to deal with an issue on which important decisions had already been taken is the most recurrent example adduced by contemporary observers and historians to illustrate the Council's absolute ineffectiveness.[35] But while it is true that the general assembly was convened after the adoption of the measures in question, it is equally true that between May and June 1931 – i.e. a few months before the promulgation of the decree on duties – all divisions of the CNC, with the exception of the liberal professions and arts, devoted special sessions to the question of foreign trade and customs policy. All of them managed to overcome internal divisions and oppositions between employers and workers and thus pass jointly approved agendas. Thus, the lengthy debate in the general assembly – in which some of the leading representatives of the employer' organisations and workers' trade unions took part – in all probability only served to cool a still "hot" topic *a posteriori*; the divisions instead prepared a real preliminary phase, helping to outline a general economic policy.

This first event highlights that it is not possible to limit oneself to observing the activities of the general assembly alone, but it is also necessary to examine its "minor" articulations, i.e. the divisions and the Central Corporate Committee.[36] As has been observed, this corresponds – among other things – to the "natural authoritarian vocation of the Fascist movement, and finds confirmation both within and outside the corporatist order in the progressive divesting of collegial bodies of authority" and "in the continuous strengthening of less representative institutions".[37]

As far as the content of the discussions is concerned, it must be noted that, in the first phase, the Council's activities were closely linked to Bottai's political initiatives. During the period in which he was Minister of Corporations, until July 1932 Bottai tried, through the corporative bodies, to find a way around the vetoes and constraints imposed by the employers' organisations. His aim was not to implement measures in favour of workers but to gain more space for the state in the economic and social sphere so as to impose the superiority of politics over economics. In the minister's intentions, even minute and seemingly marginal measures could help undermine the weight of non-state actors.

In pursuing his plan, Bottai received support from the workers' trade unions. A rather unusual alliance took shape between two subjects who had hitherto distrusted each other. In previous years, Bottai had not failed to express hostility towards the remaining autonomy of the trade unions (see Chapter 4). At the beginning of the 1930s, however, the trade union leaders found themselves converging with his view that it was necessary to increase the Fascist state's power of intervention in the economic and social fields. Both sides, albeit for different reasons, set themselves the goal of broadening the regime's base of support by freeing it from the conditioning and veto power exercised by the bourgeois elites.

The two side's motives, however, were profoundly different. For Bottai, as we have seen, the construction of a strong state, removed from the influence and power of individual components of society, had entirely political connotations that, in practice, did not exclude strongly conservative solutions in social and economic matters. His corporatist project was therefore fully compatible with the safeguarding of a strict principle of hierarchy and single command as far as the exercise of power within companies was concerned. For the trade union leaders, on the contrary, political goals were inseparable from social goals. Building the new Fascist state was tantamount to making a radical break with the bourgeoisie and liberalism, and bringing about the "Fascist revolution" meant significantly altering the balance of power in society. This was accompanied by criticism of the idea of a company as a "totalitarian" structure, closed to all worker participation.

While the positions of Bottai and the trade unionists diverged with regard to what form the Fascist state was to take, some unquestionable similarities were to be found in relation to certain basic aspects. The support that the workers' trade unions gave to Bottai's projects in discussions on corporatism often proved decisive to counter the business representatives' resistance. The Minister of Corporations not only drew up a series of measures close to the positions of the confederal leaders but at that stage was the *gerarca* most ready to defend the trade unions' role and identity.[38]

Turning to the Council's activity, we should first examine what the divisions were doing. These mainly dealt with problems related to the economic situation by carrying out preparatory work for the plenary discussions, as in the case of the customs measures. They thus allowed the confederations to influence the drafting of the more or less concrete proposal which the ministry would then submit to the general assembly for consideration. The divisions, however, also provided a forum for continuous dialogue between employers' and workers' organisations, both on specific contractual issues and on general measures. It was in the agricultural division, which was probably the most active, that the important general laws regulating sharecropping were drafted, while in the industrial division, the bill on new industrial plants was prepared and the thorny issue of reduced working hours was discussed.[39]

The Central Corporate Committee would appear to have been more effective. This body had the task of replacing the general assembly during the recesses for all urgent deliberations, except the laying down of laws, and to give opinions on questions concerning the "political orientation of trade union action" and "national production problems", as the 1930 law stated. In the Central Corporate Committee, trade unionists and employers repeatedly discussed social protection measures for the unemployed, such as new rules on unemployment benefits or the possibility of companies cutting wages to maintain employment levels. Each time, different positions emerged (the former being in favour of extending social measures, the latter of severely curtailing them), which resulted in rather heated clashes, usually resolved through compromise solutions.[40] In many cases, the Central Corporative Committee therefore provided a platform for the Ministry of Corporations to perform its function of mediating between socio-economic interests. In some situations, the ministry's intervention took the form of an attempt to limit the autocratic power of business leaders and thus acquired clear social overtones. One can include, among such cases, the decision of November 1931 to grant the industrial trade unions the right to join companies in defining piecework rates. Similar needs were addressed by another decision taken at the same committee meeting, according to which wage reductions were no longer to be applied on a national scale but only on a local and sectoral scale, and only if they met specific criteria.[41] Decisions of this kind did not significantly change workers' conditions, not least because their actual implementation was strongly opposed and gave rise to bitter disputes. But they had the merit of instilling confidence in union organisers at a time of acute difficulty for the world of work, and of providing a glimpse of the possibility of affecting power relations with the industrialists.[42]

The Central Corporative Committee also discussed and drafted two of the most important industrial laws of the 1930s, which were the real pillars of Italian industrial policy in the first half of the decade: the law on mandatory consortia – which decreed the establishment of consortia between companies within the same branch of a given economic sector in order to regulate production and competition – and the introduction of the obligation for entrepreneurs wishing to open up new industrial plants, or expand existing ones, to obtain a special authorisation from the Ministry of Corporations. These were two measures of considerable importance for industrial development and for the power structures of Italian capitalism, the implementation of which in the second half of the decade we will be discussing in Chapter 8. The Central Corporative Committee played a decisive role in the conception of these measures. It was there that the debate between the government, workers' organisations, and employers' representatives took place. These important industrial policy measures were thus entirely corporatist in origin. Paradoxically, however, they ended up not granting corporative bodies any authority by delegating all decision-making powers to entrepreneurs' associations.[43]

The disempowerment of the corporative bodies established by the two measures represented not only a clear denial of the vaunted "corporative spirit" but also a defeat of Bottai's policy. Hence the minister's explicit complaints and repeated denunciations of the "non-corporative" and "emergency" nature of the measures: On several occasions, Bottai reiterated his rejection of the "monopolistic tendency, masked by the consortia mentality" and affirmed – in full consonance with the proposals made by the workers' unions – the need for control by the corporate bodies over the consortia and the application of the law on the authorisation of industrial plants.[44]

The reform of the law on industrial property provided further proof of the Ministry of Corporations' intention to curb the excessive power of the business elite. The bill produced by the ministerial commission chaired by Senator Donato Faggella met with repeated objections from business organisations during its discussion in the third session of the general assembly. Faggella, however, defended the draft, and showing no willingness to engage in real debate with the industrialists, denied the possibility of making the requested changes to it, evidently with Bottai's support, if not directly at his behest; for the minister, on the other hand, the matter was to be considered closed even before the discussion in the Council of Corporations (a purely "technical" debate, in his opinion). Faced with such a barrier, the industrialists then had to address their grievances directly to Mussolini: in the general director of Fiat, Vittorio Valletta, sent a detailed memorandum containing criticisms of the text and the industrialists' proposals.[45]

In short, while in the first two years, the CNC's various bodies never issued any laws, they served as an instrument used – with varying degrees of success – by Bottai and the bureaucracy of the Ministry of Corporations to progressively extend the sphere of their intervention. This attempt was made by adopting a gradual approach, which nonetheless did not spare Bottai a reprimand. His stance on consortia and the law governing industrial plants, along with his handling of the "Faggella project", which earned him the open hostility of leading industrialists, played no small part in Mussolini's decision to remove him from the ministry in July 1932.[46] The attempt to weaken the economic elites' enormous influence on social and economic policies was blocked at its inception.

Meanwhile, in the same years, Bottai also sought to introduce some social policy reforms. It was precisely in this area that the Ministry of Corporations' primary measures and the most relevant debates within the Council took place. Besides, the early 1930s were the period in which the regime's intervention in this sphere was most intense, dictated by the need to contain the effects of the crisis and, at the same time, to broaden adherence and loyalty to Fascism.

Not all social welfare reforms were discussed within the Council. This is the case, for example, with the most important measure: the reform of old age pensions and the creation in 1933 of the Fascist National Social Security Institute (*Istituto nazionale fascista della previdenza sociale*, INFPS). In the case of many labour and social policy measures, the Ministry of Corporations was nevertheless able to safeguard the role of the corporate bodies in the decision-making process. It was also able to decisively influence the drafting of laws. The CNC general assembly almost invariably approved the introductory report drafted by the ministry, or rather, insofar as there was no real assessment of consensus and of the actual weight of the various factions and insofar as parliamentary-style voting was banned as it was deemed too "electoral" (a label that in the Fascist state could only have a negative meaning), the report's contents would simply be adopted by the president of the assembly, i.e. Mussolini, or in his absence, by the head of the Ministry of Corporations. The participation of employers' representatives and trade union leaders in the discussions contributed not so much to determining the content of the measures as to lending political and institutional force to the projects presented. In particular, support from the workers' trade unions was, in many cases, decisive for overcoming resistance from the business world.

The Council addressed a number of issues. At the first session of the general assembly, the topic of labour law reform was discussed.[47] According to the Ministry of Corporations, the laws in force were characterised on the one hand by "excessive fragmentation", resulting in duplications and contradictions that made full compliance more challenging and costly for companies; and on the other by the fact that the laws often dated back several years and hence referred to outdated conditions, disregarding the new legal and administrative institutions created by Fascism.[48] It was thus a question of unifying and simplifying the legislative texts, yet without "touching the substance of the laws". A special commission was therefore set up which drafted five bills: on female and child labour, on safeguarding the maternity leave of female workers, on the compulsory limitation of working hours, on Sunday and weekly rest, and on the safeguarding of occupational hygiene. Although it extended guarantees for workers, the legislation remained far behind that of other industrialised countries, mainly owing to resistance from employers' associations. Moreover, in accordance with Fascist ideology, the extension of welfare measures was neither intended to reduce inequalities nor to introduce new social rights. If anything, it was aimed at protecting the health of the body of the nation, including through forms of protection for those considered weaker.

The direct connection between social and demographic policies was made particularly evident by the law regarding the work "of women and children". The presentation of this bill emphasised the "basic need for public order, strongly understood and desired, and directly related to the preservation of the people" and the "need to protect the weaker manpower of minors and women" as a form of "demographic protection directed at the Nation's qualitative as well as numerical power".[49] In practice the bill, which was made a law in 1934, introduced a series of provisions on working hours, night work, the prohibition or limitation of certain tasks, weekly rest, hygiene conditions, and safety in the workplace. These measures introduced an extremely inadequate system of protection for female and child labour, but pandered to the regime's demographic needs: the ensuing increase in the cost of employing women ultimately encouraged their desired exit from the labour market.[50] The ministry intervened with regard to some of the most significant points once the debate was over by urging amendments and an extension of the protection measures: among other things, it proposed raising the minimum age for employment from 12 – the figure suggested by the commission – to 14.[51]

What was also lacking compared to other countries' legislation was the Consolidation Act on Working Time. The committee had refrained from presenting substantial reforms because it was awaiting parliamentary ratification of previous international conventions. The bill therefore left the pre-existing limit of 8 hours per day and 48 hours per week unchanged and also allowed, where provided for in contracts, 2 hours per day and 12 hours per week of overtime. The text, however, was considered unsatisfactory, especially by trade unionists. It did not reflect the long-term trend of reducing the working day, nor did it measure up to the increase in industrial unemployment, which was trade unionism's main weakness at that time. At the end of the debate, the CNC's general assembly approved an agenda, signed by representatives of the workers' and employers' organisations, in which they called for "the possibility of a mandatory reduction of working hours to 40 hours a week in all administrations and companies to be promptly examined, with a view to laying down precise international commitments".[52] The agenda, however, did not specify whether the reduction in working hours should be accompanied by a proportional reduction in wages or whether wages should remain unchanged.

The government, for its part, had chosen to make the adoption of binding measures conditional on the signing of an international agreement. Discussion within the CNC was combined with external interventions. In 1932, the government launched systematic measures within the ILO, unofficially aligning itself with the demands of the (anti-Fascist) European trade union movement that was united in the so-called Amsterdam International. The issue was discussed at the 16th International Labour Conference, held in April 1932, where Bottai made an address emphasising the need for an agreement signed by all leading economies, without exception, so as to establish the same conditions for everyone.[53] The meeting ended in a deadlock. A few months later, the Italian government's delegate to the ILO, De Michelis, sent a letter to the International Labour Office (the ILO's secretariat), calling for the 40-hour project to be relaunched with even greater resoluteness than the workers' unions.[54] With this move, the 40-hour issue was no longer only a workers' demand, but for the first time, received the endorsement of an important government. Not only that, but in this way, Italy distinguished itself from the other major European states, thereby confirming its image as the only state that was truly attentive to the social question – a point stressed by corporatist propaganda. This situation pleased all the factions within the country: the industrialists could hope to avoid the passing of legislative measures that would prove penalising for them compared to the laws in force in other countries; the trade unionists believed it was possible to obtain a result confirming their usefulness and relevance; and the government authorities, starting from the Minister of Corporations, saw this as an important opportunity to acquire prestige and international legitimacy.

Debate in the National Council of Corporations and international measures were not the only initiatives promoted in the country to achieve a reduction in working hours for equal pay. At the national congress of the Fascist Confederation of Industrial Workers (*Confederazione fascista dei lavoratori dell'industria*) in April 1933, the new secretary, Ugo Clavenzani, included that goal among the organisation's main demands.[55] In the following months, however, the strong resistance to this claim, and at the same time, the dramatic increase in the number of unemployed (900,000 in 1934), led many trade union leaders to fall back on demand for measures aimed merely at absorbing unemployment (a reduction in working hours along with a proportional reduction in wages), without guaranteeing a defence of wages.[56] In response, the government decided to simply ratify the Washington Convention of 1919, the terms of which had already been partly introduced in 1923 by a decree setting the limit at eight hours per day and 48 hours per week, as already indicated by the commission of the National Council of Corporations.[57]

The target of a 40-hour week was finally reached in October 1934, but only for industry, thanks to an inter-union agreement for the reduction of unemployment signed by the *Confindustria* commissioner, Alberto Pirelli, and the secretary of the Fascist Confederation of Industrial Workers, Tullio Cianetti. The reduction in working hours was implemented with a proportional reduction in wages. Provisions were made, however, for a compensatory wage in the form of family allowances, paid by a special national fund, which supplemented the income of workers who had large families and worked short hours without burdening company budgets. This was a new institution with undoubtedly modern features because, in the wake of what was also happening in other countries, it prevented wage regulation from being reduced to a negotiation between the parties involved. The agreement also established the abolition of overtime work, except in special cases, and the substitution, where possible, of female labour with male labour and of that of minors with adults. Nevertheless, the industrialists' frequent refusal to comply with these requests – which was actually often welcomed by those workers who were already employed – and the many complaints about the matter raised by the workers' unions show how difficult it was to impose a climate of collaboration in practice.[58]

Meanwhile, Italy continued to support the ILO initiative. De Michelis' letter was used by the new director of the International Labour Office, the Englishman Harold Butler (who had replaced Thomas after the latter's death in May 1932), to relaunch the plan of a 40-hour week for the same wage that was to be adopted simultaneously by all countries. The proposal was discussed at a special preparatory conference held in January 1933 ("one of the most lively and important debates in the history of the organisation", according to Butler);[59] it was then put on the agenda at the International Labour Conferences of 1933 and 1934, but the result was never achieved owing to obstructionism on the part of the employers, who always made sure not to reach the quorum so as to invalidate the vote.[60] A turning point came in 1935, partly thanks to the impetus provided by the entry of the United States into the ILO at the height of the New Deal.[61] The annual conference, held in June, finally saw the approval of a framework agreement, which was nonetheless limited to a few sectors: steel, construction, mining, glassmaking, and public works. The significant element is that the employers' front was not unanimous in opposing the agreement: the US delegate and the Italian one, Gino Olivetti, voted in accordance with the governments and the workers' representatives.[62] Italy was the only European country that succeeded in resolving the disagreements between the various social factions and to formulate a unified position: once again, it was able to reaffirm the superiority of its corporative model as the only system capable of ensuring harmony between all social groups. But despite being limited to a few sectors, the agreement did not enter into effect because many countries postponed its ratification.[63]

To return to the CNC's activities, it should be noted that the initiatives undertaken by Bottai and the Ministry of Corporations were not limited to the justification of new labour legislation. The proposal was also made to introduce the first elements of a more modern welfare and social security system. The first step in this direction was the reform of work injury legislation. The key features of the plan laid out by the ministry's offices were the extension of mandatory insurance to all workers engaged in industrial activities, the introduction of an automatic system (i.e. one not based on the drafting of private contracts by employers), the creation of a single institution to replace the range of existing insurance institutions (the *Cassa nazionale infortuni* and the various mandatory and voluntary mutual insurance unions), and the replacement of the lump-sum compensation payment with the annuity system (the payment of a monthly pension).

This ambitious plan was aimed at nationalising the welfare system and standardising workers' security across the various categories, or at least the industrial ones. However, it threatened to undermine existing mutual aid funds, the interests of private insurance companies, and employers' discretion. The upper echelons of the Ministry of Corporations were aware of what was at stake and, more generally, of the need to find a new balance between the Fascist state's professed social aims and the market's interests. This was openly stated in the ministerial report with which the plan was presented to the CNC:

> Given that work accident insurance does not have a private character, but an eminently social character, nature, essence, and purpose, the current system is in open conflict with it insofar as, although insurance is mandatory, this system allows it to be stipulated in accordance with the private forms and rules of an ordinary insurance contract, thus exposing the guarantees sought and desired by the legislator in the interest of the worker to the risk and danger of the employer's lack of diligence in the stipulation and implementation of the contract.[64]

Once again, the debates in the corporative forums – first in the divisions and then, in June 1932, in the general assembly – represented a decisive instrument in the hands of Bottai and the ministerial leadership to undermine consolidated interests. The debate clearly brought out the open opposition of the private insurance companies and all the employers' organisations. The arguments deployed constitute a veritable compendium of the business world's position vis-à-vis the extension of the social welfare system. Indeed, the risk of bureaucratisation and a consequent increase in costs was feared. It was emphasised that "only under competitive pressure can insurers be pushed to provide the best services at the lowest possible cost";[65] and consequently that a single body "acting in a monopoly regime and without the stimulus of emulation and the sting of competition would fatally settle into a bureaucratic, uneconomic life, with costs growing in proportion to its size".[66] It was also noted that the timing – the debate took place at the height of the economic crisis – was the least appropriate "to have people consider the reform project with all the necessary serenity".[67] The workers' organisations, on the contrary, fully supported the ministry's reform proposal.[68] They believed that the competition which the employers' organisations regarded as so desirable took place "not on the basis of the lower cost of insurance, but to the detriment of the injured person"; and they considered a single state institution to be the best instrument to "prevent work accident insurance from being 'branded' as a private and employers' insurance".[69]

The Ministry of Corporations' project was successfully implemented, once again, thanks to the valuable support provided by the trade unions. The National Fascist Institute for Insurance against Work Accidents (*Istituto nazionale fascista per l'assicurazione contro gli infortuni sul lavoro*, or INFAIL) was therefore established in March 1933. This institute absorbed the various bodies that had been authorised to provide protection up to that time and were aimed at industrial workers as well as nearly all state employees who were subject to the work accident law. The establishment of the INFAIL represented a significant step towards the construction of a system of social security measures based, on the one hand, on the removal of significant capital flows and profit shares from private insurance companies and, on the other, on strengthening the role of public institutions. The solution adopted was clearly statist. Indeed, it assigned the leadership of the institute to an administrative management linked to the upper echelons of the political world and to an especially constituted bureaucratic structure. The paradox of the reform was that it also came at the expense of the workers' trade unions, which had strongly supported it. Their demand to play an active role in welfare institutions remained largely unfulfilled.[70] The reform, moreover, introduced a differentiation between categories. The granting of social security protection only to private and public industrial workers, with the exclusion of agricultural or transport workers, derived from the objective fact that almost all accidents occurred in industry. Although this exclusion was also the effect of the particular focus of Fascist social policy, which only targeted individual segments of society, creating or reinforcing differentiations between categories.[71]

The consolidating acts on labour legislation developed by the Council also became state laws.[72] The only exception was the one on working hours, which was replaced by the text drafted by the parliamentary committees, consisting in the ratification of the Washington Convention, and was limited to industrial activities.[73] Except for being limited to industry, the law did not differ much – at least in its substance – from the text proposed by the CNC committee. The maximum normal working hours for manual and clerical workers could not exceed eight hours per day and 48 hours per week. According to collective labour agreements, it was possible to add to the normal maximum working hours an overtime period not exceeding two hours per day and 12 hours per week.

In all the cases examined so far, the National Council of Corporations represented the institutional setting for the dialogue between the representatives of the various interests involved: a dialogue that anticipated and, in fact, replaced parliamentary debate, which was becoming increasingly devoid of substance. The support for the ministry's projects shown by the workers' organisations proved decisive from time to time, so much so that it significantly counterbalanced the measures enacted by the business organisations, both within the corporate bodies and outside them. For the trade unions, the Ministry of Corporations' proposed social, welfare, and social security measures in the early 1930s represented partial yet significant compensation for wage reductions and exclusion from the workplace. The gravity of the employment situation produced by the economic crisis led the trade unions to strive to improve the social protection and welfare system rather than working and wage conditions.[74]

This period witnessed the emergence of a tendency that was to become entrenched with the launching of the corporations, namely: the attempt to regain on the political and legislative terrain what had inevitably been lost in the contractual field. By regulating wage dynamics from the top down and expelling trade union cadres from the workplace, workers' representatives found a new raison d'être in the construction of a more advanced welfare system. Among other things, this fully reflected the political nature of Fascist trade unionism, its function not only as a way of representing social interests but also as a political subject. Indeed, the greater attention to welfare and social security issues was justified in the name of the "Fascist revolution" and a strong state as the ultimate regulator of social conflicts.

The Council of Corporations' activities brought this irreducible complexity of the Fascist trade unions to light. While inclusion in the new corporative apparatus presupposed – in keeping with its underlying ideological principles – the abandoning of conflictual ambitions and "classist" positions, at the same time, the polarisation between workers and employers pushed union leaders to accentuate their antagonistic attitude. On the whole, however, these changes were more relevant in terms of how they redefined the trade unions' role than of their concrete results. Participation in the CNC did indeed bear significant fruits – among other things, their decisions on wages and piecework, the revision of labour legislation, and the reform of work accident insurance – but only thanks to its convergence with Bottai's steps at the Ministry of Corporations. No real alteration in the balance of power with the entrepreneurs took place, nor did trade unions acquire greater negotiating power.

Bottai was removed from the Ministry of Corporations in July 1932. From then on he played the role of the regime's main critical conscience in relation to corporatism. Mussolini himself took over as head of the ministry. Undersecretaries were appointed: Alberto Asquini (an MP and jurist) for economic services and Bruno Biagi (an MP and president of the National Institute for Cooperation) for trade union services. What further sealed Bottai's defeat was the appointment of Rossoni as undersecretary to the presidency of the Council: one of Bottai's long-standing opponents was reinstated at the top ranks of the regime, thereby also confirming trade unionism's political relevance within Fascism.

With Bottai's forced departure, the Ministry of Corporations' scope for action was clearly reduced, and with it that of the CNC, which was now called upon to deal with smaller issues. While in the first two years, the discussions had often had significant political repercussions, they now took on a purely technical character: they were no longer aimed at preparing reforms in the field of social legislation and economic policy but at ironing out legislative gaps and uncertainties or settling disagreements between the regime's bureaucracies.

In the fourth session – the first without Bottai at the head of the ministry – the general assembly discussed a proposal to reform the law regarding individual labour disputes. Disputes were becoming more and more numerous: as has been observed, "conflicts that could not be resolved amicably" were "atomised into individual disputes, with the result of emptying labour disputes of their significance in terms of class conflict as much as possible and reducing them to conflicts that were as 'isolated' and individualised as possible". Thus, "while collective disputes were drastically reduced in number and importance", "individual disputes extended to de facto include cases concerning the interpretation and application of collective agreements".[75] The issue was widely debated within trade union organisations and in legal journals. There were two major bones of contention: the scope of the labour judge's competence, which the legislation limited to relations that were subject to collective agreements, and the role of trade unions and the attempt at mediation. The general assembly almost unanimously approved the introduction of the obligation to report to the trade union – previously only imposed for disputes concerning non-compliance with existing labour contracts – and to attempt a mediation. It also decreed an extension of the labour judges' authority.

At its fourth session, the Council's general assembly was further called upon to make a pronouncement on the situation regarding the categories of workers who lacked a collective agreement because it had expired or had never been signed. The workers' unions argued that it was necessary to establish by law an obligation to draw up a labour contract for all categories within a certain period of time.[76] The ministry instead aligned itself with the position of the employers, who were opposed to introducing any obligations. The reasons given in the ministerial report are indicative of the new "post-Bottai" course: "A legislative solution seems neither indispensable nor opportune", the report stated, "since this is a field in which the parties' will is the driving principle, so to speak". Consequently, the ministry deemed it a mistake to transfer the initiative in contractual matters from trade union associations to corporate bodies.[77] A definite brake was therefore placed on the extension of the powers and assignments of the corporative bodies. The "normalisation" of the ministry and of the direction given to the CNC ended the policy of progressively opposing the business organisations' resistance that Bottai had attempted to implement.

The Council was also engaged in settling disputes between the regime's various apparatuses. Within the Fascist state's increasingly fractious institutional organisation, the trade unions constituted not only a liaison body with society but also a real bureaucratic apparatus; an apparatus intent on increasing its own power while defending the power it already had, preserving the autonomy and competencies it had acquired, and promoting the rise of its leaders. The trade unions were therefore not only engaged in negotiation with their entrepreneurial counterparts but also had to defend themselves against attempts by other bureaucratic apparatuses to remove them from certain tasks and areas of intervention. Recurrent clashes occurred with the National Fascist Party, the consensus-based organisation par excellence, and – with regard to matters of more limited importance – with the AGFPI, the Fascist Civil Service Association.

The clash between the trade unions and the PNF became particularly harsh in relation to the running of employment offices, which at the time were controlled by the workers' confederations. Intervention in the employment sector stemmed, first and foremost, from the need to cope with the high level of unemployment caused by the crisis and thus from the search for a better connection between labour supply and demand. A conflict had long been simmering between two opposing positions: the first in favour of keeping the employment offices in the trade unions' hands, the second in favour of placing them under the direct management of the state, with the participation of PNF representatives at the local level.[78]

The two positions were represented in the debate in the general assembly of January 1933 and ran through the trade union confederations themselves, dividing them between those – such as the president of the National Fascist Confederation of Bank and Insurance Employees (*Confederazione nazionale fascista dei lavoratori del credito e dell'assicurazione*) Nazareno Mezzetti – who believed that unemployment was a temporary and exceptional ill that had to be cured not through the trade unions' ordinary activities, but by strengthening the state and establishing a National Commission for Employment and Emigration, and those – such as Fontanelli and Razza – who emphasised that employment should be managed by the trade unions, as they alone had a clear view of the workers' interests.[79] At the end of the debate, while acknowledging that the PNF had a role to play, Mussolini completely endorsed the latter position. The assembly thus approved the ministerial proposal to leave the employment offices in the hands of the trade unions but called to unify the provincial offices, since up to that point each confederation had its own.

The debate between trade unions and the PNF, which the National Council of Corporations was entrusted with settling, indicates that at times the corporative institutions were called upon to perform a sort of mediating function not only between economic interests but also – purely in relation to trade union aspects – between the various bureaucracies. The Council offered them a formalised procedure for the resolution of disputes acknowledged by all parties, with the authoritative and direct endorsement of Mussolini, who had the final say. The study of corporatism is therefore linked to another relevant aspect of the regime that is decisive for understanding its actual mode of being: the polycentrism of the Fascist state, within which institutions of different kinds and different origins coexisted, based on a fragmentation of state apparatuses and an unresolved tension between the "old" institutions inherited from liberal Italy and the "new" Fascist ones.[80]

The corporatism, of course, was fully part of this institutional fragmentation. Addressing the general assembly of the National Council of Corporations on 19 October 1932, Mussolini touched on the issue in the clearest possible terms. Referring to the CNC, he stated:

> This is ours. The Senate was there and so was the Chamber, and they will remain because they fulfil their task. All those who feared that the National Council of Corporations would – as they say with a rather unfortunate turn of phrase – 'empty out' the other constitutional bodies of the State, have convinced themselves that if there is not yet glory for all, there is at least work for all.[81]

Ten years after the March on Rome, the distinction between "our" institutions – to quote Mussolini – and those that "already existed and will remain" was still relevant, and it was necessary to reiterate the need for cooperation between them.[82]

Another occasion on which the CNC was charged with resolving conflicts of purviews between different institutions emerged with the problem of classifying employees of public bodies other than the state, provinces, and municipalities. Like state employees, these did not have an employment contract but nevertheless performed functions that were not dissimilar to those performed by private employees, as in the case of savings banks or municipal companies. The civil service reform of 1923 had introduced a strict separation between the area of public employment relations and that of private employment. The National Council of Corporations, with the endorsement of Undersecretary Biagi, proposed to blur that separation and to introduce distinctions within the galaxy of public employment. In his concluding speech, Biagi argued that in the case of employment relations without "a particular legal status of a public nature", the task of adjudication should fall to labour judges rather than administrative judges.[83] At the end of the debate, Mussolini basically accepted the undersecretary's thesis, which was affirmed in the Council.[84] However, despite the commitment made by the head of government and despite the fact that the Chamber of Deputies had approved the special bill prepared by the Ministry of Corporations, nothing came of the reform. Resistance from the ministries of the Interior and Finance and, above all, from the President of the Council of State, Santi Romano, proved decisive in light of the principle of the civil service's indissoluble unity.[85]

The issue was to resurface again in the following years, albeit in a less obvious manner. The corporations, especially the credit corporation, would deal with the problem of public law bank employees, while in 1937, the Central Corporative Committee would even be entrusted with the task of preparing definitions and classifications that were useful for a unitary legislation governing the myriad of public bodies. The committee repeatedly tackled the issue for more than two years, at the end of which it reaffirmed the principle that "trade union and corporatist discipline should be extended to all public economic entities and employees" apart from "institutional public entities having the character and aims of political organisations" (such as the state, provinces, municipalities, and public charity institutions). At the end of the 1930s, therefore, overcoming the principle of the unitary nature of public employees became an issue of topical relevance again, and the need was reaffirmed to distinguish the core of the state (i.e. the ministries and central administration) from the new institutional apparatuses (first and foremost, the public companies), which were seen as having a "hybrid" nature on account of their organic and sometimes competitive relationship with society.[86] The Central Corporative Committee therefore stood out – at least with regard to economic and trade union legislation – as the institutional means to govern the Fascist state's polycentrism.

Notes

1 Santomassimo, *La terza via fascista*, 54.

2 Ibid., 56. See also Emilio Gentile, "Bottai e il fascismo", in Gentile, *Il mito dello Stato nuovo dall'antigiolittismo al fascismo* (Roma-Bari: Laterza, 1982), 205–230.

3 Giuseppe Bottai, "Intervento", in *Atti del secondo convegno di studi sindacali e corporativi. Ferrara 5–8 maggio*, vol. 3 (Roma: Tipografia del Senato, 1932), 315–318.

4 Bottai, "La concezione corporativa dello Stato", *Archivio di studi corporativi* 1, no. 1 (1930): 7–8. See also Bottai, "L'ordinamento corporativo nella costituzione dello Stato", in *Atti del primo convegno di studi sindacali e corporativi. Roma 2–3 maggio 1930*, vol. 1 (Roma: Edizioni del diritto del lavoro, 1930), 25–26.
5 This distinction is meant to echo that between "authoritarian Fascism" and "totalitarian Fascism" drawn by Emilio Gentile, *La via italiana al totalitarismo. Il partito e lo Stato nel regime fascista* (Roma: Carocci, 2001), 136–140.
6 Ugo Spirito, "Individuo e Stato nella concezione corporativa", in *Atti del secondo convegno*, vol. 1, 179–192.
7 See Cassese, "Un programmatore degli anni Trenta".
8 The experts initially appointed were Gino Arias, Rodolfo Benini, Bramante Cucini, Gustavo Del Vecchio, Giuseppe De Michelis, Alberto De Stefani, Lando Ferretti, Agostino Lanzillo, Angelo Oliviero Olivetti, and Edmondo Rossoni.
9 Luisa Riva Sanseverino, "Le norme corporative", in *Trattato di diritto corporativo*, ed. Giuseppe Chiarelli (Roma: Società editrice libraria, 1939), 860.
10 For a discussion of the powers assigned to the various corporative bodies, see Sabino Cassese, "Corporazioni e intervento pubblico nell'economia", in Cassese, *La formazione*, 63–106.
11 APC, Legislatura XXVIII, Session 1929–1930, *Discussioni*, vol. II, 1561. On Razza, see Giuseppe Parlato, "Luigi Razza tra confederazione e corporazione", *Annali della Fondazione Ugo Spirito* 11 (1999): 163–184.
12 Gherardo Casini, "La riforma del Consiglio nazionale delle corporazioni", *Lavoro fascista*, 2 October 1929.
13 APC, Legislatura XXVIII, *Discussioni*, vol. II, 1628.
14 Ibid., 1628.
15 Ibid., 1631.
16 Giovanni Gentile, "Doppia anima", *Politica sociale* 1, no. 9 (1929): 814.
17 Ibid.
18 Benito Mussolini, "Discorso del 21 aprile 1930", in *Opera omnia di Benito Mussolini*, vol. 24, 214.
19 Mussolini was to take up this issue again in the last session of the general assembly, on 14 November 1933: Ministero delle Corporazioni, *Atti dell'Assemblea generale del Consiglio nazionale delle Corporazioni. Sessione quinta* (Roma: Istituto poligrafico dello Stato, 1933), 143.
20 Sergio Panunzio, "Il processo di attuazione del principio corporativo", *Politica sociale* 2, no. 5 (1930): 431; Carlo Costamagna, "Potenza politica e giustizia sociale", Ibid., 453.
21 Filippo Carli, "Costi e prezzi", *Politica sociale* 2, no. 5 (1930): 397.
22 Giuseppe De Michelis, "Il Consiglio Nazionale delle Corporazioni e le organizzazioni internazionali", *Politica sociale* 2, no. 5 (1930): 529.
23 Anselmo Anselmi, "L'organizzazione produttiva spagnuola", Ibid., 533–540; Renato Trevisani, "Il Consiglio superiore dell'Economia nazionale in Russia", Ibid., 541–545; Riccardo Viglione, "Il Consiglio economico del Reich", Ibid., 546–549; Luigi Adolfo Miglioranzi, "Il Consiglio economico inglese", Ibid., 550–555; Ulrico Aillaud, "Il Consiglio Nazionale Economico in Francia", Ibid., 556–561.
24 Alberto De Stefani, "Un Consiglio economico e un Consiglio corporativo", *Politica sociale* 2, no. 5 (1930): 367.
25 Silvio Longhi, "L'originalità del Consiglio Nazionale delle Corporazioni", Ibid., 525.
26 Ibid.
27 Ibid., 524.
28 Giovanni Gentile, "Il sistema corporativo dello Stato", *Politica sociale*, Ibid., 415.
29 Gerolamo Bassani, "Il Consiglio nazionale delle corporazioni e alcune istituzioni affini di altri Stati", *Giornale degli economisti* 46, no. 1 (1931): 41–52; Bassani, "Istituzioni estere affini al Consiglio nazionale delle corporazioni", Ibid., 47, no. 3 (1932): 144–150.

30 Mariano D'Amelio, "L'attività giuridica del Consiglio Nazionale delle Corporazioni", *Politica sociale* 2, no. 1–2 (1930): 4; Guido Zanobini, "Le funzioni normative del Consiglio Nazionale delle Corporazioni", *Archivio di studi corporativi* 1, no. 2 (1930): 256.
31 APC, Legislatura XXVIII, *Discussioni*, vol. II, 1634, 1642.
32 See Aquarone, *L'organizzazione*, 190; Sabino Cassese, *Corporazioni e intervento pubblico nell'economia*, in Cassese, *La formazione*, 74–75.
33 See Critica fascista, "Dal Comitato intersindacale al Consiglio delle corporazioni", *Critica fascista* 7, no. 15 (1929): 289–290.
34 Ministero delle Corporazioni, *Atti dell'Assemblea generale del Consiglio nazionale delle Corporazioni. Sessione seconda* (Roma: Istituto poligrafico dello Stato, 1931), 11–25.
35 Salvemini, *Sotto la scure*, 124; Louis Rosenstock-Franck, *Les étapes de l'économie fasciste italienne. Du corporatisme à l'économie de guerre* (Paris: Editions du Centre polytechnicien d'études économiques, 1939), 208–281; Aquarone, *L'organizzazione*, 193.
36 With Ministerial Decree No. 42 of 27 January 1931, the divisions took on the name of corporations, which was to cause a great deal of confusion in 1933, when the actual corporations were established.
37 Cassese, *Corporazioni*, 99; Cassese, *Lo Stato fascista* (Bologna: Il Mulino, 2010), 121–124.
38 Giuseppe Bottai, "Intervento", 315–318.
39 Accounts can be found in *Informazioni corporative*, (1930–32) and *Sindacato e corporazione* (1933–34). On the sharecropping measures, see Ministero delle Corporazioni, *Atti dell'Assemblea generale. Sessione quinta*, 144–153.
40 ACS, PCM, Gab., 1931–33, fasc. 18.3.2752. Ministero delle Corporazioni, *Appunto per S.E. il capo del governo*, 5 October 1931; Bertini, *Le parti e le controparti*, 216.
41 "La decisione del Comitato Corporativo Centrale", *Il lavoro fascista*, 1° November 1931.
42 Cilona, *La confederazione*, 274.
43 ACONF, *Fondo Giovanni Balella* b. 90, f. 1. *Argomenti generali sulla disciplina consortile*.
44 APC, Legislatura XXVIII, *Discussioni*, session of 20 May 1930, 2753–2754; Ibid., session of 24 February 1932, 5791–5792; Ibid., session of 30 April 1932, 6764–6767; Giuseppe Bottai, "Corporazioni e consorzi", *Politica sociale* 4, no. 5–7 (1932): 361–364; g. b. [Giuseppe Bottai], "Il ricatto liberale contro il corporativismo", *Critica fascista* 11, no. 12 (1933): 223–226. See Cassese, *Un programmatore*, 200–201.
45 ACS, PCM, Gab., 1931–33, fasc. 1.1.26.2324. Bottai to Mussolini, 29 August 1931; Ibid. Beer to Perotti, 11 July 1932; Ibid. Ministero delle Corporazioni, direzione generale delle associazioni professionali. Ufficio della proprietà intellettuale al gabinetto della presidenza del consiglio dei ministri, 6 August 1932.
46 Cassese, *Un programmatore*, 199–202; Renzo De Felice, *Mussolini il duce*, vol. 1, *Gli anni del consenso 1929–1936*, (Torino: Einaudi, 1974), 289–292; Francesco Malgeri, "Giuseppe Bottai", in *Uomini e volti del fascismo*, ed. Ferdinando Cordova (Bulzoni: Roma 1980), 130–134. Bottai's dismissal was also influenced by the "incident" caused at the Ferrara conference by Ugo Spirito's thesis on the "proprietary corporation", which had generated fears and discontent in the economic world. It cannot be ruled out that Mussolini's prior approval of the report stemmed precisely from the need to weaken Bottai's position in order to facilitate his ousting: see Francesco Perfetti, "Ugo Spirito e la concezione della 'corporazione proprietaria' al convegno di studi sindacali e corporativi di Ferrara del 1932", *Critica storica* 25, no. 2 (1988): 202–243.
47 The commission consisted of Dino Alfieri, Anselmo Anselmi, Guido Antonioli, Gino Arias, Giovanni Balella, Francesco Boccadifuoco, Domenico Brunelli, Emanuele Carnevali, Guido Chiurazzi, Mariano D'Amelio, Riccardo Del Giudice, Giuseppe Girardina, Gaetano Grisostomi Marini, Giuseppe Landi, Giuseppe Pareschi, Roberto Roberti, Edmondo Rossoni, and Renato Trevisani.

48 Ministero delle Corporazioni, *Atti dell'Assemblea generale del Consiglio nazionale delle Corporazioni. Sessione prima* (Roma: Istituto poligrafico dello Stato, 1931), 57–58.
49 Ministero delle Corporazioni, *Atti dell'Assemblea generale del Consiglio nazionale delle Corporazioni. Sessione terza*, vol. 1 *Relazioni* (Roma: Istituto poligrafico dello Stato, 1932), 176.
50 Lorenzo Gaeta and Antonio Viscomi, "L'Italia e lo Stato sociale", in *Storia dello Stato sociale*, ed. Gerhard A. Ritter (Roma-Bari: Laterza, 2003), 244. On Fascist social policies and their discriminatory character in general, see Chiara Giorgi, Ilaria Pavan, *Storia dello Stato sociale in Italia* (Bologna: Il Mulino, 2021), 91–207.
51 ACS, PCM, Gab., 1931–33, fasc. 18.2.8797. *Modifiche al disegno di legge sul lavoro delle donne e dei fanciulli*, 27 March 1933.
52 Ministero delle Corporazioni, *Atti dell'Assemblea generale del Consiglio nazionale delle Corporazioni. Sessione terza*, vol. 2, *Resoconti stenografici delle sedute Relazioni* (Roma: Istituto poligrafico dello Stato, 1932), 149.
53 International Labour Conference, *Record of Proceedings, International Labour Conference, 16th session* (Geneva: ILO, 1932), 203.
54 *Letter from Mr. De Michelis to the Chairman of the Governing Bong of the International Labour Office*, 25 July 1932, in AILO, *Governing Body, Session extraordinaire du conseil d'administration du Bureau international du travail*, Geneva, September 1932, 499–500.
55 Confederazione nazionale sindacati fascisti dell'industria, *Congresso nazionale. Relazione morale e finanziaria. Roma a. XI* (Roma: 1933).
56 See *Convegno nazionale dei dirigenti dei sindacati fascisti dell'industria (Roma, 12 luglio 1934)* (Roma: Stabilimento tipografico il lavoro fascista, 1935).
57 Law of 16 March 1933, no. 527.
58 Cilona, *La confederazione*, 286–288.
59 "Note de la semaine", *Informations Sociales*, 23 January 1933, 106.
60 Franco De Felice, *Alle origini del welfare contemporaneo. L'Organizzazione internazionale del lavoro tra le due guerre (1919–1939)*, Revised and Expanded Edition (Roma: Istituto della enciclopedia italiana, 2007), 359.
61 Maul, *The International*, 85, 100–103; Ludovic Tournès, *Les États-Unis et la Société des Nations (1914–1946). Le système international face à l'émergence d'une superpuissance* (Berne: Peter Lang, 2016), 249–256; Bruno Settis, "Tra razionalizzazione e internazionalismo. Organizzazione internazionale del lavoro e Stati Uniti da Wilson a Roosevelt", *Studi storici* 62, no. 4 (2021): 967–994.
62 William Lonsdale Tayler, "The International Labor Organization", in *Contemporary World Politics. An Introduction to the Problems of International Relations*, eds. Francis J. Brown, Charles Hodges, and Joseph S. Rouček (New York-London: John Wiley & Sons-Chapman, 1939), 476, 479–480. On Olivetti's productivist culture, see Eleonora Belloni, *La Confindustria e lo sviluppo economico italiano. Gino Olivetti tra Giolitti e Mussolini* (Bologna: il Mulino, 2011), which, however, completely neglects his role in the ILO.
63 See Alessandro Brizzi, "La 'battaglia' delle 40 ore. Un aspetto delle relazioni tra l'Organizzazione internazionale del lavoro e l'Italia fascista negli anni Trenta", *Studi storici* 62, no. 4 (2021): 941–965.
64 Ministero delle Corporazioni, *Atti dell'Assemblea generale. Sessione terza*, vol. 1, 120.
65 Redenti's address, ibid., vol. 2, 78.
66 Gorla's address, ibid., 55.
67 Pala's address, ibid., 56.
68 Particularly noteworthy is Riccardo Del Giudice's address, in Ministero delle Corporazioni, *Atti dell'Assemblea generale. Sessione terza*, vol. 2, 97–99. On the definition of the trade unionist perspective, see AFSDF, *Fondo Giuseppe Landi*, b. 11. Landi's letter to Del Giudice, 24 February 1932.

69 Razza's address, in Ministero delle Corporazioni, *Atti dell'Assemblea generale. Sessione terza*, vol. 2, 105; Giardina's address, ibid., 49.
70 Giuseppe Bronzini, "Legislazione sociale ed istituzioni corporative", in *La classe operaia durante il fascismo*, ed. Giulio Sapelli, *Annali della Fondazione Giangiacomo Feltrinelli*, 20 (1979–1980), 322.
71 Paolo Frascani, "I medici dall'Unità al fascismo", in *Storia d'Italia. Annali*, vol. 10, *I professionisti*, ed. Maria Malatesta (Torino: Einaudi, 1996), 177.
72 Law of 22 February 1934, no. 370, on Sunday and weekly rest; law of 26 April 1934, no. 653, on the protection of women and children in the workplace; law of 22 March 1934, no. 654, on the protection of female workers' maternity rights.
73 Law of 16 March 1933, no. 527.
74 See Giuseppe Landi, "Il Sindacato nell'assistenza e previdenza sociale", *Politica sociale* 3, no. 1 (1931): 104–105.
75 Gian Carlo Jocteau, *La magistratura e i conflitti di lavoro durante il fascismo, 1926–1934* (Milano: Feltrinelli, 1978), 103.
76 Ministero delle Corporazioni, *Atti dell'Assemblea generale del Consiglio nazionale delle Corporazioni. Sessione quarta* (Roma: Istituto poligrafico dello Stato, 1932), 115.
77 Ibid., 38–39.
78 Stefano Musso, *Le regole e l'elusione. Il governo del mercato del lavoro nell'industrializzazione italiana (1888–2003)* (Torino: Rosenberg & Sellier, 2004), 226–230.
79 Ministero delle Corporazioni, *Atti dell'Assemblea generale. Sessione quarta*, 100–102, 104–105, 109.
80 La definizione di "totalitarismo pluralistico" è in Salvati, *Il regime e gli impiegati*, 118. Più in generale, see Cassese, *La formazione*; G. Melis, *Due modelli.*
81 Ministero delle Corporazioni, *Atti dell'Assemblea generale. Sessione quarta*, 11.
82 See Guido Melis, "Le istituzioni italiane negli anni Trenta", in *Lo Stato negli anni Trenta. Istituzioni e regimi fascisti in Europa*, ed. Melis (Bologna: Il Mulino, 2008), 100–101.
83 Ministero delle Corporazioni, *Atti dell'Assemblea generale. Sessione quarta*, 89.
84 Ibid., 91.
85 Guido Melis, "La giurisdizione sui rapporti di impiego negli enti pubblici. Nuovi documenti e quattro lettere inedite di Santi Romano (1933–1934)", in *Rivista trimestrale di diritto pubblico*, 57, vol. 2 (2007), 511–538.
86 ACS, PCM, Gab., 1934–36, fasc. 18.2.3427, sottofasc. 4. *Relazione al comitato corporativo centrale. Inquadramento sindacale di alcuni enti economici di diritto pubblico* (no date, but 1939).

7 1934

The Corporations in Action

Three years after the National Council of Corporations came into effect, despite the enthusiastic propaganda and constant intellectual fervour, the first signs of dissatisfaction began to be felt. The CNC had succeeded in carrying out some important measures, but overall it met with considerable difficulties and was relegated to a marginal position. The obstacles that the Council was encountering in claiming a genuinely proactive role for itself were beginning to be brought into focus and pointed out by certain sectors within Fascism. The most active in denouncing the disappointing failure to meet expectations were the trade unionists, who had hitherto counted on corporatism's innovativeness. Without mincing his words, in 1933 Luigi Razza wrote:

> In practice, show me a single case in which an administration, other than the Ministry of Corporations, has sought the opinion of a corporate body. At each meeting of the Council of Ministers, the Ministry of Corporations itself passes dozens of measures on industrial and commercial matters, without ever informing any corporatist organ, thus concretely demonstrating that when it comes to corporations, the watchword is: always talk and never think about it – indeed, never resort to it.[1]

The problem was exacerbated by industrial and banking bail-outs and the establishment in 1933 of the IRI – a public holding company that took control of a large share of the national production system. These measures were taken outside the corporate bodies. The problem was raised, again without any reticence, by Bottai and the editorial board of the magazine *Critica Fascista*. In 1933, Bottai wrote:

> We keep hammering away at a point on which, we are deeply convinced, the solution to many problems will one day have to hinge.
>
> What is this point? It is *the State's corporate intervention in the organisation of the national economy*. Has this intervention taken place in Italy to date? No, except for a few experiments of no great importance. In Italy, on the other hand, there have been – and still are – several cases of State

DOI: 10.4324/9781032713267-8

> intervention in economic life conducted through a non-corporative method, by disregarding trade union and corporative bodies (instruments of the same policy, corresponding to two different but converging phases) and keeping to the bureaucratic practices – let this be said without contempt – followed by all liberal and democratic states in these years of crisis. This is not a criticism. It is an observation. It is the observation of a necessary economic policy, dictated by strict and inescapable contingencies, which at least has produced and continues to produce undeniable immediate results; but make no mistake: it is not a corporatist policy.[2]

The balance of corporatism's first three years was rendered even more critical by the strident absence of the corporations, the linchpin of the new system. The fact that the National Council had found itself operating for four years in the complete absence of those bodies it was called upon to coordinate is an indication of the cumbersome way in which the construction of the new system was managed and of the obstacles it evidently encountered. According to an effective and popular formula coined *a posteriori* by Bottai himself, what Italy had was "corporatism without corporations".[3]

In this climate of ideological enthusiasm and practical disappointment, the regime decided to take another important step: the creation of the long-awaited corporations. Halfway along the institutional path that was to lead to the law establishing these bodies, Mussolini raised hopes once again for the realisation of the "corporative revolution" – implicitly responding to the discontent that was then felt – in his speech of 14 November 1933 (examined in Chapter 5):

> I shall not dwell on the conciliatory functions which the Corporations may exercise, and I see no drawback to the practice of their advisory powers. In point of fact, the various parties concerned are already being consulted whenever the Government must take measures of any importance.
>
> If consultation were to be made compulsory for certain specified matters I should see no harm in it, for everything that brings the citizen into closer contact with the State, everything that draws the citizen within the machinery of the State, is useful to the social and national aims of Fascism.
>
> Our State is not an absolute State, still less an absolutist State far removed from men and armed only with laws, inflexible as laws should be.
>
> Our State is an organic, human State, desirous of adhering to the realities of life.
>
> Even today bureaucracy is not, and will be still less in the future, a barrier between the activity of the State and the actual practical needs of the Italian people.
>
> I feel certain that Italian bureaucracy, which is indeed admirable, will collaborate with the Corporations in future as it has done in the past, whenever this proves necessary to achieve a fruitful settlement of the problems at issue.[4]

The scaffolding for the creation of the corporations had already been erected in the previous months. While not particularly long, the institutional path that led to the birth of the new bodies was extremely complex. Even a mere list of the main institutional steps reflects the complexity of the Fascist state's structure. The matter was discussed first in the trade union and corporative structures, then in the party structures, and finally submitted to Parliament's legislative authority.

The issue was quickly dealt with at the third session of the general assembly of the National Council of Corporations in June 1932. The actual process was then initiated by the Central Corporative Committee in May 1933. The confederations of employers and workers were subsequently consulted. The opinions gathered were then presented at the 18 September 1933 session of the CNC's general assembly, which was followed by meetings of the divisions at the end of September and beginning of October. Finally, from 8 to 14 November, the final round of discussion took place at the general assembly. This also happened to be the Council's "swan song".[5] From then on, this body would be completely marginalised by the corporations. On the basis of the CNC's discussions and motions, the Ministry of Corporations submitted its own bill to the Grand Council of Fascism. The latter, in turn, made further amendments, to which were added those proposed by the Undersecretary for Corporations, Biagi.[6] The last step was the parliamentary one. The draft modified by the Grand Council and Biagi constituted the starting text for the parliamentary committee entrusted with preparing the bill. The various stances on corporatism were broadly represented within the committee, which was chaired by Rocco, with Razza as the secretary.[7]

The most heated discussions, however, took place within the corporate bodies. The votes and motions expressed by the various divisions and the addresses at the general assembly offered a broadly representative picture of the orientations and views of the trade union organisations, so much so that they actually replaced parliamentary debate. During the latter, only nine addresses were recorded in the Senate – mainly apologetic and celebratory in content – and in fact, none at all in the chamber, excepting those by Rocco and Razza for the presentation of the bill.

In the course of the debates in the Council of Corporations, various grounds for dispute and contention emerged, as in some cases, employers' and workers' organisations faced off, while in others, it was different economic categories.[8] The most heated disagreements arose over the criteria according to which the new bodies should be constituted. Two contrasting proposals were made: according to the first, each corporation was to take a production sector as its point of reference and would thus be based on the existing trade union categories. The second hypothesis was instead to establish the corporations on the basis of the production cycle. In this case, there would not be as many corporations as production phases, but a lot fewer, because the production cycle encompassed all the processes required to obtain finished products, including the intermediate processes. The difference between the two hypotheses is not immediately clear. The ministerial report tried to clarify it through the example of silk: the silkworm egg was a product, the silkworm another product (i.e. the second stage in the production cycle), the silk thread a third, and the fabric a fourth; these were then followed by a fifth stage, the commercial one.

In this case, if the corporations were constituted according to category, it would be necessary to create three: one in the industrial field for reeling, twisting, and weaving; a second one in the agricultural field for silkworm breeding; and a third for trading in silk products. If, on the other hand, the production cycle criterion were adopted, a single silk corporation would be set up, with representatives of employers and workers across the various categories involved.[9]

The choice between the two criteria may seem like a technical and secondary issue. In actual fact, it had major implications. With the adoption of the production cycle system, the separation of the different sectors (most notably industry, trade, and agriculture) and the related trade union representations would disappear. This meant, firstly, that entrepreneurs' organisations in industry and other sectors would have to cooperate within each corporation to formulate proposals and choices for each type of production.[10] Such a solution would prove detrimental for industrialists, whose interests were undoubtedly the best organised and most capable of influencing the decisions of the government and administrative apparatus. This explains *Confindustria*'s opposition to the production cycle criterion and, at the same time, the favourable opinion of it expressed by the other business organisations.

Secondly, the choice of one criterion over the other was decisive in shaping the relationship between corporations and trade unions. Corporations established by professional category would be modelled on the federations and confederations, with the risk of turning the latter into mere duplicates of the corporations. The structuring of corporations by production cycles would instead make it possible to avoid an overlap between corporations and the trade union structure. In short, the category criterion risked reviving the corporatists' campaigns for the elimination of trade unions. Suffice to say that as late as at the end of 1935, Ugo Spirito sought to relaunch the goal of the "end of trade unions".[11] In the end, however, no single criterion was chosen, although most corporations were largely constituted according to the production cycle criterion.

Regardless of the choice of criteria for setting up the new bodies, the new development of the corporatist system risked coming across – like its predecessor – as a threat to trade union organisations. Once again, what the establishment of the corporations called into question was not so much trade unions as such but the confederal structure, the real bastion of trade unionism's residual political power. The question concerned, above all, workers' organisations, which were the most exposed to further fragmentation. In the speeches they gave during the phase of the corporations' establishment, trade unionists stressed precisely the confederation's "educational, highly political work" aimed at "enabling all social categories to perfectly conform to the Regime's political and economic innovations".[12]

That this was a crucial point is also evidenced by the discussions that took place at the beginning of 1934 within the parliamentary committee in charge of preparing the bill's text.[13] Rocco, chairman of the committee, championed the idea of the progressive absorption of the confederation into the state. Rocco's plan, however, met with firm and insurmountable opposition, so much so that he was forced to modify the first – and already printed – version of the introductory report for the debate in the chamber, evidently at the urging of other members. A comparison of the two versions of the text gives us a good sense of Rocco's initial idea and of his change of plans; consequently, it suggests that confederal trade unionists were still capable of defending themselves politically. The initial version claimed that "the large Confederations' tasks will now certainly *diminish*", whereas the approved text merely speaks of the need to "adapt" these tasks "to the new corporative experiences". Another phrase, even less equivocal in meaning, was instead entirely removed from the final version of the report: "The Confederations will not die: albeit with more limited tasks in terms of coordination, study, and propaganda, they will continue in their beneficial work of consolidation and synthesis".[14]

With the launching of the corporations, the question of overcoming the confederal form was essentially set aside. Not only did the new institutions not entail any further downsizing of the trade unions' presence, but on the contrary, they would afford new areas for trade union initiative and intervention. In the background of these discussions lay the even more relevant question of the new bodies' function in economic and social life. Some aimed to assign the corporations an effective role in the management of the national economy; others, on the contrary, sought to circumscribe the corporations' powers and functions as much as possible and to protect the full autonomy of private enterprise.

Once again, it was the "strange alliance" between trade unionism and that section of the PNF that looked to Bottai that promoted progress along the road to the "corporative revolution". On the trade unionist front, already in the 1933 debates at the National Council of Corporations some confederal presidents such as De Marsanich and Razza had argued the need for the corporations to take on the function of planning bodies in relation to economic activities.[15] According to De Marsanich, the corporations

> must draw up production plans for each branch of the economy, eliminating or contracting existing activities or favouring new ones; regulate production consortia and competition; and set up collective economic contracts between the production categories that supply, process, and consume raw materials and products. As this will affect all the old legal and economic relations, it is necessary to set up a corporation that dictates the rules to which individuals and businesses must submit.[16]

A few weeks after the launching of the corporations, some of the leaders of the industrial union, such as the confederal commissioner, Tullio Cianetti, and Edoardo Malusardi, reiterated their demand to make corporations the Italian economy's governing bodies, arguing that they should replace the IRI and all existing consortia and committees, or at the very least regulate their activities.[17] The hypothesis of an industrial plan that would direct companies' investments was then developed within the individual categories through studies and the first drafts of sectoral plans.[18] The debate was relaunched, with similar arguments, by Bottai's group in the pages of *Critica Fascista*.[19]

Many perceived the government's new plans as a rash move, first and foremost entrepreneurs, who feared they might limit entrepreneurial freedom and pose a threat to private property.[20] A creeping hostility towards corporatism – at least in its more radical versions – was also to be found among significant sectors within Fascism. Quite a few saw the new system as the premise for an inevitable further bureaucratisation, a dangerous slide towards socialism or a materialistic distortion of the civilisation model expressed by Fascism which might lead to the triumph of an "economicist conception of society and the individual".[21] A strongly restrictive view of the functions of the corporations was taken above all by the PNF's leadership.[22] While it is true that aversion to the regime's corporatist policy was only displayed by a few Fascist leaders – who certainly paid for that attitude politically, as in the striking case of Leandro Arpinati[23] – it is equally true that the party leaders never concealed their desire to bring corporatism back into their own sphere of influence. Corporatism was a potential means by which they could extend their power to the detriment of more conservative social forces, but it was, above all, a serious pitfall because it risked reviving the role and prerogatives of the trade unions, which in turn aspired to acquire a fully political function. The enmity between party and union leaders arose precisely from this sort of competition between bureaucracies. In this sense, as we have seen, corporatism had inevitably been a fraught field from the start.[24]

The corporations' institutional structure was ultimately to represent a compromise between these conflicting positions. After briefly passing through Parliament without further amendments, the text finalised by the Rocco committee became a law on 5 February 1934. One of the defining features of the new legislative provisions was the assigning of the presidency of the corporations to a minister, an undersecretary, or the secretary of the National Fascist Party. In addition to the government's obvious pre-eminence, the law thus enshrined the less obvious participation of the PNF, which could also count on having three representatives in each corporation.

Out of a total of 882 members across the 22 corporations, 66 were therefore members of the PNF. The largest component was obviously constituted by the employers' representatives (325) and the representatives of the workers' unions (319 – in the welfare and credit corporation, there were 6 fewer than employers' representatives). Finally, there were 114 representatives of other authorities and bodies, such as ministries and the AGFPI, the Fascist Association of Civil Servants.

As far as the corporations' duties were concerned, each would offer advice on all matters of interest to the economic sector for which it had been established whenever it was requested to do so by the relevant public administrations. Each corporation would also strive to settle collective labour disputes and draw up rules for the collective regulation of economic relations, following a proposal from the ministries or at the request of one of the affiliated associations, with the assent of the head of government. This last function, now to be fulfilled upon request from a single trade union association, represented a more extensive and less constrained version of the role formally assigned to the National Council of Corporations. The head of government then had the power to order that two or more corporations be convened together for matters concerning different economic sectors.

A few months later, with the decrees issued by the head of government on 29 May and 9 and 23 June 1934, the establishment of 22 corporations was approved, constituted according to the criterion of the production cycle, with the exception of those in the service sector.[25] The almost complete abandoning of the category criterion marked the overcoming of the classification systems for productive activities that had been designed in view of the trade union organisations.

The subsequent decree-law of 18 April 1935 extended the powers of the Central Corporative Committee, which was called upon to exercise all the functions assigned to the other organs of the National Council of Corporations following authorisation by the head of government.[26] The committee increasingly monopolised the exercise of the Council's functions, de facto becoming independent from the Council and, in particular, divesting the general assembly of its power since it was deemed unfit to operate in decisive and prompt fashion owing to its cumbersome structure.[27] This confirmed the Fascist state's tendency to progressively deprive collegiate bodies of authority, and the corresponding strengthening of less representative institutions. What remained unchanged was the weak and marginal position of the Ministry of Corporations, whose apparatus and bureaucracy the corporations had to refer to in order to fulfil their tasks.

The greatest limitation of the new institution, and of the entire corporatist system created by Fascism, was not so much its lack of power as the structural unfeasibility of representing professional interests in a genuine way – that is, through representatives selected by the members of each category – within a dictatorial and authoritarian regime. Once again, it was workers' representative organisations that suffered the most. As in the past, the presence of Fascist trade unionists in the corporative bodies was the result of an appointment from above, made by the heads of the federations and confederations, with the endorsement of the government and Mussolini.[28] The situation in the case of business interests was quite different, even more so than in the past. This was the main innovation brought about by the corporations. Owing to the substantial autonomy that the employers' associations enjoyed, prominent or top-level representatives of Italian capitalism also became members of the corporations. Scrolling through a list of the 22 corporations is revealing in this respect: to mention but a few names, we find Gino Olivetti, Franco Marinotti, and Senatore Borletti (textile corporation); Vincenzo Ardissone, Arturo Bocciardo, Luigi Orlando, Agostino Rocca, and Giuseppe Mazzini (metallurgy and mechanics corporation); Guido Donegani and Achille Gaggia (chemistry corporation); Giacinto Motta and Giuseppe Cenzato (water, gas, and electricity corporation); and Vincenzo Azzolini, Alberto Beneduce, Alberto Pirelli, and Arturo Osio (welfare and credit corporation).[29]

The entering into effect of the corporations, and the first period of their activity, was regarded by large sections of the Fascist and trade union leadership as the beginning of the final stage of the "corporative revolution". The system finally seemed to be able to progress from merely regulating labour relations to regulating economic activities.[30] Both the extension of regulatory powers, compared to those granted to the CNC, and the direct participation of trade union leaders as well as representatives of industry and finance seemed to suggest that a real change was underway.

While in Italy the analyses were largely drowned in the vast flow of propaganda speeches, abroad the planning and then creation of corporations prompted detailed and unprejudiced analyses. Corporatism had long been "one of the most fascinating aspects of the new Italy", as the Swiss journalist Paul Gentizon noted in 1933.[31]

As late as the early 1930s, reports on the matter were polarised. On the one hand, there were the numerous celebratory voices which could mainly, yet not exclusively, be traced back to Fascist or radical right-wing circles. One of the most significant texts is no doubt *The Making of the Corporate State* by the English journalist and poet Harold E. Goad, a member of the British Institute in Florence.[32] This work described Mussolini's regime as a "constructive dictatorship" capable of mobilising the vast majority of Italians, even on a spiritual level. According to Goad, through the corporatist system and inter-class collaboration Fascism in Italy had launched a campaign of national cooperation against selfish individualism and the exploitation of the weak. Despite its brazenly celebratory judgements and emphatic tones, the book attracted considerable interest, as is shown by the numerous reviews in both English-speaking and Italian magazines.

On the other hand, various observers denounced the contradictions, shortcomings, delays, and limitations in the implementation of corporatism. These were socialists, democrats, liberals, and Catholics, but also sympathisers of Fascism, such as Gentizon. Taking stock of his own Italian experience and evidently disappointed with the results of an experiment he had looked to with some hope, Gentizon stated that the Fascist corporatist state lacked coherence and still remained largely unfinished in 1933. As a result, instead of allowing general interests to prevail over particular interests, corporatism resulted in a heavily oppressive system where the individual and social forces were entirely subservient to the state.[33]

Both the celebratory and the critical speeches focused either on the general principles of corporatism (the idea of the primacy of politics over economics, the unity between the state and society, and the overcoming of social conflict), or on specific institutions, such as the legal recognition of trade unions, collective negotiation, the Labour Court, and the banning of strikes and lock-outs. In any case, the focus of analysis was the corporatism developed in the 1920s – i.e. a system for regulating relations between employers and workers. The establishment of the corporations – and the promise of an entirely new model of economic governance that this entailed – also marked a break in Fascist corporatism's transnational reception. Alongside the many apologetic and critical texts, an increasing number of detailed analyses were published that were neither celebratory nor biasedly critical. Such analyses were produced by journalists and politicians but also by jurists, political scientists, sociologists, and political philosophers, especially in Europe and on the American continent.[34] Unlike in the early years, international observers now had plenty of material at their disposal, either provided by Italian propaganda networks abroad and the anti-Fascist press in exile or collected during numerous trips to Italy: laws, speeches by political authorities, court rulings, statistical data, newspaper reports, and interviews with politicians, trade union leaders, and industrialists.[35] In many cases, these were one-sided sources or ones heavily manipulated by the

Fascist authorities. If used with the right rigour and adequate interpretative tools, however, they allowed analysis and reflection to be conducted on a more solid basis.

Among the most notable cases were a number of investigations carried out by officials and representatives of overseas governments. Two examples are particularly significant. The first is an official enquiry by the British diplomatic services. In the United Kingdom, from the mid-1920s onwards, high-ranking authorities showed an unusual interest in the advances that were being made in the Italian legal system. The annual reports that the British embassy in Rome prepared for the Foreign Office devoted increasing space to corporatism. They reflect genuine curiosity, albeit often veiled by superficiality and an inability to break free from stereotypes. The resulting verdict was therefore mixed: on the one hand, the British diplomats acknowledged the corporate states' originality and ambition; on the other, they noted the slowness and timidity with which the government was putting its proclamations into action. In 1933–1934, in an attempt to focus more rigorously on corporatism's actual impact, British diplomats conducted an in-depth enquiry based on a complex questionnaire. This was sent to their consuls in Italy, who were asked to respond in a thorough and documented manner. The embassy then collated the material received to produce a conclusive report. This document constitutes one of the most sophisticated and systematic attempts made by foreign state authorities to come to terms with the institutional and political reality of Fascist corporatism, going beyond the portrayals of it provided by intellectuals and propaganda.[36]

No less intense was the American effort to gather information and analyses. Although the Roosevelt administration officially distanced itself from the Fascist regime, various intellectuals and politicians close to the president, or in any case variously involved in the New Deal, considered Italian corporatism to be the most interesting experiment undertaken in those years. This view was expressed from many sides: by economists and officials from the National Recovery Administration (NRA), by scholars involved in foundations such as the Brookings Institution, by prestigious journals such as *Fortune*, *Foreign Affairs*, and *Annals of the American Academy of Political and Social Science*, and even by the ambassador to Rome, Breckinridge Long. It was a widely held opinion that despite the radical political-ideological differences between the two governments, there were many affinities to be found between the path taken in Rome and what was being discussed and implemented in Washington. One of the New Deal's most active and high-level advisors, the economist Rexford Tugwell, claimed to have found "Italy doing many of the things which seem to me necessary"[37] after returning from a visit to Rome in October 1934.

The subordination of particular interests to general interests and the overcoming of destabilising social conflict seemed to the Americans to be objectives shared by the two governments. More concretely, the involvement of social interests in the decision-making process, the welfare system, and the "publicising" of trade union relations, but also the use of public works as a means to boost employment and the regulating of the activities of banks and financial institutions were all areas of intervention in which US observers found unquestionable similarities with Italy. Besides, extreme pragmatism led the New Dealers to privilege the operational dimension of politics, in spite of any opposition from within the "system". Conversely, similarities between the two models were also stressed by those who opposed Roosevelt's policies – the Republicans, the economic establishment, and, in a more subtle way, the conservative wing of the Democratic Party – who sought to emphasise the authoritarian and "Fascist" character of the New Deal.[38]

In Italy too, the two experiences were made an object of comparative analysis and reflection.[39] In spite of the anti-Americanism so deeply rooted in the regime's public discourse,[40] these similarities were emphasised in numerous speeches, including some given by those in positions of authority. Returning from a stay in the United States in May 1933, Finance Minister Guido Jung reported that "in the attitude of President Roosevelt regarding the domestic problems of the United States there appears the basic Fascist concept 'everything in the state, everything for the state, nothing outside the state'".[41] Noting the positive aspects of Roosevelt's policies, however, did not mean abandoning the view of the Mussolinian state as something unique and unattainable. Fascist analyses almost invariably emphasised how the New Deal, despite its analogies with corporatism, was essentially an imitative phenomenon, and one far less successful in its practical effects – because it was democratic and not Fascist. This interpretation was reproposed in speeches for the American public, aimed at justifying the Italian experience and urging exchanges and collaboration between the two countries.

It is worth noting that the most senior members of the regime, starting from the "Duce", devoted themselves to this exercise. In a review of Roosevelt's book *Looking Forward*,[42] published by the American agency *Universal Service*, and later reprinted by *Il Popolo d'Italia*, Mussolini stated:

> In America and Europe, many have wondered how much 'Fascism' there is in the American president's doctrine and practice. One should avoid hasty generalisations. What there is in common with Fascism is the fact that the State cannot disregard the fate of the economy, for that would be tantamount to disregarding the fate of the people. Here and there in Roosevelt's book there is also a hint to the need for collaboration between all productive elements, which may remind one of the foundations of the Fascist corporation. But while Fascism has introduced profound innovations – through a genuine revolution – by creating the appropriate institutions to organically solve the kind of problems besetting the United States, Roosevelt does not address any of these problems in his book, namely the legal recognition of workers' and employers' unions, the banning of strikes and lock-outs, the Labour Court, and the national and trade corporations, which must lead the categories to self-government under the aegis of the State. Roosevelt does not go beyond the system of indirect State intervention through the measures of more or less permanent commissions of a political or administrative nature. The atmosphere in which his whole theoretical and practical system operates is certainly akin to that of Fascism, but it would be an exaggeration to push this claim any further.[43]

Mussolini nonetheless acknowledged that the American president had shown himself capable of "facing the battle with decisiveness and virile pessimism", with a style characterising "that 'way of life' which Fascism has fostered and intends to increasingly foster among the Italian people".[44]

Two years later, Giuseppe Bottai dwelled in even more detail and depth on the comparison between Fascism and the New Deal in a dense article for the prestigious journal *Foreign Affairs*. Bottai noted the successes of Roosevelt's policies and recognised the importance and originality of the National Recovery Administration. In his view, however, this was not enough. The change was still incomplete, and further developments would necessarily take place in the future. For Bottai, both a return to full economic individualism and an increase in state intervention and bureaucratic control were to be discarded. The only real solution would be for the United States to follow the Italian model. In Italy – Bottai concluded – with the creation of the corporations "an equilibrium has been established, without a complete fusion or loss of individuality, between capital and labor, between labor and the state, and between the state and capital".[45]

This interest in the American situation was no exception. In the early 1930s, Italian political, economic, and legal journals continued, even more so than in the previous period, to devote space to what was happening abroad in relation to corporatism. *Archivio di studi corporativi*, the bimonthly journal published by the Ministry of Corporations, hosted numerous articles – not all of which were disparaging – on what was taking place in other European and non-European countries. The comparison was even extended to the Soviet Union: in spite of the political and ideological opposition between the two countries, the planning system introduced by Stalin "found numerous well-informed and scrupulous observers among corporatists".[46] Within this framework, for celebrations of the first ten years of the Labour Charter in 1937, Anselmo Anselmi – a senior official in the Ministry of Corporations – mapped out the various corporatist systems for the magazine *Civiltà fascista*. He covered both authoritarian regimes and large democratic states which – in his words – "practise corporatism, even if they do so without realising it, or pretending not to realise it". The former included Portugal, Austria, and Germany; the latter included France under the Popular Front – which had introduced collective negotiation and compulsory arbitration for trade union conflicts – and the United States.[47] Alongside magazine articles were more systematic publications aimed at offering a broad and in-depth overview of what was happening abroad. One significant volume, given the context in which it arose, is *Nuove esperienze economiche*, which was published by the School for Advanced Corporative Studies in Pisa in 1935 and examined the cases of Germany, United Kingdom, the United States, the Soviet Union, Japan, Australia, and New Zealand.[48]

On the whole, these analyses reflected a well-defined thesis – already illustrated by Mussolini in his review of Roosevelt's book and by Bottai in his article in *Foreign Affairs* – according to which Fascist corporatism was exerting a strong influence on many other countries. This influence had taken on a transnational dimension and was not limited to the ideological level of theories and doctrines but also extended to the political level of government intervention in trade union relations, working conditions, and representative institutions. According to this thesis, however, no country had gone as far as Italy: neither the democratic states, which were too fragile and plagued with unsolvable contradictions, nor the authoritarian ones, which were still partly bound to the old schemes of 19th-century authoritarianism and insufficiently "Fascistised".

Nazi Germany fell into this picture as well. Numerous analyses were devoted to Hitler's legislation in Italy, and not only in those magazines and journals that were most attentive to corporatist issues. The opinions expressed were generally rather critical. As in other countries, the fundamental interpretative criterion was a comparison with the Italian model. A strongly idealised representation of it was offered which took quite literally the idea that a "corporative revolution" was underway. The criticism voiced was centred precisely on the two fundamental principles of Nazi labour ideology: the *Betriebsgemeinschaft* ("business community") and the *Führerprinzip* ("leader principle"). Regarding the former, Mario Da Silva, *Critica Fascista*'s German affairs expert, stated that Nazi legislation postulated "a corporate atomism that could reasonably be regarded as outdated" and imposed a rigidly hierarchical organisational structure. By reducing workers to mere "followers", each company, even the most advanced and modern one, was destined to "become a sort of medieval workshop". That legislation – Da Silva further observed – rested "on the fluctuation between private capitalism and statism". Consequently, it lacked "that new relationship of mediation between the individual producer and the State made necessary by over a century of struggle", the only kind of relationship allowing all the components of society to be put into the service of a higher interest, "until they coincide with the totality and unity of the national interest represented by the State, while preserving their varied individuality".[49] In *Diritto del lavoro*, Luigi Adolfo Miglioranzi criticised, in no uncertain terms, "the concept of the 'leader' (Führer) [...] at the basis of national-socialist doctrine" because it produced too sharp a fracture in the social body, leading to "the establishment of large 'barracks' [...] that might accord with German taste but certainly not with a corporative conception". By creating a relationship of "absolute subordination between leader and followers", it prevented "any expression of trade union activity".[50] In the years that followed, this critical judgement would soften somewhat, partly as a result of the rapprochement between the two countries. There always remained, however, a sense of distance, accompanied by the more or less explicit affirmation of the Italian model's superiority.

Another novelty in Fascist corporatism's international reception after the early 1930s is its extension, to a significant degree, outside Europe and the United States. In the second half of the 1930s, the Italian model held a certain appeal for radical right-wing intellectuals and political leaders in India, Japan, Argentina, and Brazil.[51] Particularly significant is the last of these cases, which has also been the focus of several studies in recent years. In the immediate post-war period, corporatism become part and parcel of the ideological baggage and political cultures of the Brazilian right wing. Theory was translated into practice with the "revolutionary" coup d'etat which brought Getúlio Vargas to power in 1930, and then with the beginning of the more properly dictatorial phase of the *Estado novo* (1937–1945).

The dictatorship's ruling class, starting from Vargas himself, was profoundly influenced both by the Italian experience as well as by Mihail Manoïlesco – who had theorised an "integral" and "pure" corporatism to be adapted to the different economic-political levels of individual countries, and which therefore seemed particularly suitable for a "peripheral" and less industrially developed reality such as Brazil's. As has been observed, "Fascist corporatism – in its multiple dimensions as the legal classification of 'the social', economic dirigisme, the organisation of the nation, and the harmonious negotiation of the capital-labour conflict – fitted perfectly with Getúlio Vargas' authoritarian and statist plan for a corporatist modernisation of Brazilian society between the two world wars".[52] In practice, corporative achievements in Vargas' Brazil took a different direction from Italian ones, except for the establishment of a single trade union under state control, which was openly inspired by the Rocco Law of 1926.[53] Throughout the 1930s, however, a debate raged in Brazil on just how profound the influence of the Italian model was: "The problem of how to adopt the cornerstones of Alfredo Rocco's corporate model without falling prey to the accusation of having imitated Fascist totalitarianism was one of the leitmotifs of ideological debate at the time".[54]

International interest did not only stem from the curiosity aroused by the creation of the corporations but also continued to be an effect of propaganda abroad. This was relaunched precisely as a result of Rocco's reform. In 1934, a special coordination office was created at the Undersecretariat (later Ministry) for the Press and Propaganda: the General Directorate for Propaganda Abroad, which was entrusted with assisting officials and militants in foreign countries, organising cultural and popularisation initiatives, and disseminating Fascist material. Corporatism continued to be the dominant theme. Not only did the publication of the *Feuille d'informations corporatives*, edited by the Ministry of Corporations, continue, but the translation and overseas dissemination of texts on corporatism was increased: speeches by Mussolini, collections of laws and institutional sources, and works on corporatist law and economics.[55] Increasing efforts were also made to foster contacts and exchanges with foreign countries by Italian intellectuals working on the topic of labour law and the corporative system. The most significant event, in this sense, was the Italo-French Conference on Corporative Studies held in Rome in 1935, which saw the participation of leading figures in Fascist politics and culture (among others, Bottai and Spirito, as well as trade union leaders such as Rossoni, Cianetti, and Capoferri) and French intellectuals with different backgrounds and orientations, most notably Emmanuel Mounier.[56] The conference was part of a series of joint cultural meetings between the two countries that took place within a few months and helped mark "the apogee of Franco-Italian cultural exchanges".[57]

This state of affairs prompted a response from the anti-Fascists. The presence of a current of interest in and sympathy for the Fascist "third way" within sectors of international public opinion that could not always be traced back to the most radical right was experienced as a problem by the regime's opponents. After having been forced to leave Italy, those intellectuals and political leaders who opposed the dictatorship had to carve out a place for themselves, as exiles and outsiders, in new contexts (especially in France, Switzerland, the United States, and the Soviet

Union). They increasingly engaged with these contexts, becoming influenced by them and establishing new contacts. Many exiles were linked to transnational organised structures, such as the Comintern or the Labour and Socialist International. The search for contacts and relations accelerated from 1933: with the rise of Nazism to power in Germany (and later with the Spanish Civil War), it became clear that Fascism had become a European-wide phenomenon which could neither be understood nor fought by remaining within national borders. Hence, considerable attention was paid to public opinion trends in democratic countries, as many of these exiles developed the conviction that Fascism also had to be isolated through a transnational battle of ideas.

Leading anti-Fascist intellectuals and journals devoted analyses and reflections to the corporate state in an effort to show its negative sides. In particular, an interpretation prevailed that emphasised abstractness and inconclusiveness: in short, the gulf between promises and actual achievements, between theory and facts. As argued, among others, by Gaetano Salvemini in *Under the Axes of Fascism*, a text published in the United States in 1936, and by Louis Rosenstock Franck – a French intellectual in close contact with Italian liberal-socialist exiles in Paris – in two volumes published in France in 1934 and 1939, the "corporative revolution" was nothing but a "fraud" or "bluff": by hiding behind the illusion and promise of a "corporative revolution", Fascism had sought to justify the elimination of free trade unions and the right to strike, favouring large capitalist groups at the expense of the workers.[58]

The bluff thesis captured an undeniably true fact. There is no doubt that the results achieved by the corporations were abysmally far from the objectives outlined by Fascist propaganda. If we look at the agendas of the meetings, we realise that we are dealing with a large apparatus that, for the most part, was mobilised for secondary and apparently insignificant matters. Even the then much-celebrated tariff and price controls produced few practical results.[59]

It seems reductive, however, to dismiss the corporations as a complete failure. If one takes a closer look at the activity they actually exercised, a number of undoubtedly interesting elements emerge. What stands out, first of all, is the profound transformation that the relations between socio-economic interests and the state underwent through the new corporative procedures. What also emerges is the often neglected participation of the corporations – with an essentially consultative function – in some important economic policy measures, which marked a break with the previous CNC experience. The most obvious change in the corporations' discussions concerns precisely the issues addressed: no longer just social and labour policies but also economic policies.[60] Besides, by 1934, the most acute phase of the crisis seemed to be over and the regime had proven itself capable of containing social unrest. Social security and welfare measures, or at any rate the celebration of such measures in a corporative setting, therefore appeared less urgent.

The corporations played a central role in the regime's autarkic policies. We will return later, in Chapter 9, to the general significance of autarky and how it fitted within the so-called "corporative revolution". Here we must instead examine the "internal" aspects of that policy, particularly interventions in industry aimed at ensuring "national economic independence". It was up to each individual corporation to draw up an autarkic plan for its own specific sector of competence, while the Central Corporative Committee – reconstituted as the High Commission on Autarky (*Commissione suprema dell'autarchia*) – was responsible for coordinating individual plans. Autarkic plans were drawn up between 1936 and 1937 and set targets for each individual production to be achieved by 1941. The corporations held a total of 45 meetings from May to September 1937; 80 already existing corporative technical committees and especially established special commissions examined the partial problems submitted to them at 310 meetings and contributed to the preparation of 40 summary reports.[61]

The trade associations' role proved decisive, especially in the initial "preliminary" phase, as they were often entrusted with the fundamental task of preparing the data collection and preliminary study of the problem.[62] Labour unions, on the other hand, were *de facto* excluded. The views of employers' organisations and the balance between the various forces within *Confindustria*, and between private and public enterprises, weighed heavily on the final result. In this case too, then, the equal representation of entrepreneurs and workers' unions was a purely formal thing, despite the effort made by Tullio Cianetti's Confederation of Industrial Workers to promote the drafting of the plans and their full implementation.[63]

The preparation of the autarkic plans was an important moment in the corporations' activity, both because of the relevance of the issues addressed and because the choices made there would help determine the direction that the state's significant financial commitment would take.[64] Very little is known, however, about the activity actually carried out, the way in which the debate unfolded, and the dialectic exchange between the various trade associations, as well as between the latter and the corporations themselves. The huge gaps in the sources unfortunately make it impossible to fill the gap in our historiographical knowledge. The one exception is the steel plan, the only one for which we have adequate documentation and a rigorous and detailed historiographical reconstruction.[65] In this case, it is clear that the sector's corporation indeed served as a forum for consultation in which the major industrial and financial groups, small entrepreneurs, and workers' unions took part. It is therefore worth following this case in detail because it provides some general insights into the role played by the corporative system in relation to autarky and the management of the industrial system.

The drafting of the autarkic steel plan became the focus of a long dispute which dragged on for several years and required a great deal of mediation. The clash pitted public and private companies against each other. At the centre of the dispute was the plan to develop full-cycle steelmaking in Italy. This is a system of producing steel directly from ore through a process that allows fuel savings and control over the entire production cycle but also requires advanced technological equipment and considerable investments. The front of the public steel industry was represented by the SIAC and Dalmine companies led by Agostino Rocca and by Arturo Bocciardo's Terni. Headed by the IRI, this front supported an ambitious programme, drawn up by Oscar Sinigaglia and Rocca, to build a large full-cycle plant in Italy that would be capable of meeting a significant share of the national demand while significantly limiting dependence on the purchase of scrap iron, which was necessary for other kinds of processing.

In order to facilitate the establishment of full-cycle steelmaking on the domestic market, the IRI's plan called for limitations on production based on other processes. On the opposite side stood large private companies and smaller northern Italian ones, which feared the loss of market shares and the drop in prices that a full-cycle plant would bring. These companies consequently did not accept the limitations on their production growth envisaged by the IRI's plan. This last point, of course, became an especially heated bone of contention. The dispute, which began with the start of the autarkic policy, dragged on until the end of the decade and required complex negotiation and mediation between the parties involved. The corporations, the corporative technical commissions, and the Central Corporative Committee, along with the trade organisations and ministerial offices, provided the forums for this negotiation. Both sides could count on some support from government representatives or the bureaucratic leadership. Each contender needed to develop a complex network of alliances, including within the corporations. The IRI leadership led by Rocca was more active and enterprising: on the one hand, it established a direct correlation between a full-cycle steel plan and the full implementation of autarky; in other words, it gave a political veneer to its production rationalisation project. On the other, it aimed to secure trade unionists' support in this battle through the prospect of increased employment in the mechanical engineering industry as a result of lower steel product costs.

As already noted, the corporative bodies were among the forums in which this negotiation took place and alliances were forged. The decisive moments were the meeting of the metallurgy and mechanics corporation in June 1937, the special commission "for steel autarky plans" which was established within its framework (and was last convened at the beginning of July), the new meeting of the corporation in September, and finally, in October, the meeting of the Central Corporative Committee, the body responsible for ratifying individual corporations' autarkic resolutions. Although the IRI and the Ministry of Finance had previously drawn up a plan – thus directly committing the government – in the process of corporate mediation, the private companies obtained important *quid pro quos*: they were able to keep all their plants in operation and maintain production levels.[66] This compromise represented a substantial defeat for the dirigiste-institutional solution designed by the IRI leadership. Indeed, the resolution approved by the corporation and then ratified by the Central Corporative Committee protected private companies, especially the largest ones, ensuring that they would not be penalised by the growing state presence. In short, the corporation functioned in this case as an institutional channel through which the most representative private groups could, to some extent, negotiate the forms that state intervention would take and their relations with public enterprises.[67]

Corporative resolutions, too, while not legally binding, played an important role. Each disputant attached great importance to formal declarations: these could lend official status and authority to their demands and could be used in negotiations with the government and the economic administrations.[68] The clash that took place on this occasion within the metallurgical corporation testifies to the strong "political" value that corporate resolutions could have in certain contexts. One can plausibly assume that such a dynamic characterised discussions not only in the steel sector but also within other corporations.

To return to the discussions in the steel sector, with the start of the rearmament policy and the consequent increase in the need for steel, the private companies were gradually able, in turn, to affirm the autarkic nature of their production processes. They were thus able to defend their market shares more strongly. In practice, they implemented a concerted obstructionist effort against the autarkic plan through consortia and the instrument of authorisations for new industrial plants and was managed directly by the special committee appointed within the corporation. The two fronts came to their final showdown in the spring of 1940. The corporation's meeting was once again the institutional context in which the different points of view found expression and the balance of power could be measured. All the contenders cloaked their arguments in the phraseology and rhetoric of the regime; all appealed to the demands of autarky and the war effort; and all drew up post-war scenarios to corroborate their theses. Once again, the corporative debate, on which the mediation of the Minister for Corporations Renato Ricci weighed heavily, marked the substantial affirmation of the private steel industry – which even managed to impose severe limits on the production capacity of the new full-cycle plant – and the downsizing of the IRI's plans. The law enacted in June fully accepted the corporation's resolutions.[69] The plan initially devised by the representatives of public enterprise, however, was to be implemented in the post-war period as the so-called "Sinigaglia plan".

It would be of little interest here, of course, to analyse in detail the contents of these proposals or, more generally, the steel policy of the 1930s or the IRI's strategies. Rather, it is worth observing how a clash between productive subjects unfolded and was addressed in 1930s Italy within the institutions themselves through the participation of all the state sectors involved and the corporative system's mediation. Indeed, it was "corporative and legislative sanctions and administrative procedures that the entrepreneurs of the 1930s [...] had to reckon with, not disregarding in turn to have recourse to them as so many instruments that they could use to assert their rationales against competitors". Consequently, "institutional" venues were "chosen by the leading actors to wage battle, circumvent obstacles, and neutralise any form of obstructionism".[70]

Similar remarks can be made for the 1936 Banking Law, one of Fascist Italy's most important economic achievements, which remained in force for over 50 years. In this case, too, as for the steel plan, the availability of more adequate documentation (the minutes of the credit corporation) and recent and detailed historiographical reconstructions allow a closer examination.[71]

The marginal role played by the credit corporation in the development of the reform is generally mentioned in the historiography as one of the clearest signs of corporatism's insignificance.[72] In parallel with the corporation's activities, and without its involvement, a small group of experts from the IRI, led by Donato Menichella, exercised a sort of pre-legislative function in absolute secrecy. Reconstructions have shown that this intervention was decisive in shaping the outline of the reform and preparing the first drafts of the text.

The welfare and credit corporation met on 12 and 13 June 1935 to discuss, among other things, the "functional and territorial distribution of credit institutions". The motion passed at the end of the meeting merely provided some guidelines for the reform, particularly in relation to the tasks of the Bank of Italy (limiting commitments to private parties on the one hand and, on the other, completing the establishment of a modern central bank) and the distinction between the various types of credit institutions. In this regard, three categories were identified: public-law institutions and ordinary savings banks, ordinary credit institutions, and institutions for long-term industrial financing.[73] The corporation decided to entrust the drafting of the reform to a special corporative technical committee, consisting of six members plus a secretary, which was to operate on the basis of those general guidelines. The IRI, however, got there first. Before the committee became operational, President Beneduce presented Finance Minister Paolo Thaon di Revel with a document containing a bill which coincided almost completely with the first seven titles of the final text. With a few marginal changes, the draft prepared by the IRI became a decree-law on 12 March 1936 and was later converted into law on 7 March 1938.

Nevertheless, while the IRI finalised the plan, the corporation fulfilled a far from the insignificant task: it offered the various interests involved the opportunity to officially express claims and proposals, thus allowing the various aspects of the reform to be calibrated in relation to the forces at play. Moreover, the corporation did not merely follow the work of the group led by Menichella, because it was deployed well before then. By mid-April, when the meeting was held that finalised the guidelines for the reorganisation of the credit system – to be followed by the IRI's operational planning – the corporation had already held two preparatory meetings, during which all the various views in the field had been voiced.[74] What emerged on those occasions were, on the one hand, a majority position, expressed in particular by the Confederation of Credit and Insurance companies (*Confederazione delle Aziende di Credito e Assicurazioni*), which supported an intervention limited to increasing the stability and efficiency of banking companies, and on the other, the position of Arturo Osio, the Director General of the Banca Nazionale del Lavoro, who advocated the public management of the credit system.[75] The IRI had therefore begun studying the plan in light of this preliminary survey of the various forces in the field and their respective points of view. The corporation's session of 12–13 June – which reiterated and clarified the views expressed at the meetings held over two months earlier – did not therefore mark this body's "debut" in dealing with the affair, but only the start of its official involvement.

The banking reform then translated the IRI's latest guidelines into a legislative text. These guidelines, however, were different from the Institute's original proposal. The initial plan differed from the one presented in December, on which the text of the decree was based, with regard both to the role assigned to the Bank of Italy and the credit supervisory system and to the distinguishing of different types of banks depending on their function (the IRI sought to draw up the reform without establishing any substantial distinctions between different juridical types of credit institution).[76] The abandonment of the original positions was undoubtedly due to the difficulty of translating those hypotheses into concrete laws comprised of articles, but also, in all likelihood, by the need to come to terms with the divergent views in the field.[77]

Having approved the banking reform, the corporation returned to the issue in February 1937. With the debate on "the functions and tasks of credit institutions in relation to the national economy's new needs", a number of aspects were addressed that the legislation had not definitively resolved, especially with regard to the distinction between short-term and medium-term financing, and hence the possibility for ordinary credit banks to exercise the latter activity as well, as they previously had. The corporation was therefore once again called upon to intervene in the reorganisation of the credit system, this time in order to negotiate between different views on the legislation's shortcomings or the need for adjustments and fine-tuning.[78]

The welfare and credit corporation also served as a forum for "minor" actors within the banking system – which had de facto been "crushed" during the drafting and implementation phase of the reform – where they could voice their demands. At its February 1937 session, the corporation dealt in particular with rural savings banks, paving the way for the approval of the consolidating act on such institutions.[79] Once again, a corporation – while far from accomplishing the "third way" – was "used" as one of the available institutional channels for negotiation to uphold specific socio-economic interests.

Notes

1 Luigi Razza, *La corporazione nello Stato fascista* (Roma: Quaderni de 'La Terra', 1933), 57.
2 Giuseppe Bottai, "Verso un piano corporativo. 2", *Critica fascista* 11, no. 6 (1933): 105.
3 Bottai, "Verso il corporativismo democratico o verso una democrazia corporativa?", in *Il diritto del lavoro* 26, nos. 3–4 (1952): 121–142.
4 Mussolini, *On the Corporate State*, 192–193.
5 Aquarone, *L'organizzazione*, 203.
6 The texts submitted to the Grand Council can be found in ACS, SPD, CR, 1922–43, b. 31, fasc. 242/R "Gran Consiglio", sottofasc. 11, inserto D. For the changes that Biagi proposed to Mussolini, and which were only partially approved, see ibid., PCM, Gab., 1931–33, fasc. 18.1.11923. B. Biagi, *Appunto per S.E. il Capo del governo. Disegno di legge sulle Corporazioni*, 20 December 1933.
7 The minutes from the meetings of the chamber's committee can be found in ASCD, *Disegni proposte di legge e incarti delle commissioni*, vol. 1305, fasc. 2059. *Commissione per l'esame del disegno di legge n. 2059.*
8 Ministero delle Corporazioni, *Atti dell'Assemblea generale. Sessione quinta.*
9 Ibid., 14.
10 Luigi Razza, "Superare la categoria", *Il lavoro fascista*, 3 October 1933.
11 Ugo Spirito, "Gerarchia del lavoro e fine del sindacato", *La Stirpe* 13, no. 12 (1935): 495–499.
12 Address by Livio Ciardi, president of the *Confederazione dei lavoratori delle comunicazioni interne*, in Ministero delle Corporazioni, *Atti dell'Assemblea generale. Sessione quinta*, 68.
13 The committee was composed of Alfredo Rocco, Giuseppe Bottai, Giuseppe Belluzzo, Carlo Costamagna, Luigi Fera, Balbino Giuliano, Ferruccio Lantini, Angelo Manaresi,

Maurizio Maraviglia, Alessandro Martelli, Giuseppe Morelli, Giovanni Pala, Sergio Panunzio, Filippo Pennavaria, Luigi Razza, Adelchi Serena, and Attilio Teruzzi.

14 The first version of the text can be found in ASCD, *Disegni proposte di legge e incarti delle commissioni*, vol. 1305, f. 2059. Commissione per l'esame del disegno di legge n. 2059; the final version can instead be found in APC, Legislatura XVIII, *Documenti, disegni di legge e relazioni*, n. 2059-A, 4–5.

15 Ministero delle Corporazioni, *Atti dell'Assemblea generale. Sessione quinta*, 71–74, 107–114. According to Renzo De Felice, it was precisely because of these views that Razza and De Marsanich lost their union positions: De Felice, *Mussolini il duce*, vol. 1, 291.

16 Ministero delle Corporazioni, *Atti dell'Assemblea generale. Sessione quinta*, 73.

17 *Convegno nazionale dei dirigenti dei sindacati fascisti dell'industria. Roma, 12 luglio 1934* (Roma: Stabilimento tipografico de "Il lavoro fascista", 1935), 10, 47. See also Tullio Cianetti, "I lavoratori dell'industria e le corporazioni", *Il lavoro fascista*, 3 November 1934.

18 This was particularly the case in the marble and cotton sectors: Confederazione nazionale sindacati fascisti dell'industria, *Atti del primo convegno dei lavoratori del marmo granito e pietre affini tenutosi a Carrara il 16–17 September 1933* (Roma: F. Damasso, 1933); "La necessità di un coordinamento corporativo dell'industria", *Il lavoro fascista*, 21 November 1933.

19 g. b. [Giuseppe Bottai], "Il ricatto liberale contro il corporativismo", *Critica fascista* 11, no. 12 (1933): 223–226; Federico Maria Pacces, "Verso un piano economico-corporativo", Ibid., 11, no. 13 (1933): 259–260; Pacces, "Lo spirito d'impresa nel sistema corporativo", Ibid., 11, no. 20 (1933): 392–395.

20 See Alberto Pirelli's address to the National Council of Corporations, in Ministero delle Corporazioni, *Atti dell'Assemblea generale. Sessione quinta*, 102–104, and the address that Pirelli made in Naples on 23 May 1934, in ACS, SPD, CO, fasc. 512.518.

21 "A noi la rivoluzione", *Il secolo fascista*, 2 (1933), 1–15 September, 289.

22 Parlato, *Il sindacalismo*, 104–106.

23 Aquarone, *L'organizzazione*, 197–198; *Leandro Arpinati. Un fascista anomalo* (Bologna: Il Mulino, 2013).

24 Cianetti, *Memorie*, 210; Pietro Capoferri, *L'ora del lavoro* (Milano: Mondadori, 1941), 125–126.

25 What follows is a list of all the corporations that were established. Corporations with an agricultural, industrial, and commercial production cycle: (1) cereals; (2) flowers, fruits, and vegetables; (3) wine-growing; (4) oil; (5) beets and sugar; (6) animal husbandry and fishing; (7) wood; and (8) textiles. Corporations with an industrial and commercial production cycle: (9) metallurgy and mechanics; (10) chemical industries; (11) clothing; (12) paper and printing; (13) building construction; (14) water, gas, and electricity; (15) extractive industries; and (16) glass and ceramics. Corporations for service industries: (17) welfare and credit; (18) professions and arts; (19) sea and air; (20) internal communications; (21) entertainment; and (22) hospitality.

26 The R.D. of 27 December 1934, no. 2101 had changed the committee's composition.

27 Aquarone, *L'organizzazione*, 207.

28 Giuliano Mazzoni, "La 'crisi' del diritto corporativo e la validità del corporativismo", *Il diritto del lavoro* 17, nos. 5–6 (1943): 131.

29 "I componenti delle 22 Corporazioni Fasciste", *Sindacato e corporazione* (1937), August, 349–374.

30 ACS, SPD, CO, fasc. 509.790. Confederazione fascista dei lavoratori dell'industria, *Rapporto dei dirigenti. Relazione del presidente*, 16 November 1938.

31 Paul Gentizon, *Rome sous le Faisceau* (Paris: Fasquelle Éditeurs, 1933), 224.

32 Harold E. Goad, *The Making of the Corporate State: A Study of Fascist Development* (London: Christophers, 1934), 126.

33 Gentizon, *Rome sous le Faisceau*, 222–226.

34 Significant, compared to previous years, are the number of analyses produced by French scholars. Among the most significant texts are: Émile Schreiber, *Rome après Moscou* (Paris: Plon, 1932); François Perroux, "Économie corporative et système capitaliste. Idéologie et réalité", *Revue d'économie politique* 47 (1933): 1409–1478; Louis Rosenstock Franck, *L'économie corporative fasciste en doctrine et en fait. Ses origines historiques et son évolution* (Paris: Gambier, 1934); Pierre Drieu La Rochelle, "La France découvre l'Italie", *Marianne*, 26 December 1934; Maurice Lachin, *La IVe Italie* (Paris: Gallimard, NRF, 1935); Carlo Valenziani, *Le Corporatisme fasciste, ses origines, son évolution* (Paris: Éditions de la Nouvelle revue critique, 1935); Georges Bourgin, *L'État corporatif en Italie* (Paris: Aubier, 1935); Maurice Prélot, *L'empire fasciste: les origines, les tendances et les institutions de la dictature et du corporatisme italiens* (Paris: Recueil Sirey, 1936); Frédéric Eccard, "Mussolini et les corporations", *La Revue des Deux Mondes* 43, no. 3 (1938): 522–548; Gaetan Pirou, *Essais sur le corporatisme* (Paris: Librairie du Recueil Sirey, 1938); and Louis Rosenstock Franck, *Les étapes de l'économie fasciste italienne. Du corporatisme à l'économie de guerre* (Paris: La Libraire Sociale et Economique, 1939). See Fiorenzo Mornati, "Le corporatisme italien vu par les économistes français des années trente", in *Les traditions économiques françaises: 1848–1939*, eds. Pierre Dockès, Ludovic Frobert, Gérard Klotz, Jean-Pierre Potier, and André Tiran (Paris: CNRS Éditions, 2000), 647–658.

35 In those years, increasing requests for material were addressed to Italian embassies, and more and more trips to Italy were made specifically in order to study the corporate system: on the British and French cases see, respectively, Mariuccia Salvati, *Camillo Pellizzi. Un intellettuale nell'Europa del Novecento* (Bologna: Il Mulino, 2021), 255; and Christophe Poupault, *À l'ombre des faisceaux: les voyages français dans l'Italie des chemises noires (1922–1943)* (Rome: École Française de Rome, 2014), 399–410.

36 On this whole project, see Marco Palla, *Fascismo e Stato corporativo. Un'inchiesta della diplomazia britannica* (Milano: Franco Angeli, 1991).

37 Quoted in Gian Giacomo Migone, *The United States and Fascist Italy. The Rise of American Finance in Europe* (New York: Cambridge University Press, 2015), 304.

38 Maurizio Vaudagna, "Il corporativismo nei giudizi dei diplomatici americani a Roma (1930–1935)", in *Studi storici* 16, no. 3 (1975): 764–796; Vaudagna, *Corporativismo e New Deal. Integrazione e conflitto sociale negli Stati Uniti (1933–1941)* (Torino: Rosenberg & Sellier), 1981; John P. Diggins, *Mussolini and Fascism. The View from America* (Princeton: Princeton University Press, 1972), 206–213; Kiran Klaus Patel, *The New Deal. A Global History* (Princeton-Oxford: Princeton University Press, 2016), 67–70, 92–93.

39 Marco Sedda, "Il New deal nella pubblicistica politica italiana dal 1933 al 1938", *Il Politico* 64, no. 2 (1999): 241–275.

40 On anti-Americanism in Fascist Italy, see Michela Nacci, *L'antiamericanismo in Italia negli anni Trenta* (Torino: Bollati Boringhieri, 1989).

41 Quoted in Migone, *The United States and Fascist Italy*, 304.

42 Franklin Delano Roosevelt, *Looking Forwards* (New York: John Day Co., 1933). The book was immediately translated into Italian: Roosevelt, *Guardando nel futuro* (Milano: Bompiani, 1933).

43 Benito Mussolini, "Roosevelt e il sistema" [*Popolo d'Italia*, 7 July 1933], in *Opera Omnia di Benito Mussolini*, *Opera Omnia di Benito Mussolini*, vol. 26, 24.

44 Ibid.

45 Giuseppe Bottai, "Corporate State and NRA", *Foreign Affairs*, 13 (1935), no. 4, 624.

46 Roberto Romani, "Il piano quinquennale sovietico nel dibattito corporativo italiano. 1928–1936", *Italia contemporanea*, 36, no. 155 (1984): 28.

47 Anselmo Anselmi, "La Carta del Lavoro all'estero", *Civiltà fascista* 15, no. 5 (1937): 347.

48 Erwin von Beckerath et al. *Nuove esperienze economiche*, preface by Giuseppe Bottai (Firenze: Sansoni, 1935).

49 Mario Da Silva, "Tra il capitalismo privato e lo statalismo", *Critica fascista* 12, no. 4 (1934): 73–74.
50 Luigi Adolfo Miglioranzi, "La nuova legge tedesca sui rapporti di lavoro", *Il Diritto del lavoro* 8, no. 2 (1934): 75. See also Delio Cantimori, "Note sul nazionalsocialismo", *Archivio di studi corporativi* 5, nos. 3–4 (1934): 324.
51 Marzia Casolari, *In the Shadow of the Swastika: The Relationships between Indian Radical Nationalism, Italian Fascism and Nazism* (London-New York: Routledge, 2020), 22–23, 75; Reto Hofmann, *The Fascist Effect. Japan and Italy, 1915–1952* (Ithaca-London: Cornell University Press, 2015), 86, 98, 120, 132–133; Angus Lockyer, "Expo Fascism?: Ideology, Representation, Economy", in *The Culture of Japanese Fascism*, ed. Alan Tansman (Durham-London: Duke University Press, 2009), 209; Federico Finchelstein, *Transatlantic Fascism. Ideology, Violence, and the Sacred in Argentina and Italy, 1919–1945* (Durham-London: Duke University Press, 2010), 52, 68; António Costa Pinto, *Latin American Dictatorships in the Era of Fascism. The Corporatist Wave* (London-New York: Routledge, 2020).
52 Fabio Gentile, "Il Brasile e il modello del corporativismo fascista", *Passato e presente* 31, no. 91 (2013): 38.
53 *Corporativismo: ideias e práticas*, eds. Marco Aurélio Vannucchi, Luciano Aronne De Abreu, and Paula Borges Santos (Coimbra: Imprensa da Universidade de Coimbra, 2023); Cássio A.A. Albernaz, "Les Conseils techniques comme des espaces de représentation dans la pensée autoritaire brésilienne (1930–1950)", *Le Carte e la storia* 22, no. 1 (2016): 62–75.
54 Gentile, "Il Brasile e il modello", 55.
55 For example: Benito Mussolini, *L'État corporatif* (Firenze: Vallecchi,1936); Mussolini, *Quatre discours pour l'état corporatif* (Roma: Libreria dello Stato, 1935); Confederation Fasciste des industriels, *L'état corporatif an 13 de l'ère fasciste* (Rome: Castaldi, 1935); CAUR – Comitati d'azione per l'universalità di Roma / Comités d'action pour l'universalité de Rome, *Du syndicat national à l'état corporatif. Les travailleurs et l'ordre nouveau* (Roma: Arti grafiche F. Canella, 1935); Bruno Biagi, *L'Ètat corporatif* (Paris: Nouvelles éditions latines, 1935); Biagi, *Desarrollos actuales y futuros del corporativismo* (Cadiz: Establecimientos Cerón, 1938); Giuseppe Ugo Papi, *La fonction economique de la propriete dans le regime corporatif* (Liege: Societe belge d'etudes & d'expansion, 1940).
56 Giuseppe Parlato, *Il convegno italo-francese di studi corporativi (1935) con il testo integrale degli Atti* (Roma: Fondazione Ugo Spirito, 1990).
57 Cristophe Poupault, "Le rapprochement culturel franco-italien et ses enjeux idéologiques (1933–1935)", in *Vers une Europe latine. Acteurs et enjeux des échanges culturels entre la France et l'Italie fasciste*, eds. Catherine Fraixe, Lucia Piccioni, and Cristophe Poupault (Bruxelles: Peter Lang, 2014), 115–130.
58 Gaetano Salvemi, *Under The Axe of Fascism* (New York: The Viking Press, 1936); Rosenstock Franck, *L'économie corporative fasciste*; Rosenstock Franck, *Les étapes de l'économie fasciste.*
59 See ACS, SPD, CO, fasc. 500.005/II. F. Lantini, *Appunto per S.E. il Capo del Governo*, 17 December 1937.
60 Sempre utile, per uno sguardo d'insieme, Rosenstock Franck, *Les étapes de l'économie fasciste*, 242–266.
61 ACS, *IRI*, *Serie nera*, b. 83. *Relazione riassuntiva dei piani autarchici al Comitato Corporativo Centrale*, November 1937 ("Riservatissima"); Alessio Gagliardi, *L'impossibile autarchia. La politica economica del fascismo e il Ministero scambi e valute* (Soveria Mannelli: Rubbettino, 2006), 125–148.
62 Mario Saibante, *Il fascismo e l'industria* (Milano: Mondadori, 1940), 46–47.
63 Ornella Cilona, "Alcuni temi di dibattito nel sindacato fascista dell'industria negli Anni Trenta: la regolamentazione del lavoro, la contrattazione nell'economia corporativa e

la riforma organizzativa (1930–1938)", *Incontri meridionali,* 3 s. 12 (1992), no. 1–2, 361–363.

64 ACS, *IRI, Serie nera,* b. 83. Ministero delle corporazioni, Segretariato generale del Consiglio nazionale delle corporazioni, *Relazione riassuntiva dei piani autarchici,* November 1937 ("Riservatissima"), tabella VIII. On the autarkic plans, see Rolf Petri, *Von der Autarkie zum Wirtschaftswunder. Wirtschaftspolitik und industrieller Wandel in Italien 1935–1963* (Tübingen: Niemeyer, 2001).

65 Franco Bonelli, Antonia Carparelli, Martino Pozzobon, "La riforma siderurgica Iri tra autarchia e mercato (1935–1942)", in *Acciaio per l'industrializzazione. Contributi allo studio del problema siderurgico italiano,* ed. Franco Bonelli (Torino: Einaudi, 1982), 217–333.

66 Ibid., 247–255.

67 Ibid., 293.

68 Ibid., 287.

69 Ibid., 307–311.

70 Ibid., 326–327.

71 Sabino Cassese, "Documenti sulla preparazione della legge bancaria del 1936", in Cassese, *La formazione,* 127–174; Cassese, *Come è nata la legge bancaria del 1936* (Roma: Banca nazionale del lavoro, 1988); Vittorio Santoro, "Separazione di gestioni tra credito a breve e lungo termine. Profili storici della formazione del 'principio'", in *La legge bancaria. Note e documenti sulla sua "storia segreta",* ed. Mario Porzio (Bologna: Il Mulino, 1981), 31–81; Gian Franco Calabresi, *L'Associazione bancaria italiana. Un caso di associazionismo economico,* vol. I, *1919–1943* (Roma-Bari: Laterza, 1997), 358–407.

72 See Riccardo Faucci, "Appunti sulle istituzioni economiche del tardo fascismo, 1935–1943", *Quaderni storici* 10, nos. 29–30 (1975): 610–614.

73 The complete text of the motion can be found in Calabresi, *L'Associazione bancaria italiana,* 620–621.

74 "Resoconto della riunione del 12 aprile 1935", quoted in full in *La legge bancaria,* 301–305.

75 Ibid; Cassese, *Come è nata la legge bancaria,* 106–122.

76 As far as monitoring was concerned, the initial proposal had been described in a detailed document issued the month before ("Osservazioni sulle partecipazioni industriali dell'Iri e sull'organizzazione di un controllo bancario nazionale", 18 November 1935, reproduced in full in *La legge bancaria,* 306–321). The point of view on the distinction between the different credit institutions is clearly expressed in the handwritten notes from a meeting held by the IRI's top managers on 3 December.

77 Santoro, *Separazione di gestioni,* 59.

78 A detailed reconstruction of this debate is provided by Calabresi, *L'Associazione bancaria italiana,* 390–401.

79 Ibid., 405–407.

8 Trade Unions, Workers, and Employers

The coming into operation of the corporations had profound effects on the trade union system. The 1934 law and subsequent decrees reorganised workers' and employers' organisations. The number of confederations was reduced from 13 to 9: the confederations of employers and workers in land and maritime communications were incorporated into the industrial confederations. Legal recognition was withdrawn from provincial unions and trade unions and granted only to national confederations and federations. The confederations were assigned powers of control, coordination, and representation vis-à-vis the federations, but only the latter were given the power to conclude collective agreements.[1] The result was the strengthening of representation by category over territorial representation and the further decline of confederal representation. In the Ministry of Corporations' intentions, this was to ensure a kind of "second unblocking".[2] The downsizing of the confederation was intended to avoid any overlap with the corporations. In practice, however, the change concerned workers' organisations and only formally employers' organisations, which managed to retain a considerable degree of autonomy. On the whole, however, the attempt to put the confederations out of business failed, and the second unblocking had limited effects. The autonomy acquired by the categories through the new statutes was insufficient to enable them to conduct their own negotiating strategy. The confederations, partly relieved of technical and contractual duties, would instead exercise functions within the corporations that could no longer be confined to the trade union sphere.

In parallel with the organisational reform, a complete turnover in the upper echelons of the workers' unions occurred. New men were placed at the head of the confederations, first as commissioners and then as presidents: Tullio Cianetti for industry, Riccardo Del Giudice for trade, Giuseppe Landi for credit and insurance, Franco Angelini for agriculture, Nazareno Bonfatti for internal communications, and Alessandro Pavolini for professionals and artists. The close link between the birth of the corporations and the reform of trade union organisations shows that the establishment of these new bodies was associated with a profound change in the practice of Italian trade unionism. New institutional methods of mediation between the government and the representatives of the various sectors of the economy and society took full shape within the corporations. This had two major consequences which were destined to mark trade union history for a long time,

DOI: 10.4324/9781032713267-9

even after the end of Fascism: on the one hand, the extension of that mediation to the entire sphere of social and economic policies, which is to say well beyond the specific boundaries of trade union relations; and on the other, the transcendence of private interests in the name of an alleged general interest.

The launching of the corporations coincided with a new phase for Fascist trade unionism, characterised by a renewed capacity for initiative and a greater power to influence the regime's policies. At the beginning of 1934, the period of substantial marginalisation that had begun with the 1928 unblocking had come to an end. Above all, between 1932 and mid-1933, the Confederation of Industrial Workers, under the leadership of Secretary Clavenzani, had managed to reassert its role. At the national congress of April 1933, the Confederation had demonstrated a new ability to confront *Confindustria* by moving beyond vacuous demagogy and resorting to polemical arguments based on serious documentation work.[3] Cianetti's appointment to the leadership of the Confederation in January 1934, first as commissioner and then as secretary, marked a further advance.[4] A similar development was also experienced by the other confederations, particularly the trade and credit and insurance confederations.

The establishment of corporations was part of this important step in the history of Fascist trade unionism. Some long-unresolved disputes were brought into the corporations. This was the case first and foremost with the long-standing issues of work from home and apprenticeship. The lack, if not absence, of contractual regulation left the field wide open to the industrialists' initiative; as a result, it left the weaker sectors of the workforce, mainly young people and women, without protection. Although trade unions had been tackling these problems at least from the beginning of the decade, they had not yet managed to achieve any significant results. The issues were therefore brought to the attention of the corporations they concerned most directly. The question of apprenticeships – whereby, in many cases, young people employed as apprentices did not receive any real vocational training but performed the tasks of adult workers for a lower wage – was addressed between March 1935 and the following January by the paper and printing, clothing, glass and ceramics, and hospitality corporations. Only in the case of the garment and hospitality corporations was an agreement reached which partly met trade union demands.[5] The issue of from home – mostly carried out by women to supplement the family budget, generally under worse conditions in terms of wages and regulations[6] – was dealt with by the clothing corporation, where the phenomenon was most prevalent. Even in this case, a partial agreement was reached, which left full regulation up to the collective agreement for this category.[7] The results were partial and limited, but they nevertheless marked a reversal of the trend and, above all, enabled the trade union to initiate more regular confrontations with entrepreneurs on those problems that remained open.[8]

The credit corporation also discussed and resolved issues of some relevance to trade unionists. This was especially the case with the problem of the unionisation of the different categories of bank clerks. The Banking Law of 1936 assimilated the employees of certain types of institutions – "banks of national interest" (the Banca Commerciale Italiana, Credito Italiano and Banco di Roma), public-law institutions (Banco di Napoli, Banco di Sicilia, Monte dei Paschi, S. Paolo di Torino, Banco S. Spirito di Roma, and Banca Nazionale del Lavoro), and savings banks – to state employees. The workers of those institutions were therefore deprived of the possibility of union membership. Although they performed the same tasks as the employees of other banks, they had fewer safeguards and guarantees. Already in the preparatory phase of the law, during the meetings of the welfare and credit corporation, the bankers' union, with President Landi at the forefront, took certain steps to ensure that all staff would be placed on an equal footing. What was at stake was the weight of the confederation – which would lose about half of its members if public banks were seen to fall beyond its scope – but also the preservation of the pay and welfare levels acquired by bank employees in previous years: the possible absence of union representation and the transfer of bank clerks to the much weaker AGFPI risked calling those achievements into question and creating strong inequalities between workers in the sector.[9] In April 1936, the confederation obtained the favourable opinion of the corporatist technical committee, and the following year achieved full success: over the course of 1937, a series of decrees recognised the right of all employees of banking institutions to join a single union, with the predictable exception of those working for the Bank of Italy.[10] The steps taken by Landi and the confederation were discussed within the corporative institutions but also – to varying degrees – in the other institutional venues concerned with the problem, to the point of directly involving the personalities with the greatest decision-making power (the ministers of Finance and Corporations; top PNF leaders; parliamentarians; representatives of the corporation and banking institutions; the trustee of the General Fascist Association for Public Employment, Domenico Sciarra; the president of the National Insurance Institute, Giuseppe Bevione; as well as that of the IRI, Beneduce).[11] As in the other situations mentioned above, an active presence within the corporations proved decisive as an essential part of a broader mobilisation.

In many cases, a considerable distance continued to separate trade union dialectics at the central level from concrete power relations in the workplace. The results achieved through corporate discussions, however, were indicative of the unions' partial emergence out of political and institutional marginalisation. In any case, as others have correctly observed, we should not forget that "with a few rare exceptions, the unions' successes were accomplished because the regime allowed them to be accomplished". What took place, in other words, was the "restitution to the trade union of moments of political and social influence that in previous years had been taken away from the trade union itself" for reasons of political stability but also to "balance the influence of the various Fascist organisations and sectors".[12]

The corporations' conciliation work coincided with the Central Corporate Committee's increased effectiveness, or perhaps helped to ensure it. From 1934 onwards, this body managed to produce significant results in the managing of labour relations. The first result was the motion for the regulation of piecework systems passed by the Committee in November 1934. This motion made the setting rates depend on collective negotiation and no longer on employers alone.[13] Although it was never fully implemented, the motion gave trade unions a new scope for action. In addition, it concretely laid the groundwork for the progressive abolition of the Bedaux system, a rigid piecework system that had been at the core of managing Italian industry in the 1930s and the focus of a heated trade union battle.[14] The mechanical engineering corporation abolished this system in the Fiat factories in Turin, while an agreement signed in May 1935 established its elimination at Pirelli.[15] The 1937 wage increases were another significant achievement. In April, the Central Corporate Committee decided on a general wage increase of 10–12%. This consolidated the trend of wage increases in industry which, since the middle of the decade, had begun to reverse the drastic cuts of previous years, albeit to a very partial extent. This was the combined effect of the trade unions' newly found combativeness and of workers' demands, especially in the major centres of the North.[16]

This new phase of corporatism did not only offer trade unionism an institutional forum in which to raise claims and negotiate with the other side. With the creation of the corporations, the trend that had already emerged in previous years, whereby trade unions shifted or broadened the focus of their initiatives from labour relations to a wider social dimension, was further strengthened.[17] It was also for this reason that workers' organisations took the lead of institutions such as municipal welfare bodies, children's holiday camps, and from November 1939, after a victorious tug-of-war with the PNF, the National Afterwork Club (*Opera nazionale dopolavoro*). As far as welfare and social security policies were concerned – after the reforms of old age and work accident insurance, and the establishment of the Fascist National Social Security Institute and the National Fascist Institute for Insurance against Work Accidents – trade unionism focused above all on sickness benefits. In this field, after numerous partial measures and lengthy discussions within and outside the Central Corporate Committee, the reform of December 1939 was finally implemented.[18]

The commitment to social policies was also combined with new ways of conceiving of wages. The introduction of family allowances in 1934 was seen by the leaders of these organisations not only as additional compensation for workers with large families but as a real transformation of wages: in other words, according to a widespread idea in the trade union world, wages would acquire a social and no longer economic nature, making it possible to develop a new conception of the economy that was no longer centred on the market and profit.[19] The way of tackling the issue of wages, as well as those of welfare and assistance, was aimed once again at making the "revolutionary" dimension of Fascism prevail, and therefore at fully realising the "ideal" of corporatism. Within the corporations, the trade unions underwent further transformation as well in terms of their role and function. In these new bodies, "the first organic attempt [was] made by a trade union organisation in Italy – albeit within a totalitarian regime – to participate in and in some way direct the government's main economic policy choices".[20] Naturally, trade unions did not abandon the path of negotiating labour contracts. However, it was economic policy that was the real pivot of the trade unions' strategy within the corporations. The idea that these should be the driving force behind planning policies oriented the efforts of the Fascist workers' organisations. By engaging in corporatist debate and economic policy-making, the trade union leadership aimed to contribute to the introduction of laws governing production that would guarantee a balance between production and consumption and – by no longer basing wage levels on automatic market mechanisms – full wage equity.[21]

To play this card in the best possible way, the confederations strengthened their statistical and study instruments. The Confederation of Industrial Workers set up an in-house economic service to study the conditions of the various industrial sectors, also on a local scale.[22] At the same time, the trade unions powerfully reasserted their presence within the company. Direct knowledge of production processes now became essential. As argued in an article published in *Il lavoro fascista*, the workers' confederations' newspaper, each union was supposed to "discuss with the employer" not only the rules concerning working conditions and wages "but also the organisation of the company, work methods, and everything in which the workers' interest and experience could be taken into account in order to correct, modify, and update production". It was necessary "to make the union penetrate the company, to make it an active collaborator of the enterprise, and at the same time to give it the possibility of showing its competence within the corporation".[23] Active participation in discussions on economic policy directions was seen by trade union leaders as a means to overcome the liberal market economy. As Landi wrote, it was also a matter of overcoming a privatistic conception of companies and encouraging the evolution of private and commercial law into a new "producers' law".[24] From the mid-1930s, trade unions therefore managed to become the central element of this composite reality, with very blurred boundaries that have been referred to as "left-wing Fascism".[25]

At the same time, the demand for a role for trade unions in economic policy and company decisions conveyed conflicting impulses that had never been entirely suppressed, namely the tendency to see the bourgeoisie and economic elites as obstacles to the totalitarian state's full realisation. Social demands could thus be associated with more general motivations and objectives, ranging from the correct application of government guidelines and directives to checking the congruity between economic and trade union life on the one hand, and the principles of corporatism and Fascism on the other. Particularly revealing in this sense is the support shown for the development of autarkic plans. Faced with bureaucratic delays and tardiness, it was precisely trade union leaders who pressed Mussolini for the rapid implementation of these plans. In October 1937, in the midst of the drafting phase of the plans and in view of an important meeting of the Central Corporative Committee, the president of the Confederation of Industrial Workers, Cianetti, wrote to the head of government arguing that only the complete enactment of the plans would make it possible to control industrial development and, at the same time, to supervise prices and the territorial redistribution of employment through the selection of plant locations. Above all, Cianetti warned Mussolini about the risk that the autarkic policy could turn into an opportunity for further enrichment for entrepreneurs. In order to avoid this, it was first of all necessary to proceed with a new increase in wages – "both in accordance with the improved economic trend in industry and, more specifically, for those categories that had suffered particular cuts in their earnings during the crisis period". Furthermore, faced with the foreseeable increase in demand for specialised labour following the autarkic policies, a body for the professional training of workers would have to be set up.[26] A year later, Cianetti presented a master plan for the distribution of raw materials, factories, and labour among the most important industrial sectors for warfare and the autarkic policy.[27] He also called for the strict control of corporations over companies.[28] In practical terms, however, the results were once again rather limited. Little consideration was shown by *Confindustria* towards the trade unions and their ambitions to "regulate production" (the public speeches of *Confindustria*'s president, Giuseppe Volpi, are revealing in this respect),[29] and Mussolini only agreed to Cianetti's demands with some delay and to a partial extent.[30]

Likewise, the corporatist emphasis on price control reflects this double motivation: on the one hand, it was linked to the defence of workers' real purchasing power; on the other, it *de facto* supported the Ministry of Corporations' anti-inflationary policies, but also the grievances made by substantial sectors of the business world regarding the excessive increase in the price of certain products.[31] In short, within the corporations, the recovery of a capacity for initiative as far as demands was concerned went hand-in-hand with the pursuit of an alleged "general interest". On several occasions, the latter clearly prevailed over the former in the trade unions' rhetoric. The corporations were supposed to impose "a permanent discipline that makes use of individual initiative, while also protecting it from the selfishness of competitors, in the collective interest of the country, including consumers", as Razza had written earlier.[32] Acting as champions of collective interests, trade unionists played the role of guarantors of the proper functioning of the measures introduced by the government and the economic institutions it had created, even in the absence of specific watchwords concerning workers' conditions. As has been written, "that was to be the moment of the full subordination of particular interests to the higher interests of the State, and the counterparts in industrial relations were to be directed towards it".[33] In opposition to *Confindustria*, the industrial trade unions rallied behind the banner of efficiency and the fight against monopolies in the name of a more balanced production system not conditioned by speculative manoeuvres, as in the case of the prolonged dispute over measures to limit competition, to which we will return later.

The credit employees' organisation led by Landi followed this line even more systematically. The confederal documents prepared for the corporation's meetings, the discussions held there, and the steps taken outside it offer repeated proof of this. The Confederation of Bank and Insurance Employees become involved, among other things, with issues such as the establishment of the Institute for the Exercise of Real Estate Credit (*Istituto per l'esercizio del credito immobiliare*) in Italian East Africa, technical aspects related to banking operations, and the collection of deposits by industrial and commercial finance companies not subject to the supervision of the Inspectorate for the Defence of Savings and the Exercise of Credit (*Ispettorato per la difesa del risparmio e per l'esercizio del credito*).[34] Each time they merely justified their intervention by resorting to generic "anti-plutocratic" statements, or ones in support of the Fascist Empire.[35] As Landi observed when preparing for a meeting of the corporation, "the Confederation of Companies has business claims to make, we have no claims to make. We can say: our opinion is this".[36]

The workers and employees' confederations, in other words, progressively invaded a space that was not their own by playing the role of "guardians of the revolution" in the economic sphere. Never before were they so close to accomplishing Sergio Panunzio's idea of a trade union inspiring revolutionary perspectives. Panunzio himself provided a particularly lucid perspective on these processes. In an article of September 1937, he wrote:

> It is not difficult to discern the almost predominantly political aspect in the current phase of the trade union. But if this generally refers to the trade union, it refers more particularly and directly to the workers' trade union. While [...] the employers' union exercises an action that is two-thirds economic and one-third political, the workers' union exercises an action that is two-thirds political and one-third economic [...] It is a matter of keeping the Fascist political spirit alive in the masses.[37]

The trade union's political activity – to use Panunzio's words – was not limited to economic policies, however. With the war in Ethiopia – and the wartime mobilisation of workers' organisations in favour of the "empire of labour" – the link between trade union activity and the regime's general policy was strengthened as never before. Evidence of this is also provided by the increasingly intense entrance of trade unionists into the PNF's ranks in the mature phase of Fascism.[38]

The changes in union activity triggered strong tensions within the confederal bodies, as even the most attentive observers in the anti-Fascist ranks noted.[39] The distance was widening between the confederal leadership, middle management, and peripheral organisers: while the first of these was focusing more and more on social and economic policy issues, the latter two had to deal with the working class's increasingly unsatisfactory living conditions and the consequent impossibility of making the "transmission belt" of consensus work. The picture was further complicated by the difficult implementation of major agreements made with the opposing side, such as the Pirelli-Cianetti agreement of 1934 on the reduction of working hours in industry. On the one hand, such agreements allowed the confederal leadership to regard certain disputes as settled; on the other, peripheral and divisional union cadres struggled to ensure the full implementation of the agreements in every factory.[40] The corporations risked being perceived by lower-level trade unionists as yet another factor restricting trade unionism proper.[41] The ineffective liaising between confederal hierarchies and provincial unions also compromised, at least initially, price control, to which the former attached strategic importance as a way of defending workers' purchasing power.[42] Even the trade union leaders, who also took part in corporate activity, did not always go along with the new course. At the congress of industrial union leaders held in November 1938, Cianetti openly urged union leaders to adopt a more proactive attitude within the corporative bodies: "the workers' organisations", he argued, "in the corporations, must not be followers, but must constitute the vanguard patrol, which it is preferable to keep in check, rather than inciting it by urging it to march on".[43]

The changes in trade unionism's nature had very little effect on the country's economic history. The workers' organisations never succeeded in seriously challenging the regime's internal balances, limiting the overwhelming power of the business front, wresting additional responsibilities from the PNF, and gaining less rhapsodic and superficial support from the government and Mussolini. Those changes, however, left significant traces in trade union history. The opening up to new social and economic issues, the adoption of the goal of strengthening the production system, and the different ways of relating to the state produced powerful changes in the nature and ways of being of the confederations that would live on after the end of the dictatorship and state trade unionism.[44]

Those changes were also part of a trend common to other industrialised countries. As we saw in Chapter 1, the insertion of trade unions into a triangular system of mediation with political authorities and business counterparts – and thus the transformation of trade unionism into an institution, to some degree – was a process that began during the First World War. With the economic crisis of the 1930s, the relationship between the state and trade unions became stronger almost everywhere.[45] The process of the "politicisation" of workers' organisations affected Fascist and pro-Fascist regimes, where it resulted in the subordination of workers' organisations to the political authorities. In such countries, workers' organisations were granted smaller margins of action than in Italy: in Germany, as we have seen (Chapter 5), this was the result of the application of the *Führerprinzip* even to labour policies, and of the consequent suppression of trade unions; in Portugal, Spain, and Romania, owing to the lower level of economic development and the fragility of the pre-existing trade union associations, the dictatorships had a more monocratic character and a weaker social dimension. Even in the USSR, consistent with the Leninist conception of the primacy of the party over the trade union, the latter was entirely subordinated to politics and confined to a role of administrative co-management in the context of planning.

In the democratic states of continental Europe, the need to cope with the decline in production, income levels, and employment rates favoured the coming together of governments (of different orientations) and trade union leaders. The economic depression reinforced the Left's statist inclinations, which had already taken root in many of its groups after 1914 or 1917. The problem of unemployment led to the call for state support measures, while the Soviet Union's appeal and the idea of a state-run planned economy also increased. Since the second half of the 1920s, Stalin's policies – and the Stalinisation of the Comintern parties – had led many communists to identify communism and revolution with state power. Among the reformists' ranks, with few exceptions, it was instead the collapse of the economy that triggered the crisis of cultures based on the self-management and autonomy of the various sectors of society. Many socialist leaders explored anti-cyclical theories and the most experimental forms of public intervention, envisaging new roles and functions for trade union organisations.

It was precisely within the framework of the encounter between the practice of negotiation between the interest organisations and the new "interventionist" economic policies that workers' organisations began to think of themselves not only in relation to the representation of interests and the stipulation of contracts but also as part of a policy of intervention and planning. Within the labour movement, it was precisely the trade unions that, in defiance of the socialist parties, conceived the possibility of "planning under capitalism", i.e. of at least partly freeing the running of the economy from market logic, without first initiating a revolutionary overthrow.[46] In France in 1934, the most important trade union confederation, the *Confédération générale du travail* (CGT), presented a labour plan – not supported by the left-wing parties – proposing both measures to launch a recovery and boost employment as well as "structural reforms" to introduce a dirigiste model of governance. Negotiation practices were then developed, albeit not without contrasts, during the Popular Front government.[47] But it was the Scandinavian countries, led by Sweden, that went furthest in developing an innovative model of economic-social management, starting with the so-called "crisis agreements" of 1933–1935. Without renouncing anti-capitalism, the trade union confederations did not regard the crisis of the 1930s as the final crisis of capitalism. To support the working classes' conditions and recover more favourable power relations, they became convinced of the need to actively intervene in the management of capitalism and to manage it differently. Hence the decision to prioritise economic growth to the detriment of immediate demands: the aim was to combat unemployment and help steer the development of the national production system, and then, in the long run, to ensure income distribution, with more favourable working conditions and a welfare system for workers and farmers.[48]

Great Britain represented an exception within this picture since British trade union organisations became increasingly detached from politics, limiting their scope of action to economic negotiation. As Donald Sassoon has observed, "continental unions were never as strong as the British ones and never relied so consistently on their strength as wage bargainers. They were also more political, in the sense that they believed they would be able to get through political means what they were unable to achieve through economic strikes".[49]

Changes in the function of Italian trade unionism must therefore be viewed within this broader framework. Stating that it managed to carve out a role for itself within the corporative state, however, does not mean supporting the thesis of its autonomy from the regime's political leadership. As a sort of "concession" from above, Italian trade unions were able to create a kind of dialectic of demands concerning social, labour, and industrial policies, but on the political terrain, they had to go along with Mussolini's directives even when they did not entirely agree with them. The most relevant example is provided by relations with Germany. The Fascist trade union milieu expressed a "deep-rooted distrust" of the Nazi world.[50] The trade union press waged an explicit polemic against the German labour law of 1934, starting with Rossoni's magazine, *La Stirpe*.[51] Trade unionists' frequent visits to Germany in the second half of the decade often engendered an attitude of suspicion and detachment. On their return, it was not uncommon for them to offer a rather negative assessment of the German social and trade union system in restricted meetings or in confidential discussions.[52] Nevertheless, Germany was by now Italy's great ally, and the regime's leadership made the clear and unquestionable suggestion that an alliance should also be formed at the trade union level: this is demonstrated by the countless meetings between representatives of Fascist trade unionism and DAF officials. Numerous visits by Italians to Germany and vice versa were organised, always with an official seal of approval; regularly celebrated in the press, these visits were attended not only by the confederations' top leaders, but also by middle management and simple card-carrying members. In Bad Schachen, on Lake Constance, in June 1937, Cianetti signed an agreement with Ley to organise a mass "holiday exchange", along with exchanging information and study trips for officials.[53]

As the years went by, this polemic gradually mellowed out and mistrust gave way to displays of enthusiasm and participation. It should also be noted that in 1937 Italy quit the International Labour Organization and the League of Nations, following the sanctions imposed by the League of Nations in response to the invasion of Ethiopia. The Fascist trade unions, as we have seen, had been subjected to constant challenges over the years by trade union representatives from democratic countries. Participation in the ILO, though, had also offered them the chance to be part of a transnational debate on social and labour policies, and to have contacts, however complex and conflictual, with international trade unionism. Leaving the organisation deprived Italian trade unionists of this possibility and consigned them entirely to the circuit of "Fascist-National Socialist internationalism":[54] the network of exchanges and relations that, in the last years of the decade, linked various social structures of European authoritarian regimes (most notably the Italian and German ones) and involved not only confederations but also afterwork organisations such as the Italian *Opera nazionale dopolavoro* or the German *Kraft durch Freude* (Strength through Joy).[55]

The employers' organisations instead largely managed to avoid these political constraints. On the one hand, *Confindustria* and other associations were actively involved in the celebration of the Italian-German alliance and participated in its related rituals. *Confindustria* leaders received their German counterparts on numerous occasions and repeatedly visited Germany. The newspapers of the business association also placed a great deal of emphasis on reporting these meetings. On the other hand, the large business groups managed to retain a certain freedom to operate on the international level. Throughout the 1930s, they succeeded in resisting efforts to impose a realignment of relations to the advantage of German companies, and in maintaining significant relations with French and British companies. At the forefront of this policy was the president of *Confindustria*, Volpi. As late as 1940–1941, tensions with Berlin were felt, as the German authorities believed they had an exclusive relationship with Italian business.[56]

The transformations that affected the employers' organisations appear more limited overall. However, the establishment of corporations marked a turning point for these organisations as well. As with the workers' unions, the organisational reform of 1934 brought about a transition from a system of representation based on territorial units to a new system centred on categories. At the same time, the confederations were first entrusted to provisional commissioners and then, in October, to new presidents. Particularly high-profile appointments were made for the

Confederation of Industry: first Alberto Pirelli was appointed as its provisional commissioner in January 1934; then, in October, its presidency was assigned to Volpi, a leading figure of Italian capitalism and one of the closest to Fascism.[57] It was precisely the confederation of industrialists, the largest and most influential of the business organisations, that benefited the most from these changes. It acquired greater political and economic weight at the expense of the other structures. Thanks to these new mergers, *Confindustria* now came to include – in addition to the industrial categories – the confederations representing craftsmen, managers of industrial companies, municipalised industrial companies, municipalised transport companies, and building owners.[58]

On the whole, the reform, complemented by the new legally approved statutes, produced a significant change in business associations. The organisational changes loosened the relationship between ordinary members and management structures. This is witnessed by the numerical difference between the overall number of companies represented by *Confindustria* and those actually enrolled: in 1936, the number of industrialists who were represented (i.e. who paid the mandatory fee) was 157,334, while there were only 82,380 associates (who, in addition to paying the fee, had enrolled voluntarily).[59]

This change was not limited to organisational structures, however. What had even greater effects was the further strengthening of the relationship between *Confindustria* and the state, which was also linked to the extension of public intervention and the measures adopted by the government to tackle the economic crisis. Within the framework of the new "autarkic-war" policies, public institutions increasingly became a privileged interlocutor for large industrial and financial groups. Bailouts, government contracts, import restrictions, the restriction of competition, and investments for the implementation of autarkic plans offered decisive support to companies, especially major ones. At the same time, the expansionist and imperialist objectives increasingly laid out in the regime's rhetoric stressed the importance of economic might: only an industrial power could aspire to play the role of a political power in the international arena.

Similar processes of increasing integration between the entrepreneurial elite – through their representative organisations – and the state are found, to varying degrees, in other Fascist and authoritarian regimes. In all of them, business organisations were able to play a role in regimentation policies without losing their ability to protect and defend the interests of the social sectors they represented. Industrial companies thus managed to retain considerable leeway in determining the forms and methods of collaboration with the regime.[60] The "dirigiste" economic policies of the 1930s profoundly altered the mechanisms of competition but did not call into question either the ownership structure or the private entrepreneurs' freedom of initiative. On the contrary, at a rather limited cost, dictatorships offered numerous advantages: not only the limiting of social conflict and the regulation of wages but also more public contracts, defence against foreign competition, and more generally mechanisms to protect against market uncertainties. Particularly revealing is what happened in Germany, where the state gained increased prominence within a more economically and technologically developed industrial structure.[61] Here, businesses and public policies were closely intertwined and business organisations played a significant role. Recent research has highlighted that the sector associations that accepted the logic of Nazi dirigisme (such as the *Verein Deutscher Maschinenbau-Anstalten*, the German Machine Builders' Association) managed to obtain numerous advantages and secure a wide margin of freedom for themselves and the companies they represented; on the contrary, those associations that tried to resist the public authorities' intrusiveness suffered negative repercussions (this was the case with the *Verein deutscher Eisen- und Stahlindustrieller*, the Association of German Iron and Steel Industries).[62]

In the shadow of protectionism and public intervention, the weight of large economic groups also increased. Much more than smaller companies, these managed to direct the decisions of political authorities and the work of public administrations to their own advantage and to steer the representative organisations. In Italy, in spite of Mussolini's rhetoric against "super-capitalism", the leadership of Italian capitalism strengthened its position. What emerged was a sort of "feudalism" or "oligarchy", in words used by one of the economic world's leading figures of those years, Ettore Conti, who in September 1939 noted in his diary:

> During this period in which the intention of getting closer to the people is affirmed on a daily basis, a financial oligarchy has taken shape that is reminiscent, in the industrial field, of ancient feudalism. Production is for the most part controlled by a few groups, with one man presiding over each. Agnelli, Cini, Volpi, Pirelli, Donegani, Falck, and very few others completely dominate the various branches of industry.[63]

As a consequence, the power of this oligarchy over the confederation and industrial federations was also strengthened, to the detriment of small and medium-sized enterprises. Among other things, this explains why small- and medium-sized enterprises often preferred direct relations with the public administration rather than the mediation of the trade organisations. If only to at least partly safeguard the existing stability and balance, the state implemented a distribution of resources (contracts, funding, imported raw materials) that tended to be fairer than that generally carried out through trade organisations.[64]

It was, above all, under Volpi's presidency that a "new" *Confindustria* emerged. His presidency openly advocated the aim of establishing more organic relations between the business world and the political authorities.[65] More systematically and consciously than in the past, the *Confindustria* leadership started pursuing different and apparently conflicting objectives: to guide the fascistisation of the entrepreneurial world, making the confederation's structures a further transmission belt for "consensus"; to defend the employers' associations decision-making autonomy against government interference; to oppose any "socialist" and "revolutionary" turn of the regime; to uphold private initiative and the full powers of company managements, which were being threatened by the more enterprising spirit of trade unions and by public intervention; and to contribute to the achievement of autary, not least in order to reap the greatest material advantages from it. Volpi safeguarded the decision-making autonomy that *Confindustria* had enjoyed in previous years. At the same time, he emphasised the organisation's formal functions by more actively involving it in the celebration of the regime's successes, especially imperial ones, and in the regime's rituals.[66] Unlike in the case of the workers' organisations, however, the economic function of representing and defending interests remained *Confindustria*'s prevalent function, as Panunzio had already noted.

On the one hand, these oligarchic dynamics therefore strengthened the political force of the major economic actors and their ability to influence government choices, even through informal contacts; on the other, relations between economic actors and political power became institutionalised. These relations increasingly passed through an organisation – *Confindustria* – that had lost its character as a private association and through special institutional bodies: the corporations. Consequently, the position of the business world towards the corporative system also changed. At the beginning of the 1930s, business associations' attitude towards the corporative apparatuses and the growing prominence of public institutions had been marked by general mistrust, as shown by the debates on – and within – the National Council of Corporations (see Chapter 6). By contrast, in the middle of the decade, after having overcome the liberalist outlook of previous years in reaction to the crisis and having verified the existence of favourable power relations, Volpi and the *Confindustria* leadership combined their long-standing mistrust of the corporations with greater willingness to use them to exert pressure on the government. They attempted to use the corporations to justify the existing situation, to get measures approved in their favour, and to promote cooperation between the various sectors of production.[67] The industrial and financial world, through its own organisations and newspapers, invoked precisely the principles of corporatism to legitimise economic institutions and choices that were not substantially different from those found in other countries.[68] This change, together with the predominance in the corporations of discussions on economic policies over discussions on social and trade union policies, accentuated the representation of "businessmen" at the expense of that of "employers".[69]

At the corporations' meetings, entrepreneurial representatives therefore adopted a pragmatic attitude: they opposed by all means the extreme steps that the most radical trade unionists and corporatists sought to take, but at the same time, they repeatedly urged the competent authorities to delegate the application of divisional legislation and the execution of procedures to the corporations themselves. Significant, if mostly indirect, traces of this are to be found in the trade press and documentation. A note addressed to the head of government by the Minister of Public Works in February 1936 is enlightening in this respect. Minister Cobolli Gigli observed (or rather, denounced the fact) that at some meetings of the corporations, the participants had not only gone out of their way to protect the categories represented – with little corporatist spirit – but had also used the institutional space to request "changes in fundamental laws" to the benefit of specific interests. In particular, the business organisations demanded that functions attributed to the executive bodies of the ministries be devolved to the corporations, possibly through corporative committees. Cobolli Gigli mentioned the cases of the compiling or revising of the contractors' register – with obvious implications for the regulation of public-private relations in the public works sector – and of public water concessions or concessions involving various hydro- or thermo-electric plants, a crucial and particularly delicate matter at a time of growing investments in the electricity industry.[70] In the latter case, rather than representing an attempt to circumvent the constraints of the legislation in that sector – particularly the December 1933 consolidating act, which was marked by "liberal continuity" – the call for a more prominent role for the corporations had a preventive character, so to speak: the corporative solution appeared to be the best alternative to a feared statist turn. In this case, however, the administration succeeded in containing the pressure from business organisations, and the change was not accomplished.[71]

This episode shows, once again, that even when the corporative bodies failed to acquire certain competencies and powers, they were still one of the main "fields of tension" in which the turbulent dialectic between the public and private sectors manifested itself in the 1930s. While informal and direct contacts with public administration officials and politicians, right up to Mussolini himself, continued to constitute the primary means of the narrow elite of big industrialists and bankers to exercise individual influence on politics and the administration, the corporations appeared to be the avenue for establishing collective "relations of influence" on behalf of an entire category.[72] In light of this, we can probably appreciate what Vittorio Cini meant when he called corporatism "the last trench of capitalism".[73]

The changes in the orientations and functions of trade unions and employers' organisations mentioned above become particularly clear when we take a close look at industrial policies and the regulating of competition. At the beginning of the 1930s, with the economic crisis underway, the government approved a series of measures to defend industrial interests. Cartels, consortia, and agreements between companies were promoted and encouraged, entry barriers were introduced, and a strictly protectionist customs system was adopted, including the use of import licences. The new legislation aimed to control production and capacity levels to cope with falling demand. In essence, companies already in the market, including less efficient ones, were protected against the entry of any new producers. The real "denial of competition" implemented by the government therefore consolidated the internal balances of Italian capitalism to the detriment of greater overall efficiency while making consumers pay the price.[74]

Although many of these measures, especially those relating to consortia and customs protectionism, were common to most of the more capitalistically advanced nations, what characterised the Italian situation was the particular intertwining of economic and political power. The denial of competition was largely favoured by state laws that were called for and not infrequently enforced by the producers themselves. Although the measures to regulate competition did not foresee the corporations' direct intervention, their implementation constituted one of the most significant tests of corporatism's real functioning, of the role assumed by the representations of socio-economic interests, and more generally of Fascist intervention in the economy. Corporatist principles shaped the implementation of the legislation on consortia, industrial plants, and import licences, even in cases where the corporations' intervention was excluded. Each of these measures provided for the state administration and public bodies to be supported or replaced by trade associations.

The real meaning of this corporatism – i.e. the goals to be pursued and the role played by each subject – was at the centre of a heated and prolonged dispute. On the one hand, *Confindustria* and the most powerful companies saw the new measures purely as an anti-crisis instrument, capable of sheltering industrial groups from the risks of excessive and unregulated competition – without, however, restricting their freedom of initiative. According to this view, genuine corporatism meant assigning the implementation of certain measures directly to the actors involved, i.e. the business organisations. In order to avoid bureaucratic encumbrances and dirigiste temptations, state apparatuses and workers' unions were to be left out. On the other hand, the trade unionists and those Fascists most committed to corporatism saw the new industrial policy and regulating of competition as a means of strengthening the state's role and to launch a form of economic planning under the corporations' control.

What lay at the heart of the dispute was therefore precisely the intervention of the corporations and, more generally, how to translate corporatism's abstract principles into reality. Disputes and tensions long marked the implementation of the main industrial policy measures launched by the Fascist government in the 1930s. It is worth dwelling on two of the most innovative and relevant ones: the system of authorisations for industrial plants and consortia. With regard to the former, the law of January 1933 assigned the state the power to authorise the creation of new industrial plants and the expansion of existing ones. The stated objectives were common to those pursued by other industrialised nations: to avoid waste and speculation; to reduce the imbalance between production capacity and market absorption capacity; to direct investments towards plants capable of facing foreign competition; and to prevent excessive falls in price levels.[75] The new legislation appeared particularly rigid and seemed to reflect the political authorities' desire to assume more extensive powers by constraining the industrialists' actions. Through it, the state administration could select which investments deserved to be supported and which had to be nipped in the bud. The law, however, was interpreted differently. While the examination of applications for permits was entrusted to a special commission at the Ministry of Corporations, the dossier was not processed by the ministerial offices but – in a generic show of deference to the principles of corporatism – first of all by *Confindustria* and the relevant sector federation. It was therefore the trade associations legally representing those who had submitted applications that would collect the required documentation and carry out an initial assessment. The industrialists' representatives found themselves in the double role of referee and player because they were called upon to express their opinion on the applications made by potential competitors. In this way, some confusion was created between the objectives set by the government and the entrepreneurs' particularistic aims, to the detriment of the former. Indeed, the representatives of the industrial trade associations could assess the applications not according to any general interest, deriving from the objectives set by the government, but in order to resolve the economic confrontation between competing producers by denying authorisations to those companies that threatened the internal balance within each sector. The commission set up at the Ministry of Corporations, in which the workers' organisations also participated, therefore played a marginal role because the opinions of the business associations largely determined the outcome of the applications.

These developments fuelled widespread dissatisfaction. Several articles in the political and trade union press were especially critical of the corporations' lack of involvement.[76] According to Bottai, the law on industrial plants represented one of the "instances of State intervention in economic life conducted with a non-corporatist method" because it "disregarded trade union and corporate bodies" and followed "bureaucratic procedure".[77] This solution was opposed above all by trade unionists, who were the keenest to combine the affirmation of the corporations' role with the battle for productivity. In their opinion, the fact of stripping the corporations of their functions – insofar as they ought to have prevented the development of monopoly conditions – reinforced the dominance of large groups by freeing them from the risks of effective competition and the possible arrival of new competitors. The limitation of viable economic initiatives also had negative repercussions on employment levels and the cost of living. Predictably, opposing arguments were instead advanced by industrialists and the government, starting with the Undersecretary for Corporations, Asquini.[78]

The system was reformed at the beginning of 1937. The commission was dissolved and the corporations were invested with its functions. The steps taken by *Confindustria* would be discussed in the corporations by the representatives of all the organisations present, and the verdict reached would be final. The role of *Confindustria* continued to be decisive, owing to the authority of its men and its "first-hand" knowledge of the situation in individual industrial sectors, knowledge from which the trade unionists continued to be excluded. The tension between the trade unions and *Confindustria* therefore did not abate. On the contrary, towards the end of 1937, an article in *Gerarchia* by Pietro Capoferri – at that time the leading name in Milanese industrial trade unionism – reignited the controversy, reviving all the accusations directed against the industrialists up to that point. The trade union leader based his denunciation on a traditional and orthodox conception of the market. In his opinion, it was necessary to prevent the law from serving as a "protective shield against the dangers of competition", to avert consumer prices from displaying "an artificiality deriving from the situation of privilege in which a branch of production" found itself, and to ensure that companies would be able to take advantage of the technological progress achieved in the most advanced countries.[79]

The industrialists, in their turn, continued to make a case for the corporatist "third way", which guaranteed the regulation of economic competition and the meeting of supply and demand through institutional procedures, and no longer exclusively through the market. In a lengthy document drafted in 1938 precisely as a response to Capoferri, the industrialists' representatives branded as "absurd the idea of framing the economic facts of the Fascist era within the laws of liberal economics". Indeed, it was necessary to abandon the "obsolete traditional schemes" that ended up "promoting the return of disavowed utilitarian postulates that are in perfect contrast to the ethical and political principles of Fascist doctrine".[80] What were also far removed from liberalism were the arguments used to defend the law on industrial plants. They reiterated the industrialists' "unchanged conviction of the need – which is a duty to the Nation – to prevent the excesses of destructive competition". The trade unions' comments regarding the negative effects in relation to employment and price levels were disputed: there was no reasonable hope of increasing blue-collar employment because production capacity by then had reached the markets' absorption capacity; it was therefore necessary to limit production in accordance with the possibilities in terms of consumption. As far as prices were concerned, it was pointed out that in the circumstances at hand not even the splitting of production among many competitors would bring any benefits.

The whole document nevertheless perfectly exemplifies the industrialists' organisation's point of view. For example, it recalled, with evident approval, that the law had been "conceived also to ensure the support of the healthy forces of production against the competition of marginal companies in an effort to defend not only private interests, but also national assets". Along similar lines, it stated: "it is evident that the concern to ensure the suitable flexibility for the industrial economy cannot cause us to lose sight of the need to avoid – for the sake of the country's economic efficiency – the waste of energy and resources that can result from the disordered activity of individuals: initiative and daring on the one hand, discipline and coordination on the other". The document is therefore a collection of statements far removed from liberal orthodoxy. It was also a far cry from the positions advocated by *Confindustria* in previous years. Indeed, in April 1930, its then president, Benni, had spoken out about the early idea of government control over the new industrial plants, arguing against it: in his view, this idea was an expression of the "deformation of the industrial spirit" and of a mentality aimed at "transforming categories into closed castes" in order to ensure "conditions of privilege and monopoly".[81]

The conflict between industrialists and the trade unions was waged not only on a directly political level – i.e. around the opposing meanings the two contenders assigned to corporate procedures – but also within the corporations. The trade unionists supported the demands of small and medium-sized companies in order to avoid the acquisition of monopoly positions by major groups. They also tried to uphold any demands that would entail employment growth and safeguard the productive balance in the areas affected by the investments. In order to wage their battle more effectively, the trade unionists also tried to have a say in the first phase of the procedure by launching parallel investigations. They attempted, in other words, to break the monopoly of information held by the industrialists by requesting data and information directly from the companies concerned. *Confindustria* denounced this "interference" on several occasions, trying to prevent the companies from cooperating, and eventually succeeded in obtaining the support of the Ministry of Corporations.[82]

The trade unions' participation in the debate within the corporations and regarding industrial policies therefore conflicted with the limited institutional means and information at their disposal. In practice, even after the partial reform, the system of plant authorisations ended up constituting – as also revealed by the post-war checks carried out by the Ministry's Economic Commission for the Constituent Assembly – an instrument for the crystallisation of market positions and, at the same time, a further advantage for larger companies, which were able to steer the business organisations.[83]

A similar disturbing and interfering action was carried out by the trade unions in relation to the consortia. At the end of 1931, with a December decree later converted into law in June 1932, the government had introduced compulsory consortia. The phenomenon of business aggregations – cartels, according to the definition used internationally – was by no means new. The 1931–1932 legislation, however, was intended to facilitate its extension and, above all, to subject it to state authorisation. The law introduced the obligation to set up a consortium when a number of entrepreneurs amounting to at least 70% of the total sector, or representing at least 85% of the production capacity, requested it. The same law provided that the government could delegate the definition of new agreements for the establishment of mandatory consortia to *Confindustria*, excluding the corporate bodies.[84] The corporatist aspect of the consortia legislation was naturally a matter of dispute. The Central Corporative Committee had finalised an initial version of the law in February 1932, tasking the divisions of the National Council of Corporations with supervising the consortia's activities.[85] During the final drafting of the legislation, though, the choice was reversed. The new version of the text, which was then finally approved, left the preparation of agreements, the striking of a balance between all interests involved, and the drafting of consortium statutes not to the corporate bodies but directly to business organisations. As with the system of authorisations for industrial plants, the law on compulsory consortia also risked constituting an element in favour of the dominant forces in each production sector and a further factor limiting competition. Leading groups could impose the establishment of a consortium on smaller companies, and consequently set the conditions for production and sales.[86]

In this case, too, both the disenfranchisement of the corporate bodies and the possible unfavourable consequences in terms of employment and prices provoked negative reactions. Bottai, who was still Minister of Corporations at the time, had openly denounced the "non-corporatist" and "emergency" nature of the measures. In his address to the Chamber of Deputies for the presentation of the measure, as well as on several other occasions, he maintained that he accepted the establishment of consortia only as a contingent and exceptional measure, affirming his rejection of the "monopolistic tendency disguised by the consortium mentality" and the need for control by the corporate bodies.[87]

Interest in direct intervention in the consortia was a significant part of the union's commitment to the corporations. Their demand for control, which would have made the cartels an instrument of industrial planning, was the focus of two congresses held in the autumn of 1933 – for the marble and cotton sectors, respectively – and of the congress of trade union leaders in March 1934, events that were all organised by the Confederation of Industrial Workers.[88] The objective of corporate control went hand-in-hand with that of combating monopolies and the manoeuvres of large groups. At the 1936 congress, the leaders of the industrial trade unions attacked the "unjustified speculation" that was taking place in some consortia and the "unjustified price gouging" made possible by the cartels to consumers' detriment.[89] Among the various indictments against the consortia's monopolistic practices and the resulting serious damage to consumers, one of the most detailed and well-documented arguments was put forward by the secretary of the National Federation of Construction Workers (*Federazione nazionale dei lavoratori delle costruzioni*), Luigi Begnotti. Begnotti strongly contended that the consortia's commercial policy led to the formation of monopolies, genuine "arbiters of the market", in clear antithesis to the "corporative economic system, where the harmony of conflicting interests must be achieved only for the purposes of the higher national interest". This lack of competition, in his view, both made it impossible to ensure the lowest prices achievable with the technical improvements introduced in the companies and prevented the elimination of the highest-cost factories: "With the Consortia policy", he wrote, "prices have become detached from production costs and thus follow their own trajectory, which is determined by the maximum profit of those who steer them – and this is still an expression of the capitalist economy".[90] Begnotti also noted that in many cases, the consortia's membership was not spontaneous: larger companies would often force smaller ones to join a consortium by charging particularly low prices in their business field. Once they joined, the smaller companies would then be deprived of any decision-making power: since they were allocated small production quotas, they could not have their own representative on the consortium's board of directors.[91]

A different view was taken by *Confindustria*, according to which consortia, whether compulsory or voluntary, constituted "the best means of curbing competition that, in many cases, taken beyond its natural limits, had manifested itself as an element of disintegration and dispersion of productive forces", especially in periods of crisis.[92] *Confindustria* therefore stood up in defence of Italian industrial legislation, which had "the regulating of production as its cornerstone", to "avoid competition when, owing to particular situations or an otherwise irreparable imbalance between resources and consumption, it manifests itself in excessive forms and turns into a real fight, which no longer amounts to noble competition or a stimulus to technical and economic improvement, but rather to the destruction of wealth and disorder on the market".[93] For the industrialists, the reference to corporatism constituted a powerful argument in favour of the measure. To those who objected that the consortia's management remained in the hands of the industrialists, the latter replied "that this remark constitutes the most evident demonstration of the fact that this is not just any measure, but the advent of the Corporative State, which realises itself in the principle of the self-regulating of the categories, as required by Declaration VII of the Labour Charter".[94]

The dispute, however, was not limited to petitions of principle. The trade unions accompanied their complaints with some specific proposals centred on asserting the need for the corporations to exercise control. In particular, it repeatedly demanded that all corporations should have their own representatives.[95] In the months of the Ethiopian War, the trade unions went so far as to demand the abolition of the consortia and their replacement by corporate technical committees.[96] As was also the case with the law on the licensing of industrial plants, pressure from the trade unions led to a symbolic result in early 1937. The law on voluntary consortia was passed in March according to which all cartels, not only compulsory ones, would have to submit balance sheets, data on prices, and the quantities of goods sold to the corporative secretariats' offices. On paper, the corporations would therefore have had sufficient data and powers to exercise effective control over the consortia, preparatory to actual policy-making. In reality, this was not the case. In several instances, sometimes even against the instructions of *Confindustria*'s leadership, the cartels did not transmit the necessary information in a timely and complete fashion.[97] The corporations also had to face the limits and vagueness of the powers at their disposal: they could not intervene in the constitution of consortia or decide on their dissolution.[98] Even further from being implemented was the provision that envisaged the possibility of consortia acquiring functions of public interest and being placed under the corporations.

If nothing else, the formal corporate controls allowed the trade unions to undertake their own study and information-gathering activities in order to gain first-hand knowledge of how consortia were set up, how they functioned, and what they achieved.[99] Despite the difficulty in accessing information, the initiatives triggered alarms from *Confindustria*, which was concerned about "interference" and "intrusive intentions".[100] One last attempt to fully accomplish the plan to subordinate the consortia to the corporations was made in October 1939, when in the Central Corporative Committee, the trade union leaders proposed to widen the scope of the consortia subject to the law, to give adequate powers to the corporations, and to strengthen the role of the corporative inspectorates. Despite Mussolini's appreciation, however, nothing came of it this time, either.[101] The trade unionists' resourcefulness – just like the demands made by those Fascists who were most supportive of corporatism – achieved very little, although their denunciations hit the nail on the head in pointing out that the existing industrial legislation was not a means for the government to impose its objectives, but rather a way for the major industrial and financial groups to consolidate their positions and get rid of unwanted competition. *Confindustria*'s fears, the need to curb trade union interference, and the frequent changes made to those regulations nonetheless show that the issue of the corporations' role in the governing of industrial development had not yet been fully settled. More generally, these elements bear witness to the presence of certain tensions between the various social forces represented and within the Fascist regime itself.

Notes

1 Aquarone, *L'organizzazione*, 206; Parlato, *Il sindacalismo fascista*, 46.
2 Ibid., 47.
3 Cilona, "La confederazione", 279.
4 On the figure of Cianetti, see Parlato, *La sinistra fascista*, 225–227.
5 "I problemi sottoposti alla Corporazione della Carta e della Stampa", *Sindacato e corporazione*, 1935, no. 3, 628–631; "I lavori della Corporazione dell'Abbigliamento", ibid., 1935, no. 5, 1454–1455; "I lavori della Corporazione del Vetro e della Ceramica", ibid., 1935, no. 12, 1064–1065; "I lavori della Corporazione dell'Ospitalità", ibid., 1936, no. 1, 89–91.

6 Working from home was considered a typically female occupation under Fascism because it made it possible to reconcile work and domestic chores: Paolo Greco, *Il lavoro a domicilio nell'ordinamento corporativo* (Città di Castello: Edizioni de "Il Diritto del lavoro", 1928).
7 Confederazione fascista dei lavoratori dell'industria, *Le corporazioni nel primo anno di vita* (Roma: Il Lavoro fascista, 1936), 177.
8 Cilona, *Alcuni temi di dibattito*, 341–342.
9 A reconstruction of the whole event is provided by Parlato, *Il sindacalismo*, 85–90.
10 See Mariano Pierro, "L'inquadramento sindacale degli Enti di diritto pubblico che hanno per fine un'attività economica", *Rivista del lavoro* 7, no. 2 (1938): 4–7.
11 Parlato, *Il sindacalismo*, 87.
12 Ibid., 84.
13 Edoardo Malusardi, "Un'ultima parola sul sistema Bedaux", *Il lavoro fascista*, 11 November 1934; Parlato, *Il sindacalismo*, 74–77.
14 Giulio Sapelli, *Organizzazione, lavoro e innovazione industriale nell'Italia tra le due guerre* (Torino: Rosenberg & Sellier, 1978, 226). Bruno Settis, *Fordismi. Storia politica della produzione di massa* (Bologna: Il Mulino, 2016), 256–257.
15 "Vittoria corporativa", *Il lavoro fascista*, 23 October 1935; Luisa Riva-Sanseverino, "Corporazione (diritto corporativo)", in *Enciclopedia del diritto*, vol. 10 (Milano: Giuffrè, 1962), 681.
16 Cilona, *La Confederazione*, 297.
17 ACS, SPD, CO, fasc. 509.790. Confederazione fascista dei lavoratori dell'industria, *Rapporto dei dirigenti. Relazione del presidente*, 16 November 1938; Franco Angelini, "Previdenza e assistenza sindacale", *Il lavoro fascista*, 23 October 1935.
18 AFSDF, *Fondo Giuseppe Landi*, b. 14. *Il Comitato corporativo centrale* (no date, but 1939). The reform's guidelines are outlined in a document drafted by the Minister of Corporations, Lantini: ibid. Ministero delle corporazioni. Direzione generale delle associazioni professionali, *Problemi relativi all'assistenza malattia ai lavoratori*, 11 October 1939. See Parlato, *Il sindacalismo*, 128–133.
19 Tra i tanti interventi sul tema, Luigi Fontanelli, "Degli assegni familiari e d'altro", *Il lavoro fascista*, 2 October 1936; Giovanni Suardi, "Dal salario economico al salario sociale", *Il lavoro fascista*, 25 October 1936; Bruno Biagi, *La politica del lavoro nel diritto fascista* (Firenze: Le Monnier, 1939).
20 Cilona, *Alcuni temi di dibattito*, 355.
21 See the remarks by the head of the economic service of the Fascist Confederation of Industrial Workers: Vincenzo Caruso, "I consorzi industriali nella economia corporativa", *Rivista del lavoro* 4, no. 10 (1935): 26–32.
22 ACS, SPD CO, fasc. 509.790. Confederazione fascista dei lavoratori dell'industria, *Rapporto dei dirigenti. Relazione del presidente*, 16 November 1938; "Come la Confederazione dei lavoratori dell'industria provvede alla rilevazione dei dati economici", *Il lavoro fascista*, 21 April 1936.
23 Z. C., "Azienda sindacato corporazione", *Il lavoro fascista*, 8 May 1934; see also Tullio Cianetti, "I lavoratori dell'industria e le corporazioni", *Il lavoro fascista*, 3 November 1934; Giuseppe Landi, "Enti pubblici ed aziende di interesse nazionale nella economica corporativa", *Rivista del lavoro* 7, no. 5 (1938): 13–23.
24 Ibid., 23.
25 Silvio Lanaro, "Appunti sul fascismo 'di sinistra'. La dottrina corporativa di Ugo Spirito", in *Il regime fascista*, eds. Alberto Aquarone and Maurizio Vernassa (Bologna: Il Mulino, 1974), 357–387; Parlato, *La sinistra fascista*.
26 ACS, SPD, CO, fasc. 509.790. Tullio Cianetti, *Alcune considerazioni sui piani autarchici elaborati dalle corporazioni*, 9 October 1937.
27 Cilona, *Alcuni temi di dibattito*, 362.
28 ACS, SPD, CO, fasc. 509.790. Confederazione fascista dei lavoratori dell'industria, *Rapporto dei dirigenti. Relazione del presidente*, 16 November 1938.

29 Ibid., fasc. 509.486/I, sottofasc. 1. Giuseppe Volpi, *Discorso sull'autarchia pronunciato all'adunata delle Confederazioni degli industriali e dei lavoratori dell'industria*, 18 November 1937.
30 Cilona, *Alcuni temi di dibattito*, 362.
31 ACS, SPD, CO, fasc. 500.005/II. Ferruccio Lantini, *Appunto per S.E. il Capo del Governo*, 17 December 1937.
32 Razza, *La Corporazione*, 33.
33 Bertini, *Le parti e le controparti*, 218.
34 AFSDF, *Fondo Giuseppe Landi*, b. 5, fasc. 4. *Istituto per l'esercizio del credito immobiliare nell'A.O.I.*; ibid., b. 17. Riunione della Giunta Confederale del 2 febbraio 1937; Ibid., b. 5. Confederazione fascista dei lavoratori delle aziende del credito e della assicurazione. *Raccolta dei depositi da parte di società finanziarie industriali e commerciali non sottoposte alla vigilanza dell'Ispettorato per la difesa del risparmio e per l'esercizio del credito. Memoria per la Corporazione della Previdenza e del credito*, no date [1939].
35 See ibid., b. 17. Riunione della Giunta Confederale del 2 febbraio 1937.
36 Ibid.
37 Sergio Panunzio, "Sindacati e partito", *Il Maglio*, 15 September 1937.
38 Parlato, *Il sindacalismo*, 107.
39 Eugenio Curiel, "Correnti e contrasti in seno al sindacato fascista" ("Lo Stato operaio", 20 November 1938), now in Curiel, *Scritti. 1935–1945*, ed. Filippo Frassati (Roma: Editori Riuniti, 1973), 212–218; Togliatti, *Corso sugli avversari*, 90–92.
40 In the face of resistance from the business front, the PNF's stance on the matter made little difference: see ACS, SPD, CO, fasc. 509.790, sottofasc. 2. PNF. Direttorio nazionale, circolare ai segretari delle federazioni dei fasci di combattimento, 2 April 1935; ibid. Carlo Alberto Berti (Confederazione fascista dei lavoratori dell'industria) a Osvaldo Sebastiani (segretario particolare del capo del governo), 10 April 1935.
41 Ibid., SPD, CR, b. 80, fasc. W/R "Biagi Bruno". Police report addressed to Mussolini, 31 August 1937; Nicola Palopoli, "Lo Stato Corporativo e la Carta del Lavoro", *L'economia italiana* 22, no. 4 (1937): 294–328.
42 ACS, SPD, CO, fasc. 500.005/II. F. Lantini, *Appunto per S.E. il Capo del Governo*, 17 December 1937.
43 Ibid., fasc. 509.790. Confederazione fascista dei lavoratori dell'industria, *Rapporto dei dirigenti. Relazione del presidente*, 16 November 1938.
44 Alessio Gagliardi, "La Cgil unitaria e la nuova costituzione economica", in *1945–1946. Le origini della Repubblica*, ed. Giancarlo Monina, vol. 1 (Soveria Mannelli: Rubbettino, 2007), 349–381.
45 Gregory M. Luebbert, "Social Foundations of Political Order in Interwar Europe", *World Politics* 39, no. 4 (1987): 449–478; *Sindacati e diritto del lavoro tra dittature e democrazie nell'Europa mediterranea e latina del XX secolo*, ed. Irene Stolzi (Milano: Giuffrè, 2019).
46 Donald Sassoon, *One Hundred Years of Socialism. The West European Left in the Twentieth Century* (London-New York: I.B. Tauris, 2010), 65.
47 Jean-François Biard, *Le socialisme devant ses choix. La naissance de l'idée de plan* (Paris: Éditions de la Sorbonne, 1985); Morgan Poggioli, "Le planisme à la CGT : Les origines d'une refonte syndicale au tournant du Front populaire", *Cahiers d'histoire. Revue d'histoire critique* 103 (2008): 27–40.
48 Klas Åmark, "Social Democracy and the Trade Union Movement: Solidarity and the Politics of Self-Interest", in *Creating Social Democracy, A Century of the Social Democratic Party in Sweden*, eds. Klaus Misgeld, Karl Molin, and Klas Åmark (University Park, PA: Pennsylvania State University Press, 1992), 56–77; Karen M. Anderson, Steven G. Snow, "Forestalling the Business Veto: Investment Confidence and the Rise of Swedish Social Democracy, 1932–1936", *Social Science Quarterly* 84, no. 1 (2003): 91–110.

49 Sassoon, *One Hundred Years*, 65.
50 Parlato *Il sindacalismo fascista*, 114.
51 Stefano Carducci, "La nuova legge del lavoro tedesca", *La Stirpe* 12, no. 2 (1934): 63–64; Alfredo Signoretti, "Involuzioni del nazional-socialismo", ibid., no. 7, 289–290; Confederazione fascista dei lavoratori dell'industria, *Convegno nazionale dei dirigenti sindacali fascisti dell'industria. Roma 12 luglio 1934* (Roma: "Il Lavoro fascista", 1935), 8; Luigi Adolfo Miglioranzi, *Elaborazioni ed esperienze di diritto sindacale comparato* (Roma: Edizioni de "Il Diritto del lavoro", 1938).
52 Parlato, *La sinistra fascista*, 117–122.
53 The bilingual text of this agreement can be found in "Das Austausch-Abkommen Ley-Cianettil. Lo scambio-operai nell'accordo dott. Ley-Cianetti", *Freude und Arbeit*, 1937, no. 9, 2.
54 Maul, *The International*, 97.
55 Daniela Liebscher, *Freude und Arbeit. Zur internationalen Freizeit- und Sozialpolitik des faschistischen Italien und des NS-Regimes* (Cologne: SH-Verlag, 2009).
56 Luciano Segreto, "Giuseppe Volpi. Il grande mediatore tra istituzioni, politica ed economia", *Studi storici* 61, no. 4 (2020): 927–928.
57 Valerio Castronovo, *Cento anni di imprese. Storia di Confindustria 1910–2010* (Roma-Bari: Laterza, 2010), 261–273.
58 Marco Maraffi, "L'organizzazione degli interessi industriali in Italia, 1870–1980", in *L'azione collettiva degli imprenditori italiani*, ed. Alberto Martinelli (Torino: Edizioni di Comunità, 1999), 161.
59 Ibid., 157.
60 *Enterprise in the Period of Fascism in Europe*, eds. Harold James, Jakob Tanner (London-New York: Routledge, 2017).
61 Adam Tooze, *The Wages of Destruction: The Making and Breaking of the Nazi Economy* (London: Allen Lane, 2006); *German Industry in the Nazi Period*, ed. Christoph Buchheim (Stuttgart: Franz Steiner Verlag, 2008); Christoph Buchheim, Jonas Scherner, "The Role of Private Property in the Nazi Economy: The Case of Industry", *Journal of Economic History* 66, no. 1 (2006): 390–416; Christoph Buchheim, Jonas Scherner, "Corporate Freedom of Action in Nazi Germany: A Response to Peter Hayes", *Bulletin of the German Historical Institute*, no. 45 (2009): 43–50.
62 Matt Bera, *Lobbying Hitler. Industrial Associations between Democracy and Dictatorship* (New York-Oxford: Berghahn Books, 2016).
63 Ettore Conti, *Dal taccuino di un borghese* (Bologna: Il Mulino, 1986), 432.
64 See ACS, SPD, CO, fasc. 500.005/I. Letter to Mussolini, 8 July 1938.
65 Sergio Romano, *Giuseppe Volpi. Industria e finanza tra Giolitti e Mussolini* (Milano: Bompiani, 1979), 206–207.
66 Ibid., 207.
67 Sarti, *Fascism and the Industrial Leadership*, 97–104.
68 Gilberto Gualerni, *Industria e fascismo. Per una interpretazione dello sviluppo economico italiano tra le due guerre*, (Milano: Vita e Pensiero, 1976), 188–189.
69 *Employers' associations* represent entrepreneurs as employers in the social sphere (i.e. in relation to trade union issues and social policies), whereas trade associations represent them as businessmen in the economic and technical sphere (i.e. in relation to issues pertaining to economic, industrial, and trade policies and anything having to do with production). In Italy the two functions have always coexisted in the same organisation without ever giving rise to specialisation: see Lanzalaco, *Dall'impresa all'associazione*, 19.
70 ACS, PCM, Gab., 1934–36, fasc. 18.2.5997. Ministro dei lavori pubblici, *Appunto per S.E. il capo del governo. Rapporto fra le corporazioni e gli organi esecutivi dello Stato*, 11 February 1936.
71 On the consolidating act of 1933 and subsequent legislative measures, see Pietro Ciarlo, "Il testo unico del 1933 sulle acque e sugli impianti elettrici, in Storia dell'industria

elettrica in Italia", vol. 3.1, ed. Giuseppe Galasso (Roma-Bari: Laterza, 1993), 61–88; Luciano Segreto, *Giacinto Motta. Un ingegnere alla testa del capitalismo industriale italiano* (Roma-Bari: Laterza, 2005), 209–228.

72 On business organisations' "logic of influence", see Alberto Martinelli, Luca Lanzalaco, "L'organizzazione degli interessi imprenditoriali e il sistema politico. La logica dell'influenza", in *L'azione collettiva*, 317–363.

73 De Felice, *Mussolini il duce* I, 291.

74 Pierluigi Ciocca, *Ricchi per sempre? Una storia economica d'Italia (1796–2005)* (Torino: Bollati Boringhieri, 2007), 204–218.

75 Ernesto Cianci, *Nascita dello stato imprenditore in Italia* (Lanciano: Carabba, 2009), 220–240; Gualerni, *Industria e fascismo*, 170–184.

76 Antonino Santarelli, "Dati e considerazioni intorno alla disciplina corporativa delle nuove iniziative industriali", *Rivista internazionale di scienze sociali* 49, no. 1 (1941): 63–64.

77 Bottai, "Verso un piano", 105.

78 See the addresses made by the former President of *Confindustria*, Gino Olivetti, and by Asquini, in APC, Legislatura XXVIII, *Discussioni*, vol. 7, respectively 7590 and 7585.

79 Pietro Capoferri, "Limiti e funzioni della legge sugli impianti industriali", *Gerarchia* 17, no. 12 (1937): 832–834.

80 ACONF, *Fondo Giovanni Balella*, b. 89, fasc. 1, *La disciplina dei nuovi impianti industriale nell'ordine corporativo*, no date (but 1938).

81 "Lettera dell'on. Benni", *Il Popolo d'Italia*, 15 April 1930.

82 ACONF, *Fondo Giovanni Balella*, b. 89, fasc. 1, *La disciplina dei nuovi impianti industriali nell'ordine corporativo*, no date (but 1938); ibid., Circolari della Confederazione fascista dell'industria alle Federazioni di categoria e alle Unioni provinciali no. 2726, 13 March 1937, no. 2995, 12 June 1937, and no. 3644/D. 25 February 1938 ("Riservata").

83 Valerio Strinati, "La legislazione corporativa sugli impianti industriali: interpretazioni e discussioni", *Le Carte e la storia* 7, no. 1 (2001): 196–208.

84 Gualerni, *Industria e fascismo*, 151–70; Cianci, *Nascita dello stato imprenditore*, 209–217.

85 ACS, PCM, Gab., 1931–33, fasc. 18.8.9114. *Schema di decreto-legge concernente la costituzione di consorzi per determinati rami di attività economica* ("riservata"), 1932.

86 Sarti, *Fascism and the Industrial Leadership*, 101–102.

87 APC, Legislatura XXVIII, *Discussioni*, 2753–2754; Ibid., session of 24 February 1932, 5791–5792; Ibid., session of 30 April 1932, 6764–6767. See also Bottai, "Corporazioni e consorzi"; g. b. [Giuseppe Bottai], "Il ricatto liberale contro il corporativismo", *Critica fascista* 11, no. 12 (1933): 223–226.

88 Confederazione fascista dei lavoratori dell'industria, *Convegno nazionale dei dirigenti 1934*.

89 Quoted in Cilona, *Alcuni temi del dibattito*, 356–357.

90 AFSDF, *Fondo Giuseppe Landi*, b. 5. Luigi Begnotti, *La produzione e la distribuzione del cemento in Italia. La situazione attuale dell'industria del cemento*, no date (but 1937).

91 AFSDF, *Fondo Giuseppe Landi*, b. 5. Begnotti, *Seguito alla relazione allegata alla nota sulla "disciplina delle produzione e distribuzione del cemento"* (letter n. 1916 del 29/4/37).

92 ACONF, *Fondo Giovanni Balella* b. 90, fasc. 1. *Argomenti generali sulla disciplina consortile*, no date.

93 Ibid.

94 Federico Chessa, "Economia controllata ed Economia corporativa", in *Annali di statistica ed economia. Università di Genova* 4 (1936): 1.

95 Confederazione fascista dei lavoratori dell'industria, *Convegno nazionale dei dirigenti 1934*.

96 Cilona, *Alcuni temi di dibattito*, 360–361.

97 ACONF, *Fondo Giovanni Balella* b. 90, f. 1. Confederazione generale fascista dell'industria italiana, ufficio disciplina della produzione, *Note per la riunione dei direttori*, no date (but 1937).

98 Gualerni, *Industria e fascismo*, 159.

99 ACONF, *Fondo Giovanni Balella* b. 90, f. 1. Confederazione fascista dei lavoratori dell'industria, direzione dei servizi corporativi ed assistenziali (servizio economico), alla Unione provinciale di Campobasso e per conoscenza alle Federazioni nazionali, 17 March 1938.

100 Ibid. Confederazione generale fascista dell'industria italiana, ufficio rilevazioni e studi, *Influenza degli accordi consortili sulla dinamica dei prezzi*, no date.

101 "Il Comitato corporativo centrale", *L'economia nazionale*, 31, October (1939): 31–33. Concerning Mussolini's support, see B. Mussolini, *La funzione dei consorzi* (1939), in *Opera omnia di Benito Mussolini*, eds. Edoardo Susmel and Duilio Susmel, vol. 29 (Firenze: La Fenice, 1966), 320–321.

9 The Last Phase

From International Corporatism to Autarky

In his numerous writings on corporatism, Ugo Spirito constantly tackled the question of the relationship between the individual and the state. Corporatism, in his view, was to enable the overcoming of the separation between the private sphere (pertaining to the individual) and the public sphere (the nation, represented by the state). Property was to remain in the hands of private individuals but would be used for general purposes that were common to the whole community rather than in pursuit of the profit of a few. Individual freedom was thus to be put in the service of the nation. The latter, in turn, was considered not as the sum of all individuals but as a collective body with its own goals, superior and transcending individuals' partial ones: Spirito himself had defined this view as the "identification of the individual and the State".[1]

Within this line of reasoning, Spirito began to argue in his writings from the early 1930s that the nation "should not be conceived anti-historically as an entity limited in its boundaries", as it "includes within itself the international world, and everything that makes up the life of this world is to be found precisely within the Nation".[2] In other essays from this period, Spirito returned to the relationship between the nation and the international system. In 1993, he wrote: "An integral corporative experience is impossible without first winning the other nations over to the corporative idea, as they are constituent elements of the single economic world. Corporatism is founded on the concepts of collaboration and organic planning".[3] Underlying this discourse was a philosophical scheme that was drawn from Giovanni Gentile and mechanically applied by Spirito. This scheme pointed to the attainment of an organic unity resulting from the recomposition of opposites, as the end point of all historical processes. The very logical structure underlying the thesis of the "identification of the individual and the State" was applied to the relationship between the nation and the international sphere. In another essay, again from 1933, Spirito argued: "Corporatism is not nationalism, and it judges nationalism to be a materialistic conception [...]. Corporatist economics, on the other hand, is truly national and therefore truly international [...]. The implementation of an integral corporatism is logically subordinated to the corporatist transformation of the entire world economy".[4] In short, in spite of Fascism's radical nationalism, the nation could not be a self-sufficient and self-contained entity, according to Spirito. Consequently, corporatism had to be conceived of not only as something functional

DOI: 10.4324/9781032713267-10

to the Italian economy but also in relation to other nations and the international economy.

At the beginning of the 1930s, Spirito was not the only one to advocate the development of a global corporatism, or to approach the issue of the reorganisation of international relations from the standpoint of "third way" principles. A prominent role was also played by the group of scholars and officials close to Bottai. This was the sector of Fascism's political and intellectual establishment that was most interested in developing projects aimed at the creation of supranational corporatist bodies.[5]

Among the first to introduce the subject was Celestino Arena, a lecturer at the School for Advanced Corporative Studies of the University of Pisa. In a 1930 article, prompted by the first signs of the economic crisis, he observed that the presence of the world market was intrinsic to modern capitalism, and that the idea of national economic autarky had proved to be purely illusory. Protectionist measures were "unsustainable in the long run because they were harmful to others and, by reflection, to oneself".[6] Each country could only achieve its own balance within a general equilibrium. Curbing the drive towards economic nationalism was not enough, however. It also appeared "increasingly urgent" to "rationalise the world economy and world politics". In order to meet this need, it was necessary to act on the national organisations representing economic and professional interests and on the international networks to which they had given rise (the international trade unions and entrepreneurs) by bringing them back into a system of harmonious relations that was marked by collaboration and subordinated to the public interest. The solution would be provided "by corporative organisation, understood in Italian terms, to be implemented within individual States and then projected abroad in official international institutions".[7] Hence, the proposal to set up an "international economic council" with regulatory powers within the League of Nations, following the example of the Italian National Council of Corporations [8] Arena relaunched his idea the following year. After pointing to the "lack of co-ordination" between the various branches of economic activity within each country, as well as across countries, as the cause of "misdirection when it comes to finding appropriate solutions to get out of the current morass", he reiterated the need for "close contact" between "national economic technical bodies" and "international bodies" (including both existing bodies and those yet to be created).[9]

It was Bottai who attempted to translate the idea of a global corporatism into more explicitly political terms and to relaunch it through supranational institutions. Addressing the Second Committee of the League of Nations Assembly in September 1931, the Minister of Corporations revived the analysis outlined by Arena. The crisis was "not merely cyclical but structural, and new methods were called for, both in economic policies of the several States and in international economic equilibrium". Far from providing a solution, protectionism and economic nationalism could worsen the situation. Precisely to counter the growth of national selfishness and the conflicts triggered by protectionist policies, Bottai "suggested the desirability of closer association with the work of the League of those bodies which had been set up in a number of countries in and outside Europe since the war under the general name of National Economic Councils". He then went on to list the main Councils, among which the Italian CNC obviously stood out.[10]

Bottai relaunched his idea the following year, this time within the International Labour Organisation. On that occasion, he affirmed:

> on behalf of my Government I proposed in September 1931, at the Second Committee of the League of Nations Assembly, that national economic councils representing the State, the employers and the workers should take a part in international economic organisation. Such an idea is most appropriate to the International Labour Organisation which, like the Italian corporative system, rests on the collaboration of States, employers and workers. It is absolutely necessary to establish permanent co-ordination between the economic competence of the League of Nations and the social competence of the International Labour Office, for this alone can ensure unity of direction. Such unity is the only means of definitely overcoming the crisis which Italy is facing resolutely and frankly, thanks to the sentiment of solidarity that animates the institutions which Mussolini has given her.[11]

Bottai's project had little follow-up. Apart from the approval of a resolution by the League of Nations' assembly, neither supranational bodies nor other governments gave serious consideration to the idea of global corporatism. Instead, the discussion continued among specialists in corporatist issues in Italy.

Filippo Carli brought up the subject at the Second Conference of Trade Union and Corporate Studies in Ferrara. After analysing – with an abundance of data – the economic crisis' most relevant features and highlighting the strong influence of international processes on international economies, he concluded by calling for the establishment of "international corporations reporting to a supranational body – such as the League of Nations – capable of directing individual economies".[12] Arnaldo Volpicelli, an associate of Spirito, addressed the issue from a more philosophical perspective. While on an internal level corporatism was intended to bridge the gap between the individual and the state, on an external level, it was seen to serve the purpose of overcoming both nationalism – understood as the existence of separate legal systems, as was typical of the liberal age – and socialist internationalism.[13] Volpicelli therefore called for the establishment of "an international organisation" capable of reconciling the "partial" sovereignty of the state with the "totality" of the international system, thus breaking down the "great walls of national autarkies".[14] Stemming from this was his rejection of war "as a purportedly legal, economic, and ethical way of solving international conflicts and forming an international will".[15] Once again, autarky was an explicit polemical target: a few years later, when that word became one of the symbols of Fascist politics and propaganda, such talk would prove unthinkable in Fascist Italy.

In *Critica fascista*, the magazine directed by Bottai, Mario Gianturco – an official of the International Labour Organisation's information division – instead linked the export of corporatism to the preservation of international peace. Only by building full "social solidarity within", between all categories could one pursue "international solidarity".[16] In Gianturco's case, too, this reasoning translated into a strongly critical stance towards any idea of autarky, i.e. towards any policy tending to reduce ties with other countries.

The most systematic and intellectually ambitious proposal was put forward by Giuseppe De Michelis, the Italian government delegate to the International Labour Organisation.[17] De Michelis was the author of *La corporazione nel mondo* (*The Corporation in the World*), a text which envisaged a European cooperation policy based on a corporatist system of regulation by interweaving corporatist theory, economic analysis, demographic studies, and geopolitical issues. Published in Italy in 1934, the book was soon translated into English and French.[18]

De Michelis set out from the idea that the economic crisis had revealed the unsustainability of the old order: capitalist development and mass production had ended up generating profound imbalances, while the integration of economies based solely on the free market had created tensions and instability. As in the case of the other authors already encountered, autarky and the closure of nation-states were considered not a possible solution, but on the contrary, the source of new and further problems. In order to achieve a new equilibrium that was capable of ensuring economic development and social welfare, it was first necessary to take note of the unequal distribution of resources between states and to favour forms of exchange that would promote a more balanced distribution. De Michelis suggested, "a new systematisation wherein it is intended that the three factors in the production of goods – labour, land and raw materials, and capital – shall be associated internationally and combined with a view to the maximum return".[19] More specifically – if we can talk about specificity, given the generic and, at times, vague nature of the proposal – this reorganisation of international relations revolved around three axes: internationalism, neocolonialism, and corporatism.[20] The first axis implied cooperation – which until then had been nearly absent – between the three main supranational organisations: the League of Nations, the International Labour Organisation, and the International Institute of Agriculture. The second consisted in initiating new forms of economic collaboration among world powers, which relied on a revitalisation of the colonization of the African continent. The imperial projection of European states constituted a source of strength – for accessing raw materials and expanding markets – that had to be governed and bolstered by new principles in the interest of both the colonisers and the colonised populations.

The most significant element in De Michelis' speech was the third one, corporatism:

> The corporative system contains elements fruitful for the coherent and elastic regulation of the world market [...]. The nations form to-day the parts of a single great economic undertaking: not a transitory necessity, this, but rather the expression of the inherent law of the enlargement and integration of markets.
>
> The vast international market is to-day what the single market of a nation, formed out of the rudimentary local markets, was only a few decades ago. [...] the principle of international co-ordination will overcome and will

> absorb the national units while at the same time respecting their political autonomy.
>
> Thus the fundamental principles of the corporative plan of co-ordinating the action of the groups are susceptible of being readily carried out in international economy: the principle of the limitation of property and of individual initiative, of the adaptation of productive forces to the needs of consumption, the duty of making all the available economic energies co-operate to that end, and, lastly and above all, the principle of protecting in the most effective and the most productive way the unorganised mass of consuming population.[21]

The reference to the principles of corporatism was what distinguished De Michelis' proposal within the international debate on the new world economic system. That element gave Italy a centrality and primacy that would otherwise have been unthinkable. De Michelis sought to treat the issue with great caution, not least so as not to upset his foreign readers. He specified that "there is nothing specially and exclusively Italian in this system of economic policy. Uniquely and pre-eminently Italian is, however, the sagacity of having divined it and positively constituted it with the firm intention of carrying it into practice".[22] Despite this display of understatement, however, the book closed with a celebration of Fascist Italy, the corporate state, and its role in the world:

> In Italy and in the Italian corporative system live and operate the spiritual germs of this escape from the economic pressure which afflicts mankind and throws the nations one against the other; they exhibit the expansive virtue of their own supreme principle, of the rational co-ordination of social forces and social activities for a comprehensive aim of prosperity and of power.
>
> There can be no doubt that by applying them on the international plane in a vaster sphere of action the mission of the great industrial countries of Europe will be fulfilled by assuring to the world another century of prosperity.[23]

De Michelis' broad project did not arouse particular interest abroad. It went "almost completely unnoticed both within the ranks of the European right and within the ILO", of which he was one of the most active and experienced delegates.[24] Indifference was certainly also due to the threatening and destabilising position on the international order that Mussolini was then taking. Instead, as was to be expected, it had more substantial echoes in Italy. Here, the book aroused very mixed reactions, ranging from the enthusiasm of those who saw it as a "profoundly Mussolinian" proposal[25] to those who considered corporatism inextricably linked to the nation-state and therefore considered its extension to the global scale inconceivable.[26]

Aspirations to establish an international corporate community suffered a drastic reduction in the mid-1930s. The turning point brought about by the Fascist war in Ethiopia and the transformation of the foreign policy situation it entailed put an end to any hypothesis regarding the creation of supranational institutions inspired by the Fascist corporate model. From then on, the theme of the Empire became the dominant propaganda motif. Even in this phase, however, corporatist discourse continued to serve as a reservoir of ideas for Fascist politicians and intellectuals. Among the countless books and articles on the governing of the new possessions, many were devoted to the project of exporting the corporatist order to the colonies. The image of universal corporatism found new expression, at least to some degree, within the discourse on what was defined as "corporatist colonialism", which was aimed at creating a labour community based on cooperation between all productive subjects, both in the motherland and in its possessions.[27] The theme had already been outlined at the beginning of the decade, at the time of Libya's "reconquest", and was relaunched after the conquest of Ethiopia and the establishment of Italian East Africa.

The main contribution to corporatist colonialism's cultural and institutional development came from experts on colonial issues, mostly officials of the Overseas Administration: among the most active were Gaetano Napolitano, Mario Scaparro, Giambattista Castelbarco, Guido Fornari, Alberto Giaccardi, Mario Gianturco, Gennaro Mondaini, Italo Papini, and Fernando Valenzi. As a result, the debate mainly unfolded in the pages of periodicals linked to the colonial ministerial apparatus, such as *Rivista delle colonie italiane, Notiziario corporativo della Libia*, and *Rassegna economica delle colonie* (from 1937 *Rassegna economica dell'Africa italiana*), as well as through the three congresses organised by the *Centro studi coloniali* (Centre for Colonial Studies) in 1931, 1934, and 1937.[28] On several occasions, however, the subject was addressed outside the confines of specialist colonial studies and found room in important journals devoted to politics and ideological deliberation also involving some prominent figures in Fascist culture, such as Sergio Panunzio, Volpicelli, and Paolo D'Agostino Orsini, one of the main exponents of the Italian geopolitical school.[29]

This debate combined several crucial issues. First of all, it concerned the legal establishment of a new economic and social order in the Italian colonies. Several authors saw corporatist colonialism as the means both to enable the institutional and legislative modelling of the colonies on the metropole and to frame – within a system based on collaboration – the juridical dichotomy between colonists and colonised, that is, between metropolitan citizenship and colonial subjecthood.[30] It was argued that by creating a more harmonious system, the corporations would aid the achievement of the colonial project's objective: the economic and demographic "development" – that is, rational exploitation – of the African possessions.[31] Corporatist colonialism also intersected with a more general issue, namely the self-representation of Fascist imperialism, which the regime's rhetoric presented as a historical experience that was different from all other colonial models, both past and present. With remarkable skill at mystification, some authors even spoke of a "moral imperialism" aimed at achieving the "highest social justice" among peoples.[32] Moreover, they defined Fascism's colonial conception as "profoundly spiritual" as opposed to the "purely individualistic and capitalist" one of liberal states.[33] Rhetorical statements such as these served a mostly propagandistic function. More significant in terms of theoretical elaboration were those contributions that intertwined the discourse on the exporting of corporatism to the colonies with the debate on international relations and the search for a different geopolitical balance. Referring to De Michelis' book, Gennaro Mondaini argued: "A corporative colonial policy [...] could [...] not only benefit the mother country and colonies, but perhaps open up new horizons for colonial systems and colonial relations between nations, since both are struggling to adapt to the new moral and economic requirements and the new political tendencies among peoples".[34] More specifically, the topic was developed by the theorists of a geopolitical current that envisaged the creation of a "great space" extending across the two shores of the Mediterranean, "Eurafrica", from which the "plutocratic" powers would be expelled in order to create a new international order that would give a prominent place to Fascist Italy.[35]

The exporting of corporatism to the colonies was also viewed as an opportunity to relaunch the corporatist project in the motherland. As we shall soon see, in the second half of the 1930s, signs of disappointment had begun to surface with respect to the failed achievements of the so-called "corporative revolution". According to Sergio Panunzio, the exporting of the corporative order to the African possessions would make it possible "to push this vast and complex movement to its maximum degree of efficiency and effectiveness", thus bringing "the whole corporative social and economic system to maturity in the kingdom as well". The colonies promised to serve as an ideal laboratory for the syndicalist and corporatist experiment since the "demolishing [of] the old feudal system" in Africa had created a "social vacuum" in which "no limits" were to be found "and no resistance based on pre-existing rights and organisations".[36] The "virgin land" theme was widespread in publications about the colonies in the 1930s, where it was theorised that the economic, family, social, and mental framework of the subject populations provided optimal conditions for the realisation of the Fascist project since it was not polluted by the individualism of European societies.[37]

The debate among specialists was accompanied by some institutional achievements, which occurred after the conquest of Ethiopia and the establishment of the Empire. Overall, the result was a complex and non-linear institutional structure. At the centre were six Corporative Colonial Councils (*Consulte coloniali corporative*, later named *Consulte corporative dell'Africa italiana*), which were established (by Royal Decree no. 1872 of 21 August 1936) for as many economic sectors – agriculture, industry, trade, construction, communications, credit, and insurance. In 1939, these Councils were reorganised by production cycles and their number was increased to ten. The Councils included representatives of the Ministry of Italian Africa and other state bodies, the PNF, trade unions, and corporations. Their task was to offer opinions on programmes for the "development" of the colonies and on all topics that the ministry deemed useful to submit for their consideration. The Colonial Councils of the Corporative Economy (*Consigli coloniali dell'economia corporativa*, Royal Decree no. 1932 of 1 July 1937) operated in the colonies instead: they were present in each of the territories that made up Italian East Africa and were entrusted with assisting the governor in dealing with economic issues and working conditions.[38] In addition, confederations of workers and employers were established exclusively for Italian settlers.

The results fell far short of expectations. Corporate colonialism was stifled by the bureaucratisation that had always characterised the administration of the Italian colonies. The new institutions were overwhelmed by the countless offices and bodies operating between Italy and its possessions, often resulting in overlaps and conflicts. Furthermore, the plan to implement a corporatist system of collaboration between all components was never implemented because any recognition of African labour was ruled out. From the colonial subjects' perspective, all rhetoric aside, the Fascist Empire was characterised by an authoritarian, violent, and discriminatory practice of domination: "The manifest breach of international law and the war crimes committed by Italian troops made any talk about the cooperative and non-exploitative nature of Italian colonialism look absurd and propagandistic".[39]

The project of corporatist colonialism did not ultimately turn the Fascist overseas territories into an innovative model of imperialism: the outcome was "undoubtedly disappointing", even for workers from Italy.[40] It did not even succeed in making up for the abrupt decline of the idea of universal corporatism, or indeed in masking the first signs of fatigue and disappointment that were beginning to appear among the advocates of the Fascist "third way".

The war against Ethiopia, the sanctions imposed by the European powers, and the establishment of the Empire marked a break, and not merely with respect to the country's international position. On 23 March 1936, when inaugurating the second corporative assembly at the end of the first cycle of corporative activities, Mussolini announced the beginning of "autarky". In the words of the Fascist leader, this was the "beginning of a new phase in Italian history"; a new phase dominated by the goal of "achieving as much autonomy as possible in the economic life of the nation in the shortest possible time".[41] The new catchword of autarky and the theme of national economic independence soon became rampant in the regime's publications, overlapping and, to some extent, replacing discourses on corporatism. Many Fascist intellectuals were quick to speak of a "transition" or even a "corporatist pause", since the new policy of trade and investment to replace imports would inevitably take resources away from welfare policies.[42] *Critica fascista* was at the forefront of this debate. One of the young members of Bottai's group, Agostino Nasti, wrote that "action for power" had to "take precedence over action for social renewal" and that corporatism had proved to be an inadequate instrument for the attainment of power objectives.[43] By contrast, Ernesto Bassanelli argued that corporatist life was being stifled by an increasingly intrusive centralised state, while the "heavy trappings of war" were "too closely reminiscent of the schemes of State socialism".[44] Mario Rivoire instead denounced the "widespread laziness" and "pervading silence" surrounding the assertion of foreign policy's primacy over domestic policy.[45] Naturally, this did not mark the end of Fascism's anti-capitalist, social, and populist demands. Indeed, these experienced a revival in the anti-bourgeois campaign of 1938. However, towards the end of the decade, they came to be increasingly disengaged from the corporatist framework, which was now deemed an inadequate means to ensure real social change.[46]

International interest also began to wane, although it did not die down completely. A few in-depth studies were published which sought to remove the subject from the contrasting gaze of opponents and apologists. Of particular note among these were the works of George Lowell Field, William Welk, and Carl T. Schmidt, published respectively by Columbia, Harvard, and Oxford University Press.[47] Even the more widely circulating press continued to discuss the subject from time to time: in the spring of 1938, a lavish *Life* article reminded American readers that "inside Italy there is also 'The Corporate State'", and that the Labour Charter was the "kernel of Fascism".[48] The hype had passed, however, and the interest in corporatism as a topic had apparently cooled down considerably.

With the turning point of autarky, the first assessment of the "corporative revolution" was drawn in Italy. With the beginning of the second cycle of corporations in March 1936, the trial stage could be said to be over. The direction taken by the new bodies appeared clear to observers, yet it was bound to cause discontent in those sectors of Fascism that had hedged their bets on corporatism. The changes in terms of social representation and of the way in which the relationship between socio-economic interests and the state was managed constituted significant novelties but could hardly be considered sufficient and satisfactory proof of the existence of a new system.

Voices of disappointment began to surface in this climate. Once again, corporatism proved to be a topic that could be discussed in a relatively open way; and once again, *Critica fascista* stood at the forefront. Among others, Federico Maria Pacces wrote in 1937: "Still divorced from the administrative order of the State, the corporations meet, discuss, and approve 'declarations', while companies continue to produce as before and ministries continue to collect [...] paperwork as before". The doctrine, for its part, "stands by, somewhat mortified, and looks on; or else, ethereal and irresponsible, it roams the clouds of utopia".[49] Articles such as these foreshadowed themes, tones, and arguments which many leading figures would adopt in the post-Fascist era, giving rise to a literature of regret and missed opportunities in which Bottai would play an absolutely leading role.

In the second half of the 1930s, the various sectors of the "Fascist Left" would cling precisely to corporatism's original myth. They saw corporatism not as a system in the making – one at least already partially realised that, if anything, needed to be recorded, fine-tuned, and interpreted – but rather as an objective that was still far from having been achieved. The pursuit of this objective meant reviving the languishing revolutionary spirit and opposing the conservative and "bourgeois" character acquired by the Fascist regime. It was this radicalisation of positions and the increasingly evident distance from Mussolini's guidance and the regime's leadership that gave rise to so-called "frondist Fascism" (*fascismo di fronda*); this took shape in the second half of the decade and was carried forward by groups of young people and certain sectors within the trade union movement.[50] The so-called "frondists" (*frondisti*) called for a "new wave" based not on detachment from Fascism but rather on the building of a different kind of Fascism, with more social, more Mussolinian, and more dictatorial features – in other words, a kind of Fascism capable of expressing an acceleration in a totalitarian sense.[51] The anti-bourgeois campaign launched in 1938 would fuel the "frondists" hopes for some time.

Disappointment was also felt among Fascism's more institutional sectors. Right from the start, the Undersecretary (from January 1935) and then Minister (from

June 1936) of Corporations Ferruccio Lantini did not conceal his disillusionment. Speaking at the national conference of the Confederation of Industrial Workers in October 1936, he admitted that few issues had been resolved and that many motions had been formulated in vague terms. For corporatism to work, "it is not enough to enshrine it on an altar so that it may be admired it from afar, possibly through the praises, criticism, and various interpretations of intellectual speculation". A remedy might emerge over time, Latini argued. However, the situation which had arisen presaged yet another setback in corporatism's realisation: with the beginning of autarky – Lantini acutely noted – some "even saw in the corporations a hindrance to the attainment of so-called economic independence, while others embraced the autarkic ideal in the hope of pushing corporatism into the background until it could be buried for good".[52]

In the second half of the 1930s, speeches highlighting the distance between the "third way" project and the corporations' actual functioning led to the formulation of some reform proposals. In some cases, the "disappointed" themselves presented Mussolini with reform plans for reorganising the institutional framework of the corporative structures and the attributions of power. The most systematic project was undoubtedly the one put forward in the trade union sphere by the President of the Confederation of Industrial Workers, Cianetti. This project was drawn up in the spring of 1937 as part of the then ongoing discussion on the reform of the state structure with the aim of giving it a corporatist imprint. Cianetti's project constituted an expanded and sharper version of the report that the Confederation had submitted to the Solmi commission at the end of 1936, and which had been tasked with drawing up a constitutional reform centred on the transformation of the Chamber of Deputies into a corporatist chamber.[53] Cianetti's 1937 text provided for the amalgamation of the corporations, which were to be reduced from 22 to 9 and to be constituted exclusively according to the production cycle's criterion. It assigned to the new chamber the power to issue – through the corporations – "corporative norms concerning the self-governing of categories in economic matters". It proposed a reorganisation of the ministries that had competencies in economic, social, and trade union matters. Above all, the text identified the specific functions to be assigned to the corporations, namely:

a the legislative and regulatory function;
b evaluating and controlling the economic performance of companies, consortia, and industrial groups and entities operating in the economic sector; controlling compliance with the laws and corporate regulations issued; and applying sanctions;
c the attempt at mediation in labour relations, both in contractual stipulations and in collective disputes;
d the formulation of motions aimed at setting guidelines for economic development.[54]

Cianetti's project therefore aimed to redefine the corporations' work by assigning them extensive and well-defined powers and making them the focus of economic planning. These proposals were not taken into consideration by Mussolini. Cianetti repeated this attempt – again to no avail – a couple of years later, in August 1939, when immediately following his appointment as Undersecretary of Corporations he sent the head of government a new programme to reorganise the corporate and trade union system.[55]

Another reform project, much more limited and circumscribed, was outlined by Minister of Corporations Lantini. It aimed not to change the whole corporative system but, more modestly, to revitalise the role of his ministry. By the mid-1930s, the Ministry of Corporations appeared to be drowning in routine and low-profile bureaucracy, as it had been supplanted by more recently established institutions and lacked significant powers. The ministry was even weaker politically and institutionally compared to its early years. With Bottai's departure, the activity of study, cultural intervention, and political and institutional planning had grown increasingly fruitless. The failure of attempts to gain control over the had confirmed the marginal role played by the Ministry in Industrial Policy, while the emergence of the corporations had reduced its functions in the trade union field. Finally, with the beginning of autarky, the ministry had been stripped of its significant foreign trade competencies, as almost the whole Directorate General for Trade (*Direzione generale per gli scambi*) – including both its staff and management – had now been transferred to the Undersecretariat for Trade and Currency (*Sottosegretariato per gli scambi e le valute*). Lantini decided to make one last attempt at revitalisation through the autarky campaign. In a memorandum addressed to Mussolini in July 1939, he proposed setting up an undersecretariat for industrial and autarkic services tasked with ensuring the autarkic plans' implementation. Latini suggested Agostino Rocca, the person in charge of managing the public steel industry, to be this new institution's head.[56] This last proposal was dropped by Mussolini as well, however.

Despite these unsuccessful outcomes, the projects drawn up by leading representatives of the trade union and corporative institutions such as Cianetti and Lantini bear witness to the tension that continued to characterise corporative planning even in the second half of the 1930s, at least among certain sectors of Fascism. The constitutional reform of the representative system was finally initiated in parallel with these attempts. The aim of replacing the Chamber of Deputies with a new chamber, based on corporatist principles, had been an objective of Fascism from the outset. The idea had resurfaced, albeit fleetingly, in the parliamentary debate on the establishment of the National Council of Corporations. It was then gradually re-proposed by various party and institutional leaders.[57] The goal of creating a Chamber of Fasces and Corporations (*Camera dei fasci e delle corporazioni*) was finally announced by Mussolini in his March 1936 speech on "national economic independence".[58] In November, the Grand Council of Fascism appointed a special commission to formulate proposals for the new chamber's formation and functioning. This commission, known as the Solmi Commission after its rapporteur Arrigo Solmi, completed its work in July 1938.[59] On the basis of the results achieved, the Chamber of Fasces and Corporations came into being at the beginning of 1939, replacing the Chamber of Deputies. At the same time, the reform of the National Council of Corporations was approved: the composition of the council changed, as it now consisted of members of the Central Corporative Committee and full members of the corporations.

The approval of the Chamber of Fasces and Corporations marked the end of the elective principle. Its members were not elected, not even through the plebiscitary "fiction"; rather, they became such automatically by virtue of the role they held in the party or in the corporative organisations, and as soon as they lost such a role, they ceased to hold office in the new assembly. The Chamber of Fasces and Corporations consisted of the head of government and members of the Grand Council of Fascism, the National Council of the National Fascist Party, and the National Council of Corporations. The last council made the most significant contribution: it accounted for as many as 525 of the total of 682 national councillors, as the members of the new chamber were referred to. Fascist political leaders and the representatives of the various corporative categories thus became direct representatives of the nation without any form of mediation. The corporative principle thus acquired constitutional significance – although this was mitigated by the coexistence of the political and party principles.

The new chamber became the focus of what little hopes the disappointed corporatists still harboured. The challenge now was no longer to create a form of planning guided and promoted by the corporations but to build a genuine representative system based on the productive categories: a system capable, according to Mussolini, of "guaranteeing direct representation for the people through those men who are most directly in contact with it and who are therefore in a position to know its needs and aspirations with greater certainty".[60]

In this case, too, however, hopes were destined to be dashed. While the new chamber's way of operating – through legislative committees which could approve bills instead of the plenary assembly – made the approval of laws swifter and less cumbersome, thus apparently suggesting a revival of the assembly's role, on the constitutional level, the reform actually marked the definitive abandonment of the distinction between legislative and executive power, with the complete subordination of the former to the latter. The founding law explicitly stated that the Chamber of Fasces and Corporations would collaborate with the government in the drafting of laws, *de facto* making the government the source of all legislation. Moreover, it reaffirmed the head of government's position of absolute pre-eminence within the executive, even as far as the issuing of legislation was concerned.[61] The constitutional reform, which was intended to celebrate corporatism as a new political and institutional system and thus enshrine the Fascist State's corporative nature, ended up confirming and further strengthening Mussolini's charismatic dictatorship and the overriding role of the "Duce of Fascism".

Notes

1 Ugo Spirito, "Individuo e Stato nella concezione corporativa", in *Atti del secondo convegno*, vol. 1, 179–192.

2 Ugo Spirito, "La nuova economia", in Ugo Spirito, *I fondamenti della economia corporativa* (Milano: Treves, 1932), 27.

3 Ugo Spirito, "La crisi del capitalismo e il sistema corporativo", in Ugo Spirito, *Capitalismo e corporativismo* (Firenze: Sansoni, 1934), 80.
4 Ugo Spirito, "L'economia programmatica corporativa", Ibid., 119.
5 Fabrizio Amore Bianco, "Le corporazioni oltre lo Stato. Progetti di corporativismo internazionale nell'immaginario del fascismo", in *Genealogie e geografie dell'anti-democrazia nella crisi europea degli anni Trenta. Fascismi, corporativismi, laburismi*, ed. Laura Cerasi (Venezia: Edizioni Ca' Foscari, 2019), 247.
6 Celestino Arena, "Le associazioni professionali nella politica internazionale", *Archivio di Studi Corporativi* 1, no. 1 (1930): 182.
7 Ibid., 195–196.
8 Ibid., 193–195.
9 Arena, "La corporazione nei suoi riflessi internazionali", *Lo Stato* 2, no. 9 (1931): 655.
10 UN Archives, League of Nations Official Documents, Item A-C2, Minutes, 1931, EN. *Records of the Twelfth Ordinary Session of the Assembly. Meetings of the Committees. Minutes of the Second Committee (Technical Organisations)*, 1931, 30.
11 Giuseppe Bottai's address in International Labour Conference, *Record of Proceedings, International Labour Conference, 16th Session* (Geneva: ILO, 1932), 204. See also Giuseppe Bottai's address in International Labour Conference, *Record of Proceedings, International Labour Conference, 11th Session* (Geneva: ILO, 1928), 218–219.
12 Filippo Carli, "Le crisi economiche e l'ordinamento corporativo della produzione", in *Atti del Secondo Convegno*, vol. 1, 233.
13 Arnaldo Volpicelli, "Corporazione e ordinamento internazionale", *Nuovi Studi di Diritto, Economia e Politica*, 7, no. 6 (1934): 357–359.
14 Ibid., 364.
15 Ibid., 362–364.
16 Mario Gianturco, "Funzione internazionale della Corporazione", *Critica fascista*, 11, no. 21 (1933): 406.
17 On De Michelis' life, see Maria Rosaria Ostuni, "Giuseppe De Michelis", in *Dizionario biografico degli italiani* [Italian Dictionary of Biography], vol. 38 (Treccani: Rome, 1990), 639–644.
18 Giuseppe De Michelis, *La corporazione nel mondo* (Milano: Bompiani, 1934) [translations: *World Reorganisation on Corporative Lines* (London: Allen & Unwin, 1935); *La corporation dans le monde* (Paris: Denoël et Steele, 1935)]. See Jens Steffek, "Fascist Internationalism", *Millennium. Journal of International Studies* 44, no. 1 (2015): 3–21.
19 De Michelis, *World Reorganisation*, 234.
20 Steffek, "Fascist Internationalism", 13.
21 De Michelis, *World Reorganisation*, 212–213.
22 Ibid., 211–212.
23 Ibid., 246.
24 Pasetti, *L'Europa corporativa, Una storia transnazionale tra le due guerre mondiali* (Bologna: Bononia University Press, 2016), 228.
25 Alberto Donini, "La corporazione nel mondo", *Critica fascista* 12, no. 17 (1934): 340.
26 Giulio Colamarino, "La corporazione nel mondo", *Nuovi problemi di politica, storia ed economia* 5, no. 5 (1934): 662–665.
27 Matteo Pasetti, "Un 'colonialismo corporativo'? L'imperialismo fascista tra progetti e realtà", *Storicamente* 12, no. 38 (2016). https://storicamente.org/pasetti_colonialismo_corporativo#nt-4; Gian Luca Podestà, "Il colonialismo corporativo. Politiche economiche e amministrazione coloniale nell'Africa orientale italiana", in *Governare l'Oltremare. Istituzioni, funzionari e società nel colonialismo italiano*, eds. Gianni Dore, Chiara Giorgi, Antonio M. Morone, and Massimo Zaccaria (Roma: Carocci, 2013), 59–70.
28 Centro di studi coloniali, *Atti del primo Congresso di studi coloniali. Firenze, 8–12 aprile 1931. IV sezione: Giuridica* (Firenze: Giuntina, 1931); Centro di studi coloniali, *Atti del secondo Congresso di studi coloniali. Napoli, 1–5 ottobre 1934. IV sezione:*

Giuridica (Firenze: Giuntina, 1935); Centro di studi coloniali, *Atti del terzo Congresso di studi coloniali. Firenze-Roma, 12–17 aprile 1937. II sezione: Giuridica* (Firenze: Sansoni, 1937).

29 Pasetti, "Un 'colonialismo corporativo'?".

30 Italo Papini, "La condizione giuridica delle popolazioni nelle colonie italiane", *Rivista delle colonie italiane* 8, no. 2 (1934): 82–96.

31 Gaetano Napolitano, *Problemi del corporativismo fascista nell'Impero e nelle colonie* (Cedam: Padova, 1939), 40–54.

32 Pietro Vertecchi, "La giustizia sociale sul piano internazionale", *L'Ordine Corporativo* 3, no. 4 (1936): 3–5.

33 Luigi Genzano, "Colonialismo corporativo", *Conquiste d'Impero* 6, no. 22–23–24 (1938): 308.

34 Gennaro Mondaini, "Colonie e corporativismo (Parte II)", *Rivista delle colonie italiane* 8, no. 12 (1934): 1005.

35 Jens Steffek, Francesca Antonini, "Toward Eurafrica! Fascism, Corporatism, and Italy's Colonial Expansion", in *Radicals and Reactionaries in Twentieth-Century International Thought*, ed. Ian Hall (New York: Palgrave Macmillan, 2015) 145–169; Mario G. Losano, *La geopolitica del Novecento. Dai Grandi Spazi delle dittature alla decolonizzazione* (Milano: Bruno Mondadori, 2011), 145–146.

36 Sergio Panunzio, "I sindacati e l'organizzazione economica dell'Impero", *Rassegna economica dell'Africa italiana* 26, no. 4 (1938): 554, 557.

37 Mondaini, "Colonie e corporativismo", 998.

38 Gian Luca Podestà, *Il mito dell'impero. Economia, politica e lavoro nelle colonie italiane dell'Africa orientale 1898–1941* (Torino: Giappichelli, 2004), 265–269.

39 Steffek, Antonini, "Toward Eurafrica!", 162–163.

40 Pasetti, "Un 'colonialismo corporativo'?".

41 Benito Mussolini, "Il piano regolatore della nuova economia italiana", in *Opera omnia di Benito Mussolini*, eds. Edoardo Susmel and Duilio Susmel, vol. 27 (Firenze: La Fenice, 1959), 242.

42 Luciano Zani, *Fascismo, autarchia, commercio estero. Felice Guarneri un tecnocrate al servizio dello "Stato nuovo"* (Bologna: Il Mulino, 1988), 119.

43 Agostino Nasti, "Direttrici politiche del regime", *Critica fascista* 15, no. 25 (1937): 2–3.

44 Erba [Ernesto Bassanelli], "Corporativismo e autarchia", *Critica fascista* 16, no. 9 (1938): 132–134.

45 Mario Rivoire, "Il perché del silenzio", *Critica fascista* 15, no. 28 (1937): 52–54.

46 Santomassimo, *La terza via fascista*, 232–235.

47 George Lowell Field, *The Syndical and Corporative Institutions of Italian Fascism* (New York: Columbia University Press, 1938); William G. Welk, *Fascist Economic Policy: An Analysis of Italy's Economic Experiment* (Cambridge: Harvard University Press, 1938); Carl T. Schmidt, *The Corporate State in Action: Italy under Fascism* (New York: Oxford University Press, 1939).

48 "Fascism. Inside Italy There Is Also 'The Corporate State'", *Life*, 9 May 1938, 31–42.

49 F. M. [Federico Maria] Pacces, "Sbloccamento delle Corporazioni e riorganizzazione corporativa dei ministeri", *Critica fascista* 15, no. 5 (1937): 67.

50 The standard reference work is Ruggero Zangrandi, *Il lungo viaggio attraverso il fascismo* (Milano: Feltrinelli, 1961). See also Vito Panunzio, *Il «secondo fascismo» 1936–1943. La reazione della nuova generazione alla crisi del movimento e del regime* (Milano: Mursia, 1988).

51 Santomassimo, *La terza via fascista*, 227.

52 Ferruccio Lantini, "Funzionamento delle corporazioni", *L'Economia italiana* 33, no. 11 (1936): 832–833.

53 The full text has been published in Francesco Perfetti, *La Camera dei fasci e delle corporazioni* (Roma: Bonacci, 1991), 247–250.

54 ACS, *Carte Cianetti*, scat. 6, fasc. 76. *Contributo agli studi per la riforma costituzionale*, no date [but 1937].
55 Ibid., fasc. 75. Ministero delle corporazioni. Il sottosegretario di Stato, 31 August 1939.
56 ACS, SPD, CO, fasc. 500.001. *Appunto per il duce del ministro delle corporazioni Ferruccio Lantini*, 7 July 1939.
57 "Fine del Parlamento?", *Critica fascista* 11, no. 10 (1933): 192; Silvio Longhi, "Integrazione parlamentare", *Il Popolo d'Italia*, 15 April 1933.
58 Mussolini, *Il piano regolatore*, 242.
59 See the exhaustive account in Perfetti, *La camera dei fasci*, 174–95, esp. 239–398, which includes the commissions' proceedings.
60 APC, Legislatura XXIX, *Disegni di legge e relazioni*, vol. XXVI, no. 2655, 2.
61 Aquarone, *L'organizzazione*, 277–279.

Epilogue

With the outbreak of the Second World War, and particularly with the beginning of Italian participation in June 1940, various Fascist politicians and intellectuals came to believe in the possibility of relaunching the "corporative revolution", both domestically and on an international scale. Cultural, political, and institutional tensions were no doubt channelled towards wartime needs and myths. At the same time, however, two new ideas emerged in this scenario which seemed to be creating the conditions for the implementation of the Fascist "third way". The first was the idea of "revolutionary war", according to which the ordeal of the conflict would lead to a palingenetic transformation of society, for which the traditional elites and the "parasitic" classes would pay the price. The second idea was the emergence of a European "New Order" entailing not only the complete geopolitical rearrangement of the continent but the establishment of a European "great economic space" resting on continental autarchy and the construction of a "new economy".[1]

The debate on corporatism was therefore rekindled in relation to both the role corporations were to assume in the Italian economy and the theme of exporting social justice, the redistribution of resources among world powers, and thus universal corporatism.[2] Alongside the revival of arguments and proposals from the 1930s, some theories were put forward that marked a break with them. Some thinkers theorised the need, within the framework of a post-war European "new order", to decouple corporate institutions from the state and the nation by creating supranational structures. This also led to a call to reform the corporatist order established on a national basis.[3] In this period, the "failure of corporatism, or at least the fact of its not being fully realised" became a topic of open discussion for many intellectuals.[4] After the conflict's first phase, however, these themes faced a steady and progressive decline. The ever more pressing demands of war production left little room for talk of "revolutionary war", while the rediscovery of the nation helped to undermine the idea of a "New Europe" and plans to establish supranational and continental institutions. Once again, even when reformulated within a wartime perspective, the debate on universal corporatism produced no concrete results. The situation at home was no better. When Italy joined the War, the realisation of corporatism definitely took a back seat. The corporations were deprived of their powers and the Ministry of Corporations ceded powers to the Ministry of War Production. Social policy disappeared from the government's agenda, while economic policy was managed directly by Mussolini in traditional dirigiste and centralist fashion and according to the needs of war. Trade union policy was instead limited to a very partial defence of the industrial workers' negotiating power. Even the latest creation, the Chamber of Fasces and Corporations, thus ended up representing a "ridiculous failure", as Cianetti observed.[5] It was precisely Cianetti who came up with the last futile attempt to reform the corporative institutions. A few weeks after his appointment as Minister of Corporations in April 1943, he presented a new project that not only assigned a central role to the corporations but was also intended to relaunch his ministry, which among other things was to take control of the Institute for Industrial Reconstruction (IRI) – a long-standing rallying point for left-wing Fascism.[6]

Corporatism's trajectory officially ended shortly after 25 July 1943 and Mussolini's overthrow: with the legislative decree of 9 August 1943, the Badoglio government suppressed all corporative bodies. Nor did corporatism regain space in the Italian Social Republic of Salò. The socialist character that Mussolini intended to give the new state, as reflected in its name, had little to do with the ideas and achievements of previous years. References to corporatism were meagre and fleeting in official publications as much as in political addresses and legislative texts. Indeed, no mention of corporatism was made in the 18 points of the Verona Manifesto, the ideological document that launched the Social Republic. It is true that a Ministry of Corporate Economy was established on the ashes of the Ministry of Corporations.[7] Its mandate, however, did not envisage the operation of corporative bodies, as these had been dissolved and never reconstituted, but rather – in addition to the management of the system of production in northern Italy – the realisation of the completely different and far more radical goal of "socialisation". The pursuit of class harmony and the equal representation of interests was thus replaced by a direct attack on private property and the industrial bourgeoisie.

Socialisation, however, even more so than corporatism, was an idea destined to remain unfulfilled: it proved an unrealistic attempt that was largely improvised and completely out of step with the course of events. The plans drawn up by the Minister of Corporative Economy, Angelo Tarchi, "envisaged an arrangement that was absolutely respectful of private property and capitalist hierarchies".[8] Even the reconstitution of a single workers' confederation in November 1943 (long hoped for by Fascist trade unionists) gave confederation leaders some hope in the short run, but all in all, it was not followed by any concrete steps in the direction of either full political empowerment of the trade unions or of some compensation for the labour world.[9]

Salò's extreme "anti-capitalist" demagogy bears witness to the disrepute into which the idea of corporatism had fallen and the impossibility of reproposing it outside the Fascist regime. Yet, despite this, post-war Italy's liberation from the legacy of the corporatist "third way" was neither immediate nor straightforward. The debate within the Constituent Assembly provides numerous testimonies of this. The issue of corporatist representation was at the centre of a comprehensive project presented by the Catholic constitutionalist Costantino Mortati. Far from echoing Fascism's ideology and institutional framework, it envisaged transforming the Senate into a corporatist chamber based on the representation of interest groups, professionals, and trade unions. The draft of this project was approved by the commission, with the abstention of the left-wing parties, only to be soon discarded – not least by the Christian Democrats – in the plenary assembly.[10]

Couched in democratic terms, other aspects of corporatism – such as public recognition, having a single trade union for each sector, and the presence of joint bodies with the power to direct social and economic policies – also exerted unexpected, yet not always hidden, influences both on trade unionism (e.g. the unitary *Confederazione Generale Italiana del Lavoro*, Italian General Confederation of Work) and on the work of the Constituent Assembly's third sub-committee.[11] The very construction of the new trade union system was influenced by the enduring corporatist legacy: the impossibility of reproposing a system such as the one built in the first two decades of the century, which had been based on the reciprocal autonomy of the state and those organisations for social representation, as well as the presence of legislation that included interest groups in those decision-making processes pertaining to economic and social matters, made an engagement with the Fascist experience unavoidable.

The immediate post-war years and the drafting of the new Constitution therefore appear to be marked, from this point of view, by a progressive and non-linear liberation from corporatism's institutional and cultural legacy. We may regard this, however, as a sign of the kind of lingering influence that inevitably accompanies transitions from one political regime to another and of the forms of continuity that inevitably arise even in situations of radical change. It certainly cannot be regarded as the re-emergence of the corporatist legacy in Republican Italy. Corporatism, after all, was intrinsically defined by the enshrining of rigid identities, the centrality of "producers", the social and cultural irrelevance of consumption, and a very close integration of the state and society. Not even a redevelopment of corporatism in a democratic sense could make it relevant in post-war society, which was opening up to political pluralism, the autonomy of social subjects, an emphasis on participation rather than decision-making, and the new dimension of consumption. Most importantly, in the eyes of all of democratic Italy's political cultures, corporatism seemed inseparable from the ideological and political model designed by Fascism; as such, it could only be unconditionally rejected.[12]

Notes

1 Fabrizio Amore Bianco, *Mussolini e il 'Nuovo ordine'. I fascisti, l'Asse e lo 'spazio vitale' (1939–1943)* (Milano: Luni, 2018).

2 Fabrizio Amore Bianco, "Le corporazioni oltre lo Stato. Progetti di corporativismo internazionale nell'immaginario del fascismo", in *Genealogie e geografie dell'anti-democrazia nella crisi europea degli anni Trenta. Fascismi, corporativismi, laburismi*, ed. Laura Cerasi (Venezia: Edizioni Ca' Foscari, 2019), 254.

3 Federico Maria Pacces, "Appunti per servire l'idea di una Nuova Europa", *Critica fascista* 18, no. 20 (1940): 323–328, and no. 21: 340–345; Pacces, "Verso un'economia corporativa europea", *Critica fascista* 19, no. 1 (1940): 6; Mario Gianturco, *Il volto corporativo della nuova Europa* (Milano: Fratelli Bocca, 1943).

4 Mariuccia Salvati, *Camillo Pellizzi. Un intellettuale nell'Europa del Novecento* (Bologna: Il Mulino, 2021), 319.
5 Cianetti, *Memorie* cit. *Tullio Cianetti,* Memorie dal carcere di Verona, *ed. Renzo De Felice* (Milano: Rizzoli, 1983), 281.
6 Ibid., scat. 5, fasc. 56. Cianetti (ministero delle corporazioni), *Appunto per il Duce*, 15 May 1943. Cianetti's "long-term project" is reconstructed in detail in Parlato, *La sinistra fascista*, 225–288.
7 Marco Borghi, "Dal ministero dell'Economia corporativa al ministero del Lavoro", *Rivista di storia contemporanea* 22, no. 2–3 (1993): 357–392.
8 Luigi Ganapini, *La Repubblica delle camicie nere. I combattenti, i politici, gli amministratori, i socializzatori* (Milano: Garzanti, 1999), 14.
9 Ibid., 390–452.
10 Fabrizio Astolfi, "Democrazia corporativa. La proposta di Costantino Mortati in Assemblea costituente", *Italia contemporanea*, no. 239–240 (2005): 225–247.
11 See the classic Gino Giugni, "Esperienze corporative e post-corporative nei rapporti collettivi di lavoro in Italia", *Il Mulino*, no. 1–2 (1956): 3–17. I shall also refer to Alessio Gagliardi, "La Cgil unitaria e la nuova costituzione economica", in *1945–1946. Le origini della Repubblica, vol. I, Contesto internazionale e aspetti della transizione, Comitato Nazionale 1945–1946 alle origini della Repubblica,* ed. Giancarlo Monina (Soveria Mannelli: Rubbettino, 2007), 349–381; Gagliardi, "Le forze sociali tra cambiamento e restaurazione", in *Dal fascismo alla Repubblica: quanta continuità*, eds. Marco De Nicolò and Enzo Fimiani (Roma: Viella, 2019), 131–169.
12 Very different observations apply to the complex apparatus of public bodies that prospered over the following decades, as this was undoubtedly connected to the corporative system and culture, yet cannot be identified with them: see Mariuccia Salvati, "The Long History of Corporatism in Italy: A Question of Culture or Economics?", *Contemporary European History* 15, no. 2 (2006): 223–244.

Index

For Product Safety Concerns and Information please contact our EU representative GPSR@taylorandfrancis.com Taylor & Francis Verlag GmbH, Kaufingerstraße 24, 80331 München, Germany

Printed and bound by CPI Group (UK) Ltd, Croydon, CR0 4YY
30/09/2026
02225125-0007